Social Development in Indian Subcontinent

Social Development in Indian Subcontinent

India, Pakistan and Bangladesh

H.Y. Siddiqui

RAWAT PUBLICATIONS
Jaipur and New Delhi

ISBN 81-7033-840-9

Published by
Prem Rawat for *Rawat Publications*
Satyam Apts., Sector 3, Jawahar Nagar, Jaipur 302 004 (India)
Phone: 0141 265 1748 / 7006 Fax: 0141 265 1748
E-mail: info@rawatbooks.com
Website: www.rawatbooks.com

Delhi Office
4858/24, Ansari Road, Daryaganj, New Delhi 110 002
Phone: 011-23263290

Typeset by Rawat Computers, Jaipur
Printed at Chaman Enterprises, New Delhi

Contents

Preface

We have witnessed a historical event recently, the end of a whole century. Looking back scholars differ in their views about the important changes that could be termed as events of the century. The debate is likely to continue, as each subject specialist would attach more significance to changes in her/his field. Long for example, an economic historian highlighting economic changes as by far the most significant, felt that the real living standards of the masses have changed but the elite has largely appropriated the gains of technological innovations and economic development. Life expectancy and literacy have improved even though incomes have remained stagnant. Amartya Sen indicated that the greatest event of the century has been the development of democracy. Sociologists have enumerated that the most significant feature of the twentieth century, has been the growing acceptance, that self-actualisation of the individual is a greater goal than loyalty to any group such as family, religion, race, ruling dynasty or nation. Now looking at these opinions it is obvious that the important societal concerns are located around three important dimensions of human society, economic, political and social. A fair evaluation of social development would include all three in its scope.

One way of summing up these changes during the last century could be that while the democratic forms of governance expanded and developed, it still could not help the common people to get a reasonable share out of the economic development process. Further, while the democracy as a form of governance

Preface

We have witnessed a historical event recently, the turn of a whole century. Looking back scholars differ in their views about the important changes that could be termed as events of the century. The debate is likely to continue, as each subject specialist would attach more significance to changes in her/his field. Bradford de Long for example, an economic historian highlighting economic changes as by far the most significant, felt that though the living standards of the masses have changed but the elite has largely appropriated the gains of technological innovations and economic development. Life expectancy and literacy have improved even though incomes have remained stagnant. Amartya Sen indicated that the greatest event of the century has been the development of democracy. Sociologist Peter Burger enumerated that the most significant feature of the twentieth century, has been the growing acceptance, that self-realization of the individual is a greater goal than loyalty to any group such as family, religion, race, ruling dynasty or nation. Now looking at these opinions it is obvious that the important societal concerns are located around three important dimensions of human society, economic, political and social. And any evaluation of social development would include all three in its scope.

One way of summing up these changes during the last century could be that while the democratic forms of governance expanded and developed, it still could not help the common people to get a reasonable share out of the economic development process. Further, while the democracy as a form of governance survives, the polity created to serve the society dominates it. The attitudes are becoming more individual in orientation in consonance with the economic values rather than promoting social caring. The self-realization of the individual is a greater goal than loyalty to any group such as family or a nation. Is there a contradiction in these developments? In other words is economic development promoting social development or more specifically social cohesiveness of society? Further, has democracy as a political system failed to ensure the people centred development? If yes, then what is the alternative?

Berlin is more focused in his assessment that in the twentieth century the development of natural sciences and technology on the one hand, and the ideological shifts on the other, have changed the lives of millions of people. Science and technology have accomplished far reaching changes in shrinking the world and producing immense material resources to help create a glittering world which is unprecedented. However, the discovery of a technology to structure the social attitudes and norms remains so far a cherished dream. In other words as yet it is not possible to control the human mind to produce an ideal social environment. The problem is that all goods do not complement each other, if you pursue one, you miss the other. As Machiavelli discovered virtues such as humility, acceptance of suffering, unworldliness, the hope of salvation in an afterlife, will not lead to a strong nation state. Those who live by the percepts of morality are bound to be trampled on by the ruthless pursuit of power on the part of men who alone can recreate and dominate a republic. The economic and the social, or more simply the individual and collective goals also do not go well together. As Rousseau, Tolstoy and more recently Gandhi believed that the moral universe of peasants was like that of children, not distorted by the conventions and institutions of the civilization, which sprang from human vices – greed, egoism and spiritual blindness.

What the last century has without doubt accomplished is making it clear in no uncertain terms that the ultimate goal of all societal development is economic, the rest is secondary. If you do not have the material resources you are underdeveloped and a risk to the development of others. The options before you are, all out efforts for economic development as part of a global economy. But political compulsions of democracy for the developing countries are not compatible with this approach. The millions of people in the world, who are not part of mainstream economic development, are getting restless. The democracy has made them more vocal and active. The point is we now know where the last century has taken us, the question is what the new millennium will deliver?

One way to seek an answer is to look at the history of the last five decades of the three nations, that earlier were one. Have they achieved the goals that these nations so passionately wrote in their constitutions and planning documents? What lies ahead for them in future? Do they have any theory to help them structure the future? Do these nations have the social system to deliver the goods as planned? Is there an alternative as is fashionable to predict at the end of a treatise? Whether there is one or not the quest for development would go on, irrespective of the fact of what it delivers.

I have not followed any specific outline in narrating the history. I have only visited Pakistan once and have seen Bangladesh only through the eyes of many different scholars including novelists. The data referred to have been taken from different sources, generally national or governmental in nature. The data by international institutions such as World Bank and UNDP have been used as well. I am aware that it is rather an ambitious task to explore the development in three countries. But I am confining myself to present the economic, social and political scene, rather than providing any explanation for the same. I am indeed grateful to all the persons and institutions whose findings have been used to describe the current situation in these countries. All sources have been duly acknowledged.

I would like to express my thanks to my family, wife Farida, son Eraj and Victoria, my daughter-in-law and Seema, the rebel, my daughter, who is determined to discover her own pathway. Their support though granted grudgingly has helped me to work long hours that it takes to complete any writing assignment.

H. Y. Siddiqui

1

Introduction

Problem of Conceptualizing Social Development

The term 'social development' is more popularly used now to refer to the process of inducing changes in societies termed as under developed or poor. The earlier terms used to refer to the same objective were 'development' or 'economic development'. The term 'development' reflects a preference for the direction of change, while change is a neutral term. Some changes are considered as development while others are considered as a decline. It is obvious that a change is termed as development or otherwise, depending upon the value framework used to evaluate it. Such evaluations differ within a society and between societies. Girls taking up employment is seen by some as the writing on the wall for the dooms day, whereas others view it as a positive change. In a village some 60 kilometres away from New Delhi, the daughter of the head of a village was forced to withdraw from school as the community still consider it undesirable for girls to continue their schooling beyond a point, particularly after they enter their teens. The individual freedom similarly is viewed by some as a sign of development while others consider it a sign of decline of social values. The quest for creating an ideal human society is as old as human history itself. The difference is that earlier it used to be the task of philosophers to ponder on the subject but by the middle of the last century, the idea has become a worldwide political concern.

The indicators for measuring the level of social development is a matter of debate, but generally education levels, employment and income levels, expectation of life at birth, child mortality rates, maternal mortality rate, availability of safe drinking water and toilets, etc., are taken as important indicators of social development. The perception of an ideal society, however, is a much more complex issue and has created major conflicts within and between societies. Both religious and political sentiments have dominated the movements to win the popular support to legitimize one or the other framework. As is obvious the debate will go on as there can never be a consensus on the issue.

After the end of the Second World War many new nations emerged on the world scene, including India and Pakistan. These nations were economically categorized as poor and socially rated as backward. The cold war between the capitalist and the communist blocs was dividing the world in different camps to pursue their future development. The importance of international relations and the fact that the world was shrinking and becoming a global village was gradually being realized. The interdependence of modern day societies on each other and design of powerful nations to control other nations, to promote their own economic and political values was emerging as a global trend. Yet, it was becoming evident that it would be difficult to politically control the culturally diverse nations of the world. The new strategy to control was discovered in the form of economic development and modernization. The project development was designed to change the entire life style of people the world over. A model composed of economic development on the one hand and a democratic polity on the other was projected. Western scholars around the middle of the twentieth century defined development as a process of becoming 'modern', beginning with modernization of economy. The industrialization was expected to change the rural into urban habitats, improve the rate of economic growth by improving the productive capacity of the society and the individual actors in it. The economic prosperity was expected to slow down the rate of population growth and generate more employment to achieve a condition of full or nearly full employment. Along with these economic changes the modernization process was expected to develop democratic institutions in the society. These institutions such as a free press, judiciary and legislatures besides grassroots organizations, women's groups, youth groups and other democratically elected bodies, were to ensure wider participation of the people in designing the social arrangements necessary for ensuring an adequate share for every household in the development process. It was considered the key for the smooth functioning of the economy to ensure a minimum level of socio-economic need fulfilment for all. The modernization theory therefore assumed that economic growth would uniformly spread to all segments of the society. That greater economic resource in turn would change the social values and attitudes of the people in general. The belief for example in ascribed status and the traditional hierarchies leading to predetermined patterns of economic occupations, etc., would be replaced by more democratic arrangements. It would open the way for a belief in equal opportunities for economic development and political participation for all members of a society. It was also expected to dilute the religious passions and create a more secular approach to the day-to-day affairs in the society.

The prescriptions for economic development and modernization of society were developed and perfected in major US universities and other academic institutions, just after the end of Second World War. The Truman Doctrine, as it was called, simply stated that any political/economic/social development not in line with the US should not be allowed to prosper (Preston, 1986). However, the possibilities created by Keynes theoretical work, where the state could play a central role in economic development saved the situation. It offered the development experts the opportunity to cater to both, the popular sentiments for radical reforms and the US philosophy to oppose any radical changes leading to total domination of the state. As Streeten (1995) argued that discussion of 'development' had its origin in (a) problems of resources and people, and (b) the cold war.

The phenomenal growth of science and technology,

however, helped in generating faith in development projects. The technology helped in raising the economic growth in different nations across the world including the developing countries. However, all models to redistribute growth among the poorer sections have not been very successful. The theory of producing a desired set of social structure also remains as elusive as ever. This, some have acknowledged as the failure of sociology, while others like Isaiah Berlin, who believed in the historical inevitability, were from the beginning critical of the possibility of creating an ideal society. It is worth acknowledging that all movements began with ideas about what relations between men have been, are, might be and should be; and have succeeded in introducing changes in societies. Such ideas are the substance of ethics as Berlin pointed out. The relations between the state and the members of a society remain the centre of debate. Various models based on the ethical values, about how life should be lived, to suit the need and aspirations of different societies have so far been tried. These range from total domination of the state to relegating the state into the role of an arbitrator to correct the mutual relations between the members, while leaving them as free as possible. But as is obvious all such efforts so far succeed in introducing changes but have not succeeded in constituting an ideal society.

Development efforts aimed at promoting economic growth supported by foreign aid both from the USSR and USA and a number of other countries were launched in many new nations around 1950. By far the liberal democratic model which gave a lot more freedom to individual members vis-à-vis state was more prevalent than the communist model which gave primacy to the state to control the relations between members by curbing their rights to economic gains. By now things are moving in the other direction where the state is being pushed into the background as far as the economic matters are concerned. The more significant development is the international pressure on individual states to give up their territorial controls as far as the trade is concerned and be governed by an international order.

This is likely to have far reaching significance in the context of social development of the smaller nation states. The prime concerns in an ideal society are – that majority of the members attain a satisfactory standard of living, though these standards may differ from society to society, and that all members abide by certain norms to promote collective well-being, in other words they respect their differences and allow each other enough space to function freely without in any way exploiting the other. The term social development in a sense refers to achievement of these objectives. It could also be called political philosophy or ethics applied to society. These tasks pose different issues depending upon the current levels of economic, political and social levels of a society. The economic development addresses the first concern whereas political and social development address the second.

Arthur Lewis (1955), a prime architect of the liberal democratic model, defined development as widening choices, in other words, greater economic prosperity to provide greater material comforts. The assumption was, as we stated earlier, that the growth would spread through the market forces and the state would provide social services and undertake other programmes to push the growth downwards. It was assumed that the fate of the poor should not be a matter of concern during the initial stages of development and once the stage of mass consumption arrives poverty would disappear. Some though could see that it was too ambitious a goal particularly in the context of poor countries like India with a huge population, and that the poorest 20 per cent were beyond the reach of economic growth through any development planning (Pant, 1974). The assumption that economic prosperity would lead to more democratic and secular trends in society is a dream. The expansion of economic wealth is expected to redefine the need, and the consequences may adversely affect the functioning of the democratic institutions. The ability of the state to develop the social services to expand education, health and employment and thereby bridge the already existing economic and social disparities is a crucial issue for debate. The use of new found economic and political power to end social discrimination is another important issue. The containing problem of the population growth coupled with mass illiteracy, economic deprivation and providing opportunities for economic participation are considered prime objectives of social development.

After nearly two decades of development efforts, Gunnar Myrdal (1968) and some other studies noted that the growth did not trickle down, the unemployment remained high despite economic growth, the population continued to grow at a high rate, the health and education standards were low and the growth of industrialization was leading to development of slums in the cities. As Streeten noted no theory helped in meeting adequate standards of nutrition, health and education, as it is not known precisely which financial, fiscal and human resources and policies produce these desirable results (Streeten, 1995: 340). The discovery of these trends generated a lot of debate at different levels including international institutions. The objectives of development were restructured to focus on achieving the goals of education for all, health for all, employment and housing for all and finally human rights for all by the turn of the century. This is what came to be defined as the process of social development, and was meant to divert attention from a pure economic approach to give a little more space to social and political development in the overall agenda of development. However, this did not mean that the importance of economic growth declined in the overall efforts at development of an ideal society.

The modernization theory expected economic growth to translate into democratic trends in the society in all institutional arrangements including political governance. The political development was expected to widen the participation of common man in the efforts for social development and lead to greater economic and social equality among different segments of society. The political development was, therefore, expected to provide a method of putting in place a democratic power structure capable of not only providing good and effective governance but social justice as well, by following people friendly strategies of economic growth. An analysis of experience of political development efforts in different countries would indicate to what extent the modernization theory delivered these goals. The nature of state in developing countries provide a rich variety and the state followed a variety of economic strategies to address the problem of social development. These strategies varied from an open economic approach, where the state did not attempt to regulate the economy for example in Pakistan, to where the state played a key role in regulating the economy for example in India. It would be interesting to look at the trends of economic development in these countries. Has the democratic political structure been more successful or a dictatorial regime? What approaches have been successful in delivering good governance or social justice? Since the advent of the social sciences the relationship between the economic and political change has attracted scholars and practitioners alike. The central theme has been the correlation between individual freedom and economic development on the one hand and economic institutions and the political structure on the other. As a result a number of theories were advanced to explain these relationships. However, it is obvious that there is a relationship between the economic and political institutions of a society. Yet, is it possible to discover universal laws to create ideal political structures to produce desired economic indicators seems to be a central concern in social theory. As Mosse David et al. (2001) noted, a development site is complex and unpredictable. It consists of a complex interplay of cultural and political factors. Relationships between these factors have been under study and so far have not yielded any definite theory to control the outcome of development efforts.

Social development is conceived simply as an attempt to convert the rural populations into urban human settlements. The historical struggle to civilize the native is what it is often termed. The general idea is to help people to produce and consume more and keep this cycle going. Is it logical, natural or desirable and finally is it feasible, are some of the key issues involved in development debates. The terms such as 'underdeveloped' and 'developed', which dominated international debates in classifying societies or nation states on this continuum during the 1950s, were based on the state of economy in these countries. If for example, the main stay of the economy was agriculture, it was considered underdeveloped. It meant a large rural population and low per capita GNP. The consumption levels were low. These societies are therefore rightly described as economically underdeveloped. But are they socially underdeveloped as well, is an issue which has generated a lot of debate in the past. The theory of orientalism developed by Edward Said simply indicates that it is the framework which is decisive in terming people socially backward or otherwise.

Difficulties in Defining the Ideal

The construction of economic, political and social arrangements to create an ideal society has evoked immense debate. For example, the economic arrangements vary from total freedom to individual to pursue any economic goal to complete state domination of economic sector. Tolstoy, Gandhi and Rousseau believed that the ideal economic society was that of small peasants, characterized by spiritual beliefs, while others believed in the scientific rationalism in industry and ever growing material wealth. While some would refer to theological texts to evoke principles on which the ideal would be constructed while others would pursue a more rational and scientific approach. However, it is interesting to note that the common point in both the approaches is that it is possible to construct the ideal. Yet, despite some idea about the general direction the specifics remain vague. For example, key words in social analysis and policy, such as participation, emancipation, empowerment, social justice have rarely been clearly defined. Does empowerment refers to a change in the power position of different actors or a change in the concept of power? What is freedom, how can one attain it? Is education a liberating factor? What is meant by emancipation, is it emancipation from political exploitation or from the material world? Social justice is another difficult concept not easy to comprehend. It is not difficult to find a large segment of public opinion favouring a highly segregated society, as some feel it serves the larger interest of the society in ensuring stability and good governance. The ultimate objective of economic development is seen as to bring about an improvement in the economic status of the general population of a society, which is seen as crucial for human well-being. Though, now even World Bank experts are realizing that economic wealth may not necessarily lead to peace or happiness. The primacy of economic and individual centred goals is rooted in western philosophic tradition, whereas Indian philosophy emphasizes the negation of self. In Weberian terms, the former is materialist in orientation whereas the latter is idealist. The developing societies are characterized by social values where 'group', (family/caste/community) well-being, is still considered primary as compared to individual well-being. The construction of 'self' and the 'other' is the key to survival of relationships in groups. Economic development affects this process of social construction. The economic man is likely to be more self-centred, thus leading to conflicts in-group. One of the indicators to study the impact of economic development in the society could be to monitor what happens to the institutions of family and marriage in a society. The changing nature and frequency of conflicts internal as well as external may serve as a good indicator of social development in a society for some.

Yet another indicator of social development as we indicated earlier is to measure the political development of a society. What political institutions have been evolved over the years and how stable and accessible are these? The concept of power and how it is defined and how widespread it is, are all good indicators of social development. The initial efforts at economic development in the so called underdeveloped countries like India, Pakistan and Bangladesh, were aimed at achieving economic development on the one hand and helping the common man to participate in the process of political development to share in the construction of future social policies. It is a far more complex task to devise arrangements to share power. It is difficult even in a group where more intense relationships are in place, such as family, to ensure democracy. It becomes impossible to think of democracy in plural societies. The concept of power generally refers to control over others rather than control over self. The ideas about who should control are very specifically dealt within theological texts and in secular constitutions. And both exist side by side in a democratic society. It creates a paradox as Vasudha Daghamvar (2003) recently pointed out in the context of female emancipation. The feminist assertions of equality and theological texts of various kinds preferring and keeping in place patriarchy as the popular ideology of gender construction make the social construction a task beyond redemption.

According to western scholars, it is one of the greatest achievement of the last millennium that individual freedom and orientation has increased. The sociological hypothesis is that development promotes a process of modernization, which replaces the traditional social values, norms and institutions and restructures human relationships. In a 'socially developed' society, the roles are not ascribed but acquired and offer greater scope to individuals for self-fulfilment. The growth of individual freedom is seen to result in a change of earlier institutional arrangements. For example, two major features of a socially developed society are doing away with gender and caste restrictions. The individual is expected to have greater freedom vis-à-vis the state and other institutions of social control leading to greater human satisfaction. Thus, the current approach to development assumes a positive correlation between economic development and social development. The term social development in this sense include such diverse issues as – reducing economic disparities between various social groups based on caste, religion or ethnicity, promoting gender equality, ensuring political participation of different segment of population, and above all reducing conflicts and promoting cooperation both within and between societies or nation-states.

Problems in Creating the Ideal

The mechanism identified to ensure popular participation in development is a widespread network of education. The underlying assumption was and still is that education promotes democratic values and attitudes. Such persons actively participate in the political decision-making process, and are more open, transparent and just. With the spread of 'education', society then is expected to become more cohesive, conflict free and consequently more social and moral in character. The question is does education liberate? Has the spread of education made man more others oriented and social or has it lead to a higher achievement orientation and greater individualism, and which would be considered as liberation? This is where the direction of change is assessed in relative terms depending on the value framework of the culture.

During the past five decades, data from the developing countries suggest that the level of education has gone up somewhat. The availability of health services or more precisely modern medicine has improved and political and social participation of women and other vulnerable groups has increased marginally. The state expenditure on social services has not declined, and it may continue at its present level in future. The point, however, is has it ensured a wider participation in the economic development process, and has it altered the social environment? What is the social impact of improvements in income, education and health? Have these societies become more 'modernized' and cohesive? Or the advancement of education and awareness has aggravated tensions and conflicts? Will economic development lead to social development? Is a cohesive, conflict-free and caring society a mere utopia? It may be worthwhile to ponder upon these issues to look at the future implications of development.

The development models seem to begin with the following assumptions:

— It is necessary to generate more economic resources to increase the per capita availability of material goods and services;

— The technological development and global market is capable of generating adequate economic growth in developing countries;

— Social development is a by-product, which could occur on its own or through enlargement of the social service net work; and

— The availability of more goods and services leads to greater social cohesiveness and social development.

The process of influencing the so-called 'poor' or 'developing' countries to adopt a more global market friendly approach has accelerated in recent years. The question often asked is, is there a link between the collapse of the communist block and the 'development' – to be defined as a glittering world of new technology, high rise structures defining the skyline, and a market full of consumer goods. Is it likely to undermine the autonomy of nation states? What are likely to be its implications to promote social development signifying increased access to health and education for more, if not all, and a wider participation in the process of economic development? It is, therefore, significant to note what political changes are likely to happen and the future role of the state vis-à-vis individual welfare or entitlement. The current thinking is that the state has become an obstacle in case of both economic and social development. The state responsibility, therefore, should be replaced by community or family responsibility. Social development as we have argued earlier is multi-dimensional in nature and in fact refers to a process of economic, political and social development of a society. The studies of development over the years have indicated that political, social and economic developments in a society may not keep pace with each other, and instead of supplementing each other, in fact may negate each other. Economic development alone will not ensure social development. The current review of social development tries to look into the details of what has happened in the countries under review. The subsequent chapters would look at the process of economic, political and social development in India, Pakistan and Bangladesh. The crucial issues are, has economic growth been as widespread as it was expected, has it effected the political and social development in these countries. Or has it lead to group, community or regional differences and conflicts, in the process distorting the political process of development. The secular and democratic values are not easy to acquire as the very process of socialization in many societies ensures the opposite, for example to firmly believe in categories and hierarchies. To learn to dominate is a value more generally sought among male and to obey among the female rather than an attitude of mutual respect. Have these trends been reversed by the project development?

The economic has become more crucial at the present juncture, as the poor developing countries find themselves in a bind, having made a lot of promises to large populations, on the one hand and having borrowed enormously from financial institutions on the other. However, the interpretation and opinions on what has happened will differ. Sociologically, what is significant is, to ponder over the question of the possibility of future social change efforts and to take note of the changes that are likely to occur in view of the new global economic and political environment.

It may be relevant at this juncture to take a more closer look at some of the assumptions giving primacy to economic development.

Economic Development

As indicated earlier, development is generally seen as an economic phenomenon. This generally is measured in terms of the following indicators:

Levels of Living

The usual description in textbooks on development begins with highlighting the fact that in developing nations, general levels of living tend to be low for the vast majority of people. This is true not only in relation to their counterparts in rich nations but often also in relation to small elite groups within their own societies. These low levels of living are generally indicated in the form of low incomes (poverty), inadequate housing, poor health, limited or no education, high infant mortality, low life and work expectancy, and in many cases a general sense of malaise and hopelessness.

The conclusion is drawn with reference to the materialistic framework of an industrial albeit 'modern' society. It assumes that people should live in urban areas, in houses with modern sanitation facilities, access to modern school education and modern health facilities. They must live for as long as possible and should continue to achieve higher and higher levels of material comforts. Those not able to qualify are termed underdeveloped and poor, suffering from malaise and hopelessness. An alternative way of looking at the same reality could be that a majority of people is living a nature friendly life by using minimum of the natural resources. The truth is that a sizable segment of third world population lives in rural areas and have very simple and nature friendly life styles. Further, a sizable section of these people may not be looking forward to living in urban areas and adopting a more 'modern' or western lifestyles. It is equally true that economic theory so far has not discovered a way to distribute incomes within or between countries in a more equitable manner. A more important issue is the impact of further economic growth both within nations and internationally.

Per Capita National Income

The per capita gross national product (GNP) is often used as a summary index of the relative economic well-being of people in different nations. The GNP itself is the most commonly used measure of the overall level of economic activity. It is calculated as the total domestic and foreign value additions claimed by a country's residents without making deductions for depreciation of the domestic capital stock. The gross domestic product (GDP) measures the total value for final use of output produced by an economy, by both residents and nonresidents. Thus, GNP comprises GDP plus the difference between the income residents receive from abroad for factor services (labour and capital) less payments made to non-residents who contribute to the domestic economy.

As an illustration of the per capita income gap between rich and poor nations, in 1997, Luxembourg had a per capita income of $28,010 compared to Sierra Leone with a per capita income of $159. The least developed countries have an average of $245 per capita as compared to $908 in case of all developing countries and $17,618 in the developed countries (HDR, 1999: 155-58). In other words a person in Luxembourg had more than 176 times the per capita income of one of the world's poorest countries, Sierra Leon, and more than 60 times that of one of the world's largest nations, India. There are similarly significant gaps between per capita income between rich and the poor in the same country.

The fact remains that in countries with a lower per capita income compared to industrialized nations people can live happily. The problem begins when linear inequality increases and a small population starts consuming more and also advertising the fact that the central purpose in life is to live like a king. The effort to expand the needs is perhaps the real problem.

Slower Growth Rates of National and Per Capita Incomes

Another very important fact according to development experts is that many Third World countries are growing at a slow rate. In some cases for example in Pakistan and Bangladesh the growth may be slower than the growth rate of the population. As many studies pointed out, growth slowed considerably during the 1980s and, real per capita GDP actually declined by 0.2 per cent in

1990 and 0.12 in 1997, despite planned development efforts. Although Asian countries continued to grow at a slower pace during the 1980s, negative economic growth in Latin America and the Caribbean averaged –0.4 per cent and in Africa –1.7 per cent.

Country	*GDP per capita*		*Avg. annual change per cent*
	1975	*1997*	
Malaysia	1,253	3,387	4.6
Thailand	557	1,870	5.7
Philippines	568	652	0.6
Saudi Arabia	8,970	5,057	-2.6
China	109	564	7.8
Indonesia	265	785	5.1
India	251	465	3.1
Pakistan	222	417	2.9
Bangladesh	134	218	2.2
Sri Lanka	278	551	3.2

Source: Human Development Report, 1999: 155-57.

During the 1980s and 1990s, the income gap between rich and poor nations widened at the fastest pace in more than three decades. The income levels of the richest 20 per cent of the world's population grew much faster in comparison with the poorest 40 per cent. In 1960 the income ratio between the rich and the poor was 30 to 1, at the end of the 1980s it became 60 to 1 and by 1995 it had become 82 to 1.

The new rules of globalization, privatization, liberalization and tighter intellectual property rights are shaping the path of technology, creating new risks of marginalization and vulnerability. Tighter control of innovation in the hands of multinational corporations ignores the need of millions. For poor people the technological progress remains out of reach (HDR, 1999: 68). New patent laws pay scant attention to the knowledge of indigenous people, leaving it vulnerable to claim by others. These laws ignore cultural diversity in creating and sharing innovations. The result is the silent theft of centuries of knowledge from developing to developed countries (Ibid, 68).

Since 1980 there has been a dramatic growth in some 15 countries, bringing rapidly rising incomes to many of their 1.5 billion people, more than a quarter of the world's population. Over much the same period, however, economic decline or stagnation has affected 100 countries, reducing the incomes of 1.6 billion people, again more than a quarter of the world's population. In 70 of these countries average incomes are less than they were in 1980 – and in 43 countries less than they were in 1970.

The world has become more polarized, with the gulf between the poor and rich of the world widening in recent years. In the past 30 years, the share of the poorest 20 per cent of the world's people in global income declined from 2.3 per cent to 1.4 per cent, while the share of the richest 20 per cent rose from 70 per cent to 85 per cent. The ratio of sharing of the richest and the poorest went up from 30:1 to 61:1. Economic growth in promoting human development, in identifiable instances has become the source of human misery and frustration. The instances are: jobless growth, ruthless growth, voiceless growth, rootless growth and futureless growth.

Yet as the latest version of the Human Development Report (1999) itself noted, globalization, the most recent prescription for speeding up economic development, is creating new threats to human security in both rich and poor countries alike. The relentless pressures of global competition are squeezing out compassion, invisible heart of human development. Poor people and poor countries risk being pushed to the margin in this proprietary regime that is controlling the world's knowledge. After nearly five decades of efforts about 840 million people are still malnourished. A vast majority of them are to be found in India, Pakistan and Bangladesh. The overall consumption of the richest fifth of the world's people is 16 times that of poorest fifth. Nearly 1.3 billion people live on less than a dollar a day and close to 1 billion cannot meet their basic consumption requirements. The share in global income of the richest fifth of the world's people is 74 times that of the poorest fifth. As Sen

(1999) noted the complex reality about human development and deprivation remains a mystery even now. The world GDP increased from 3 trillion to 30 trillion in the last 50 years, but the share of poor countries fell from 20 per cent to 10 per cent (HDR, 1999: 25). Is this also true for rich and the poor within a country and if so what are likely to be the implications for the future?

The world is shrinking. Contacts between people have been growing. Technology has bridged the distances between cultures across the world. This exposure could be exciting for some, disturbing for others. There is an element of imbalance in how this exposure affects the materially poor countries. The glitter of the industrialized world, and the elite within their own countries confuses them. They start worrying about their material poverty more than they had previously. Is this change in attitude likely to affect the social structure in the societies under review?

Distribution of National Income

The growing gap between per capita incomes in rich and poor nations is not the only manifestation of the widening economic disparity between the world's rich and poor. To appreciate the breadth and depth of Third World poverty, it is also necessary to look at the growing gap between rich and poor within individual low development countries to use the World Bank terminology.

In 1960, the 20 per cent of the world's people in the richest countries had 30 times the income of the poorest 20 per cent, in 1997 it has increased to 74 times. The worst deterioration among the income inequality among the Organization for Economic Cooperation and Development (OECD) countries was in Sweden, United Kingdom and in United States during 1980s and 1990s. In United Kingdom families below the poverty line rose by 60 per cent and in Netherlands by 40 per cent in 1980s. Net worth of world's 200 richest people increased from $440 billion to more than one trillion in four years, from 1994-1998 (HDR, 1999: 36-7).

The gap between rich and poor used to be generally greater in less developed nations than in developed nations but now the inequality in some of the richest nations is as great as in some of the developing nations. For example, if we compare the share of national income that accrues to the poorest 20 per cent of a country's population with that of the richest 20 per cent as an arbitrary measure of the degree of inequality, we find some very interesting trends. In only four countries of the world for which data has been published by the World Development Report, 1999-2000, the share of the richest 20 per cent was less than 35 per cent, and in no country the share was less than 30 per cent. In case of 8 countries including South Africa and Mexico the share of the poorest 20 per cent was less than 3 per cent and in the case of 28 countries including Malaysia, Chile, Nigeria, Russian Federation and Zimbabwe it was less than 5 per cent. In only 5 countries the share of the poorest 20 per cent was 10 per cent or more. India, Pakistan and Bangladesh despite their low per capita level and mass poverty, still provide 9 per cent or more to the poorest 20 per cent of the population. The lowest Gini index a measure of inequality (0 reflect perfect equality) was 19.5 in Slovak Republic, followed by 23.1 in Austria. The most disturbing fact is that the 225 richest people in the world have a combined wealth of over $1 trillion, equal to the annual income of the poorest 47 per cent of the 2.5 billion people. The wealth of 32 richest people exceed the combined GDP of South Asia (HDR, 1998: 30).

Distribution of Income

Country Gini index	*Poorest 20 per cent*	*II 20 per cent*	*III 20 per cent*	*IV 20 per cent*	*Richest 20 per cent*
India 29.7	9.2	13.0	16.8	21.7	39.3
Pakistan 31.2	9.4	13.0	16.0	20.3	41.2
Bangladesh H 28.3	9.4	13.5	17.2	22.0	37.9

WDR 1999-2000: 238-39.

The highest income inequality is in Sierra Leone as the Gini index is 62.9 and the richest 20 per cent consume 63.4 per cent of the national income, the richest 10 per cent 43.6 and the lowest 10 per cent just 0.5 per cent, followed by South Africa with a Gini index of 59.3. The richest 10 per cent in South Africa consumes 45.9 per cent and the poorest 10 per cent 1.1 per cent of the national income. In countries like Brazil, Chile, Mexico, Lesotho, Mali, Nicaragua, Niger, Guatemala and some other Latin American countries the Gini index is above 50 and in all these countries the richest 20 per cent consumes more than 50 per cent of the national income. The other notables where the rich consume more than 50 per cent of the national income, are Thailand, Malaysia and Zimbabwe. In most of the countries – only in four countries they consume less than 35 per cent – the rich consume more than 35 but less than 50 per cent including United Kingdom, United States, China, India, Bangladesh and Pakistan. Moreover, there is no obvious relationship or correlation between levels of per capita income and degree of income inequality as Bangladesh with the same low per capita income as India, has a much better record of inequality than the US. It underlines the point that economic development cannot solve the problem of inequality. It is important to look at how the income is distributed among the population and why.

The HDR, 1999 noted that uneven globalization is bringing not only integration but also fragmentation – dividing communities and nations into caste/class/regional identities, of which some are integrated and others are excluded giving rise to growing demands for an increase in their share of benefits, opportunities and power. The report noted that social tensions and conflicts are ignited when there are extremes of inequality between the marginal and the powerful. Recent studies show inequality rising in most OECD countries during the 1980s and into the early 1990s. The net worth of world's 200 richest people increased from $440 billion to more than $ 1 trillion in just the four years from 1994 to 1998. The assets of the three richest people were more than the combined GNP of 48 least developed countries (HDR, 1999: 37).

Poverty Measurements

The Human Development Report, 1997 introduced the concept of Human Poverty Index (HPI) to measure the different dimensions of poverty. It is important to remember that the concept of human poverty is much wider than the problem of its measurement. The HPI is calculated on the basis of percentage of people not expected to survive beyond the age of 40 years (P1), the percentage of adult illiterates (P2), and P3 which is calculated on the basis of percentage of people without access to safe drinking water, health services and percentage of moderately and severely underweight children under five years of age. The P3 is calculated by taking an average of all the three:

$$HPI - I = [1/3\ (P1 + P2 + P3\ ]1/3$$

The problem is that data in respect of these indicators is not easily available and that the definitions of undernourishment and access to health services continue to change. For example, the claim that a health centre is available within a distance of a kilometre or within easy reach do not necessarily indicate access to proper medical care. The same is true for the doctor-population ratio. The magnitude and extent of poverty in a country depend on several factors but economists are concerned with – the average level of national income and the degree of inequality in its distribution. During the 1970s, as interest in problems of poverty increased, development experts devised a series of concepts of poverty and developed elaborate techniques to measure its magnitude within and across countries by attempting to establish a common poverty line. They went even further and devised the concept of absolute poverty. It is meant to represent a specific minimum level of income needed to satisfy the basic physical needs of food, clothing, and shelter in order to ensure continued survival. Despite the efforts the estimates of world poverty are only estimates. The central concern today is to see whether poverty howsoever defined is increasing or declining.

Continuation of Absolute Poverty: Its Economic and Human Dimensions

Human poverty calculated in terms of HPI revealed that HPI ranges from 3 per cent in Trinidad to 62 per cent in Niger according to HDR 1998. The HPI was more than 50 per cent in Mali, Ethiopia, Sierra Leone, Burkina Faso and Niger despite various efforts at development and in 32 countries it was around 33 per cent. Unemployment among youth aged 15-24 was 32 per cent among women and 22 per cent among men in France, 39 and 30 per cent in Italy and 49 and 36 per cent in Spain (HDR, 1998: 26-27). More than 100 million people are homeless in rich countries.

In 1989, almost 1.25 billion people, or 23 per cent of the world population, were living in absolute poverty. In 2000 the number of poor people in the world has increased to 33 per cent or around 1.9 billion people. In terms of the proportion of Third World populations, the absolute poor comprised almost one out of every three persons.

Low Levels of Productivity

Development projects highlight the relatively low levels of labour productivity in the developing countries. This is generally explained in terms of a number of basic economic concepts as explained in subsequent paragraphs.

High Rates of Population Growth and Dependency Burdens

Of the world's population of approximately 5.7 billion people in 1997, about 4.5 billion live in developing countries. The total fertility rate in case of the least developed countries was 6.6 per cent as compared to 5 per cent in all developing countries, and 1.9 per cent in developed countries (HDR, 1999: 200). The average annual population growth rate was 2.5 per cent in the case of the least developed countries compared to 2 per cent in all developing countries and 0.6 per cent in developed countries. In South Asia, the total fertility rate is 3.3 per cent. The dependency ratio is 84.8 in the case of the least developed countries compared to 62.5 in all developing countries and 49.7 in developed countries. In South Asia it is 68.1.

Death rates (the yearly number of deaths per 1,000 population) in materially poor countries, because of improved health conditions and the control of major infectious diseases, as a result of economic development during the past fifty years, have declined substantially. As a result, the average rate of population growth is much higher compared to the population growth of 0.6 per cent per year in the industrialized world. A major implication of high birth rates is that children under the age of 15 comprise almost 40 per cent of the total population in these countries, as opposed to less than 21 per cent of the total population in the developed countries. Thus, in most developing countries, the active labour force has to support proportionally almost twice as many children as it does in richer countries. The problem has been created by a steep reduction in the death rate in recent years, while the efforts to control the birth rate failed despite the development projects aimed at achieving the same.

Indicators of Social Change

Myrdal (1968) in his classic study of development in several developing countries noted, that economic growth has not helped the poor segment of the population within nations. It was then proposed that the future thrust of development projects should focus on improving the accessibility of common person in the economic development programmes. The key indicators for such an approach were improvement in health, education and employment of people in general with particular emphasis on vulnerable groups such as minority population groups, women and other socially deprived groups.

Health

The well known indicators of health status are life expectancy at birth, child mortality rates, female mortality rates, births attended by trained manpower, nutritional status, immunization coverage etc. In the least developed countries of the world, life expectancy in 1997 averaged only 51.7 years, compared to 64.4 years in case of all developing countries and 77.7 years in developed nations. In sub-Saharan Africa, it is only 48.9 years. Infants mortality rates (the number of children who die before their first birthday out of every 1,000 live births) average about 104 in the least developed countries, compared with 64 in all developing countries and 6 in developed countries in 1997 (HDR, 1999: 171).

In the mid-1970s, more than 1 billion people, almost half the population of the developing world (excluding China), were living on diets deficient in essential calories. In both Asia and Africa, over 60 per cent of the population barely met minimum caloric requirements necessary to maintain adequate health. Moreover, it has been estimated that this caloric deficit amounted to less than 2 per cent of the world cereal production. Malnutrition therefore is not due to an imbalance between population and food supplies, it is more due to inequality in world income distribution. Thus, malnutrition and poor health in the developing world are more a matter of unequal distribution than of food production. Nearly one-third of the world population were without access to health services, 1.33 billion did not have access to safe drinking water, 2.25 billion (more than half the world population) lived without sanitation facilities. Nearly 180 million children under age 5 were malnourished. The percentage for under weight children in all developing countries was 18 per cent compared to 22 per cent in least developed countries and 6 in developed countries.

According to Human Development Report (1999), 28 per cent of the population in all developing countries, 41 per cent in least developed countries, 50 per cent in sub-Saharan Africa did not have access to safe drinking water. The figure for lack of sanitation facilities is given as 57, 63 and 56 per cent for the same regions, and the figure for underweight children is given as 31, 40 and 32 per cent.

The importance of access to clean drinking water, which is one of the most important measures of health, cannot be overemphasized. Market-friendly development efforts have been promoting the sale of safe drinking water, soft drinks and alcohol pouches in these places to combat water-borne diseases, responsible for more than 35 per cent of the deaths of young children in Africa, Asia and Latin America. Cigarette consumption with 1970-72 = 100 as base, had become 160 per adult in case of all developing countries and 156 in case of least developed countries (HDR, 1999: 175). In the case of developed countries it is 88 and in South Asia 134.

The data reveal that in 1997, the number of doctors per 100,000 people averaged only 14 in the least developed countries, compared with 253 in the developed countries. Most of the medical facilities in developing nations are concentrated in urban areas where only 25 per cent of the population resides. In Bolivia, only one-third of the population lives in cities, but 90 per cent of the health facilities are found there.

Education

Access to quality education is considered an important aspect of social development in the developing nations. Literacy levels are taken as an indicator along with enrolment at schools particularly female enrolment. For example, among the least developed countries, literacy rates average only 44.7 per cent of the population in 1997. The corresponding rates for all developing countries and the developed countries are approximately 64 per cent and 99 per cent, respectively. Currently, it is estimated that more than 300 million children have dropped out of primary and secondary schools, and of the estimated 1 billion illiterate adults, more than 60 per cent are women. However, the quality of education of children who do attend school regularly and its relevance has not received due attention. Further, the impact of education particularly in the rural areas and among the women remains grossly under-researched.

Access to Employment

Development specialists indicate that the labour force in the developing countries is underutilized on account of underemployment – people, both rural and urban, working less than they could (daily, weekly, or seasonally), and unemployment – people who are able and willing to work but are unable to join the labour force. Many experts have suggested better education facilities for promoting proper utilization of labour force. Unemployment among young people aged 15 to 24, many of whom are educated, is estimated to be typically almost twice as high as the overall average. When the underemployed are added to the openly unemployed and when 'discouraged workers' – those who have given up looking for a job – are added in, almost 35 per cent of the combined urban and rural labour force in developing nations is estimated to be not utilized or under-utilized. World Bank experts now admit that the economic growth is not helping in the growth of employment.

Political Development

Political development aims at creating a system of distribution of power to take collective decisions which has implication for the society as a whole and to enforce them, through a transparent, participatory and legitimate process. The legitimacy here means that people in general have participated in expressing their opinion about who should govern and how. In other words a system of democratic institutions is put in place, which is sustainable and functional. Many developing countries including India, Pakistan and Bangladesh continue to face enormous problems in sustaining a democratic system of governance. Despite economic development, the process of state formation frequently gets off the track. Frequent change of constitutions and use of violence to capture power continue to take place under the very nose of the United Nations. The problem has become more pronounced with the growing awareness of the link between political power and economic growth, after the colonial rule in many of these countries came to an end. This is not to suggest that colonial rule was more democratic and the system of governance more peaceful or egalitarian, but to suggest that the colonial rule has unleashed a process of change to generate conflicts in these societies. The territories, which were fragmented before the colonial rule and later came to be called nation states, are trying to come to terms with their new found freedom. The current state of these societies is best summed up by title of a book, *New Nations and Old Societies*.

The first stage in the process of political development is to define the relationship between the state and the people and between people. The product is called the constitution of the country which specifies the rules of conduct for all the stakeholders and set up institutions for governance and delivering justice. The problem is that it is easy to debate and evolve a constitution but it is extremely difficult to translate the provision of ensuring equality, liberty and justice on the ground. Most political systems have failed to survive, since the process of defining the claims of different stakeholders in a society is a never ending process, particularly in the context of expanding economic choices.

The process of developing a constitution is a good indicator of political development in a country. The process of making subsequent changes in it is more important than the constitution itself, because only this provision can save the original document. For example, the constitution has survived in India as the provision to make changes rest with a collective body, unlike the provision in Pakistan, where the power rests with an individual. The other indicator of political development is, how frequently the transfer of power takes place according to the constitutional provisions. The political stability of a state is of prime importance in the development process. The degree of trust that other states and international financial institutions and the big corporations repose in a country, depends on how stable a state is. The final indicator of political development is how well the people in general participate in the political process of state formation. There are several indicators for measuring this, the most important being a free press and an environment of transparency. It raises several other crucial issues about the role of the state in the political development. The issue has become centre-stage as there are frequent examples of the process of state formation getting distorted, after nearly 50 years of experiments in different countries, underlining the fragility of political development.

It would therefore be interesting to analyze the level of political development in the countries under review and its implication for their future economic and social development. Has the constitution and the institutions and principles it originally devised survived and how well have the people participated in the political process? How effective the state has been in providing good governance and a fair deal to the common man? These issues are likely to influence the future development debates in these societies.

Prescriptions for Change

Theorists of the 1950s and early 1960s viewed the process of development as a series of successive stages of economic growth through which all countries must pass. It was primarily an economic theory of development in which the right quantity and mixture of savings, investment, and foreign aid were all that was necessary to enable a developing country to proceed along an economic growth path that historically had been followed by the more developed countries. Development thus became synonymous with rapid, aggregate economic growth. This linear-stages approach was largely replaced in the 1970s by two competing schools of thought. The first, which focused on theories and patterns of structural change, and the second, focusing on international linkages of development. It viewed underdevelopment in terms of international and domestic power relationships. Emphasis was placed on the need for new policies to eradicate poverty, to provide more diversified employment opportunities, and to reduce income inequalities. It did not work, as the income inequality within and between nations grew further. The continued failure of development efforts lead to another revolution in economic thought which emphasized the beneficial role of free markets, open economies, and the privatization of inefficient and wasteful public enterprises. Failure to develop, according to this theory, is not due to exploitative external and internal forces as expounded by dependence theorists. Rather, it is primarily the result of too much government intervention and regulation of the economy. Disenchantment with traditional neoclassical models of economic growth intensified during the late 1980s and early 1990s as the debt crisis escalated and it became increasingly clear that traditional theory was at a loss to explain the dramatic disparities in economic performance across countries.

The early naive illusions of development as an endeavour in social engineering towards a brave new world are still there. It is now being propagated that economic progress is an essential component, but it is not the only component. The new slogan is development is not purely an economic phenomenon. Development should therefore be perceived as a multi-dimensional process involving the reorganization and reorientation of entire economic and social systems. It would be interesting to see what has been done and can be done to put this new perspective in the countries under review. India, Pakistan and Bangladesh under the guidance of international financial institutions are still experimenting with different models. It typically involves radical changes in institutional, social, and administrative structures as well as in popular attitudes and, in many cases, even customs and beliefs.

Development and Environment

An important aspect of social development is to ensure that economic development in particular do not compromise the general ecological balance. The ecology refers to the respective share of different living and non-living elements on earth. The protection of the environment is an essential part of development and without adequate environmental protection, development is undermined. During the past two decades this awareness has grown. It has been suggested that poverty and environmental degradation is caused by greed. Excessive material consumption may lead to a self-perpetuating process whereby, communities may inadvertently destroy or exhaust the resources, needed for their survival. Pressures on environmental resources can have severe consequences for self-sufficiency and peaceful co-existence. Environmental degradation can also result in severe health hazards and may impose high costs.

Damage to soil, water supplies, and forests resulting from unsustainable methods of production would greatly reduce the chances of long-term national productivity. Rapid population growth and expanding consumption of natural resources are likely to do extensive environmental damage.

Development economists have adopted the term sustainability in an attempt to clarify the desired balance between economic growth on the one hand and environmental preservation on the other. Although there are many definitions, sustainability basically refers to "meeting the needs of the present generation without compromising the needs of future generations". Implicit in this statement is the fact that future growth and overall quality of life are critically dependent on the quality of the environment. The natural resource base of a country and the quality of its air, water, and land represent a common heritage for all generations. To destroy that endowment indiscriminately in the pursuit of short-term economic goals penalizes both present and, especially, future generations.

It would be important to see how attempts at social development are looking at these issues in India, Pakistan and Bangladesh.

2

The Politics of Modernization and Development

The history of a small area, where development efforts were carried on covering nearly hundred years, by two distinct forms of state, colonial and indigenous, is used here to argue:

(a) 'Development' is a vague term.

(b) The relationship assumed between economic change and social change in a society is neither uniform in nature nor very specific.

(c) Development projects conceived primarily in terms of economic development, are never able to accomplish what they claim.

(d) Finally, it is an effective strategy to control the poor and legitimize the elite.

Divi Seema, a cyclone-prone area, is located on the east coast of India. Canal irrigation was introduced into Divi Seema in 1907. As a result of improved irrigation, big landowners came from the mainland and took over the land as absentee landlords pushing the previous dryland cultivators towards the coast. Between 1907 and 1937, the irrigation system was extended, further marginalizing the indigenous inhabitants and pushing them into the dangerous coastal strip where only fishermen had lived previously. Mangrove forests had once protected the coastal strip, acting as windbreaks to cyclones and a deceleration zone for the storm surges accentuated by the delta's extensive offshore shallows. By the mid-1930s most of the mangroves had been cut down and by the early 1940s overpopulation of the coastal strip had led to their total destruction. The British, aware of the increasing physical threats of cyclones and flooding on the expanding population, and seeing the problem in terms of physical safety, built the first coastal earthen bund in the late 1930s to protect property and save the repetitive costs of replacing infrastructure. At the same time, they built embankments on both sides of the river Krishna together with land drainage and associated works. None of these works, however, prevented the low-lying areas from periodic waterlogging.

In the late 1950s, the state government, in accordance with the government of India's First and Second Five-Year Plans (1947-60), set up Primary Agricultural Cooperative Societies and transferred 20,000 acres of government land in the coastal strip to fishermen, cultivators and landless labourers. However, by the mid-1960s the land had been taken over by big landlords, as the intended beneficiaries could not get credit from the banks for land development and the big landlords and their allies had appropriated the agricultural inputs. They working closely together with the merchants and traders, control the agrarian economy of Divi Seema. They have connections with local politicians, irrigation engineers and banking officials, ensuring that nearly all government resources go to them. The two most important resources are water supply, and credit. Very little development was carried out in Divi Seema after the collapse of the co-operatives and it remained cut off during the rainy seasons, retaining its reputation as a wild place populated by undisciplined people (Winchester, 2000).

Between 1907 and 1977 the population of Divi Seema doubled. The uneven distribution of economic resources principally in the form of landownership continues. Ninety per cent of the population is dependent for their staple food and employment on a handful of large landowners. The banks lent only to those who owned land or other major assets as collateral and tended to write off loans at election times – a practice that is widespread all over India, but irrelevant to the poor (who have no bank loans). The poor had no choice but to continue to go to the moneylenders (mainly the big landlords, shopkeepers and traders), whose exorbitant rates kept most of them in debt for life. The informal market had many other destructive features; one being the system of interlocked contracts, in which lenders set conditions on the borrowers to provide their labour and/or produce at disadvantageous terms to the borrowers; another was the arrangement whereby those with rice surpluses offered rice loans preceding the harvest on condition that they were repaid immediately after harvest at the rate of two bags for one (ibid).

In 1977, aquaculture (prawn and fish farming) was introduced in Divi Seema, into areas previously under rice cultivation. To make use of poor-quality agricultural land the government promoted aquaculture in the late 1980s and encouraged banks to give larger loans for aquaculture than for rice cultivation. As a consequence, the area under agricultural cultivation in Divi Seema has decreased by more than 80 per cent, while the number of landless labourers increased by more than 50 per cent. Rice production thus went down with a commensurate decline in agricultural employment. This resulted in migration to other dangerous coastal areas land for grazing became scarce and affected the animal husbandry – as a supplementary occupation for agricultural labourers (ibid). The flora of the area was destroyed during the period as well, the coastal strip is now fully exposed to wind damage and flooding. Half the area is now permanently under water, and may lead to spread of water-borne diseases. In mid 1990s a disease almost destroyed the fish and prawn stocks, the worst affected again were the poor. Winchester, then goes on to document the role played by NGOs in Divi Seema. The NGOs attempted to establish self-help groups to provide loans and other subsidised agriculture inputs, health care and education. He concludes that despite the intention, the NGOs failed to organize the villagers and the entire programme collapsed as soon as the NGOs withdrew. The result was no different than the collapse of government programmes in an area as soon as the collector or any other senior officer managing the programme is transferred.

To cut a long story short, Winchester concluded that

successive efforts at development failed to bring about any significant change either in the economic or the political situation of the poor.

The Myth of 'Development'

The central concern in the formulation of 'development' is to promote economic development, to improve the general availability of economic resources for meeting human needs. The process is expected to initiate a change in the social structure and attitudes posing hurdles in bringing greater economic progress. The process of development attempts to modernize the 'traditional', 'primitive', 'underdeveloped' societies.

The central thesis of 'development' is that social change occurs according to a pre-established pattern, the logic and direction of which are known. Social science has been viewed as the science to provide the logic, direction, and technology of social change. Immense resources have been spent and continue to be spent on both theory building and project management of development. The myth of the modernization continues since the human societies in recent times have undergone rapid transformations such as the rise of the nation state, industrialization, urbanization, secularization, bureaucratization, rapid expansion of human knowledge, though these transformations have been unequally distributed in different societies. The difficulty lies in assuming that these transformations have modernized the human societies and that any of these transformations can be replicated and in turn will lead to similar results in all societies. The theory construction to explain 'modernization' albeit 'development', poses serious problems since the very concept theoretically is untenable. A variety of development models are an indicator of the problem one faces in the universal application of these models. Further, the economic theory can hardly be expected to change social attitudes, norms or institutional arrangements in society.

There could only be two possible explanations, for the popularity of the development agenda despite the severe criticism it has evoked in recent history. Firstly, the elite is still optimistic beyond doubt that the modern technology would help in resolving both the economic and the social problems and secondly, they know that to generate hope is to continue to posses the power of defining and dominating. The characteristic of 'modern' Europe and in particular of England, Smith argued, is that liberty and security are to be extended to the poor and the landless, and for providing this the state must be empowered. The liberty was defined as the liberty to live as per the 'guidelines' provided by the state. The liberty meant to work for wages, act as obedient citizens and to continue to be governed peacefully. The power of the dominant takes over in the interest of promoting the commerce and making the poor civilized. The process once initiated to define the poor in England is thus extended to still other poor globally. In doing so the well-meaning elite not only benefits in economic terms, it acquires the legitimacy to govern as well. The similarity of the development project in the post-independent India and other newly emerging nation states in the middle of the present century, therefore, was highly predictable. As was the response of the new ruling elite in these nations, who were the logical links to the colonial past. The preference for promoting industry and commerce by Nehru as against the Gandhian dream of a rural India was thus only a logical extension of the dominance of the 'modern' European over the subaltern.

The Myth of 'Modernization'

Tipps (1973) in his critique of modernization theory noted that the popularity of the notion of modernization must be sought not in its clarity and precision as a vehicle of scholarly communication, but rather in its ability to evoke vague and generalized images which serve to summarize all the transformations of social life in the wake of the rise of industrialization and the nation-state in the late eighteenth and nineteenth centuries. He traces the origins of modernization theory to the international setting of post-second world war era, in particular, the impact of the cold war and the emergence of Third World societies. In the US at that point of time substantial intellectual interest and resources were invested to study the newly emerging nation-states in Asia, Africa and Latin America. At that point of time very little was known about the socio-economic institutions of these societies. It was, however, very important for the justification of the American system of liberal democracy that these nations accept the notion of democracy, and progress as was the case in the west. The social sciences were used as a vehicle to study, diagnose and prescribe models for development of these societies. The motivation for promoting development, first economic then social was not difficult to understand. As Rothschild noted, social development was not inimical to but rather a condition for the development of commerce (Rothschild, 1996:332). An argument which in the twentieth century was to become the logic of welfare state in Europe and for developmental projects in the 'less developed' nations.

The manner in which economic theorists tend to approach the agenda of change in non-western societies is deeply rooted in the notion of development, which was a product of western social science. This western thinking about social change has persisted from the pre-Socrates through eighteenth and nineteenth centuries of progress and social evolution to contemporary social science. The concept of development embodies a wide range of substantive interests and definitional varieties, yet the critique of development should focus on the development as an idea system *per se*, rather than attempting a piecemeal analysis of one or the other version of development. The unit of analysis is the national territorial state which is of critical significance, even though the assumption is largely implicit.

Tipps, in his critique of modernization, begins by dividing the theories of modernization in two categories. The critical variable theories of modernization which equate modernization with a single type of social change, e.g., industrialization, or rationalization. The second set of theories of modernization he categorizes as dichotomous theories, which explain modernization in the context of tradition or as opposed to traditional. The development then becomes a series of transformations from primitive, subsistence economies to technology-intensive, industrialized economies. From feudal state to democratic state, from ascriptive systems to achievement oriented systems, from religion to secularism and from joint or extended to nuclear family system oriented etc. Tipps argues that in critical variable theories of modernization the term modernization is being used as synonym for already relatively well established terms and as such performs no useful function and hence should be abandoned. It is sociologically more appropriate to say that the society is undergoing a process of industrialization rather than modernization.

In Divi Seema, economic growth or other development inputs including transfer of resources failed to produce any significant social change either in the structure of family or in the structure of economy or in the political power sharing in the society. Within the family, the family hierarchy has remained unchanged, including the gender relations. The caste hierarchy similarly has remained intact. The efforts at change in Divi Seema are economic in nature and as such can at best be described as economic changes. The economic change may or may not result in other changes. A rise in income of the household may not result in a change in the family hierarchy. Further, the scope of economic change may remain confined to some groups and not the entire society, as is generally the case in India, Pakistan and Bangladesh where economic benefits have not reached the poorer sections of the population, despite an effort made in that direction, both by government and by NGOs.

Tipps pursues his critique of dichotomous variety of modernization theories at three levels, the ideological, the empirical and the methodological or meta-theoretical. The ideological critique begins with the often-quoted argument of, it being the product of an essentially ethnocentric world view, and rooted in the self-confidence of ethnocentric achievement of the western countries. The terminology of the contemporary discourses on modernization depicts an improvement, as reflected in the use of the term modernity rather than civilization, and tradition rather than barbarism. Yet, it continues to evaluate the progress of nations, by their proximity to the institutions and values of western, and particularly Anglo-American societies. In other words, 'modern' refers to conformity with western values, without the onus of dependence on the West.

Combining strains of rationalism, progressivism and liberalism modernization becomes a liberal utopia rather than an analytical construct. This utopia does not concern itself with the ambivalence toward modern industrial societies exhibited by Marx, Weber, Durkheim earlier as theorists and Gandhi more recently as one concerned with the culture of common people. People in general either rich or an ordinary fisherman or labourer in Divi Seema are generally happy being religious, and have so far not felt the need of a change in social arrangements such as marriage and family, despite the change in the economy of the area. This is true of the entire society in India, Pakistan and Bangladesh. However, as Tipps pointed out, even though the modernization may be absolved of the charges of American or western expansionism, the limited cultural horizons of the theory, appear to be a subtle form of cultural imperialism, an imperialism of values which superimposes American or more broadly western cultural choices upon other societies, as is the tendency to subordinate all other considerations to the technical requirements of economic development (Tipps, 1973). The notion of modernization postulates that the selection of the spouse is an individual right, whereas in Divi Seema it is still considered to be the right of the family. Further, the marriage is also not seen as a one to one relationship, it has more wide-ranging social implications involving not only the families concerned but also the community at large. Community sanction of marriage is essential. A slightly indigenous model of 'modernization' or development in Divi Seema may mean marriage at a slightly older age, to ensure better health for women and balancing the power relations within the family but without promoting individualism. Even this limited change remains largely a distant goal and a utopia.

Tipps asserts that there is in principle no reason to assume that the notion of modernization itself is inherently incompatible with a variety of ethnocentrism or that a revolutionary or socialist version of modernization theory could not be developed. Even if one rejects the idea of western version of modernization and substitutes it with an alternative version, it would be no less subject to these or other ideological distortions. In other words the myth of development or modernization as a critique can be applied to all varieties of development theories and models.

The critique at the empirical level begins with the difficulty of explaining the change on account of 'western impact'. Any theoretical framework which ignores other variables such as the impact of war, conquest, colonial domination, international political and military relationships or international trade and cross-national flow of capital, etc., cannot hope to explain either the origins of these societies or the nature of their future struggles or problems. Other difficulties are raised by the notion of traditional society, as modernity and tradition are essentially asymmetrical concepts. Moreover traditional societies also do not conform to a homogeneous category. Diversity may be found within as well as between traditional societies. The dichotomous approach by ignoring this diversity which contributes to the determination of the specific character of their development, as illustrated by alternative courses of economic change in China and Japan. The emergence of a hybrid society which is neither 'traditional' nor 'modern' or which is economically poor or rich, nor agricultural or industrial in nature, also create difficulties, though the usual explanation is a transitional phase between 'tradition' and 'modernity'. However, the transitional stage as an explanation cannot hold ground when the process endured for a number of generations. And finally the proposition that tradition and modernity represent two mutually exclusive, functionally inter dependent clusters of attributes. Or more specifically as Tipps argues to assert that attributes of tradition and modernity are not mutually exclusive. To assume so is to impose an imperialism of categories. Once it is conceded that tradition and modernity are not mutually exclusive and the first is not a precondition for the other, then the assertion that each constitutes a closed, functionally interdependent system of attributes, also becomes suspect. Use of modern economic technology may fail to produce modernity as such. Traditional may be rational and may facilitate change as well. Modern medicine, the transistor and television and a modern bureaucracy are all modern traits, however whether or not such modernization implies eventual modernity is problematic. Rapid social change in one sphere may serve only to inhibit change in others. And as Whitacker argued if modernization is not an-all-or-nothing process, i.e., if it does not either displace tradition or fail, then it nullify the supposed significance of the terms, namely that they identify distinguishable classes of societies (Whitacker, 1967: 190-2).

To sum up his argument he takes up the critique at the methodological or meta theoretical level. He refers to the tension between the logical requirements of comparability and those of explanation, i.e., the concern for extending the applicability of the concept to large number of cases and to increase specificity to enhance its power of discrimination. These difficulties are evident in accepting modernization as a theory. Such conceptualizations that technical, economic and ecological changes ramify through the whole social and cultural fabric, stretch the limit of applicability too wide and other concepts like modernization is a multifaceted process involving changes in all areas make possibility of a theoretical construct impossible. It is the tendency to mistake concept for a fact that Tipps concludes to be the central problem which is characteristic of all developmental theories of change. He concludes that the real and imaginary create difficulties for the social sciences. The history of social sciences remains a continuous struggle to attempt to order reality analytically through the construction of concepts and looking for universal theories to explain human behaviour without much success since it cannot acquire the scientific rigour of physical sciences as humans are self programming and unpredictable.

Tipps, suggests to continue the efforts of comparative studies to develop an alternative paradigm (Tipps, 1973: 224). Pieterse (1992), on the other hand, noted that comparative method served as an adjunct to evolutionism, and that cross-cultural comparisons had never been culturally neutral, by implication to hope for anything better is simply put fragile optimism.

As Pieterse pointed out developmentalism is the truth from the point of view of the centre of power; it is the theorization (or rather ideologization) of its own path of development, and the comparative method elaborate this perspective. He further noted that the dispute in western social science has not been between developmentalism and an alternative but between different strands of developmentalist thought, such as liberal and radical, and now between market friendly and people-centred. Development is conceived in primarily economic terms whereas modernization is more concerned with eighteenth century's political rationalism.

There has been a crisis of universalism because, since the end of 1970s, the trans-cultural nature of concepts derived from western discourse is increasingly becoming doubtful and hence rejected. Comparative analysis cannot lead to a causal relationship it can only be interpretative. Thus, the prioritization of economic development in development and modernization thinking assumes that economic factors are equally important everywhere and that the relationship between economics and politics will show a similar pattern everywhere. However, the myth of a grand theory combining economic and political has come in for a severe attack from different quarters. Thus neither universalism, nor relativism provides adequate answers (ibid).

The Myth of 'Economic Redistribution'

A major concern in the development projects has been in achieving some measure of redistribution of economic wealth and power relations in a society as we noted earlier. As earlier models of economic development failed to deliver, various modifications in the models were attempted. Terms were changed from economic development to social development, sustainable development, development with a human face and so on. Reviewing the development experiences of last five decades, therefore, as Streeten (1995:333) observed, the change in the thinking about development appears like a comedy of errors, a lurching from one fad to another.

The development thinking started in 1950s, influenced by Arthur Lewis (1955) and others who prescribed economic growth as the key to poverty eradication and development of all aspects of society. It is significant to note that in 1950 development was defined as widening choices by Arthur Lewis and in 1999 by Human Development Report. The key ideas in 1950 were that the growth would spread through the market forces and the state would provide social services and undertake other programmes to push the growth downwards, however the fate of the poor should not be a matter of concern during the initial stages of development. Some planning experts have very categorically argued that the poorest 20 per cent were beyond the reach of economic growth. It is again interesting to note that Lewis right in the beginning has tried to keep the economic growth functions out of the purview of the state, while in actual practice in many nations particularly in India, state did play a major part in promoting economic growth. Secondly, many scholars have anticipated the limits to growth and its implications for the poor. As has been discovered in hindsight, so far no model to redistribute the benefits of growth has succeeded. The disparities as the data continue to show have increased between the rich and the poor both within a nation and between nations.

As an illustration, the per capita income gap between rich and poor nations, in 1997, Luxembourg had a per capita income of $28,010 compared to Sierra Leone with a per capita income of $159. The least developed countries have an average of $245 per capita as compared to $908 in case of all developing countries and $17,618 in the developed countries (HDR, 1999: 55-58). In other words a person in Luxembourg had more than 176 times the per capita income of one of the world's poorest countries, Sierra Leon, and more than 60 times that of one of the world's largest nations, India. There are similarly significant gaps between per-capita income between rich and the poor in the same country.

Gunnar Myrdal (1968) noted that the growth did not trickle down and that the concept of employment and unemployment were very different in Asia when applied to self employed subsistence farmers, landless labourers, artisans, traders, educated young people, saffron clad monks, beggars, caste conscious Brahmins, or women. Nutrition, health and education were identified as important factors in promoting better labour utilization, and providing opportunities for the common man to participate in the economic growth process. But, as Streeten noted, we do not have any model for meeting adequate standards of nutrition, health and education. It is not known precisely which financial, fiscal and human resources and policies produce these desirable results (Streeten, 1995:340).

The efforts to provide an equal opportunity to people for participating in economic development has by and large failed and irrelevance of egalitarianism and redistribution efforts were exposed. Having conceded the fact that economic gains of poor cannot be substantial, basic needs was the next logical step in development thinking. The basic needs approach also called for participatory community involvement and non-governmental efforts in designing and implementing the development projects. The projection of minimum help and community participation appealed to members of the national and international community and therefore succeeded in mobilizing resources. (ibid:342). Human development and sustainable development followed and continue to be the latest key words in the development thinking. These slogans and change of shifts more than anything else prove the point, a large segment of population in many developing countries remain outside the scope of main stream economic development process.

In Divi Seema, several development strategies, transfer of resources, credit, change in economic activity, inputs in health and education, etc., did not result in any meaningful change in the lives of the poor.

The Myth of 'Democracy and Social Responsibility'

The modern national state was conceived as an important organ of a democratic society and was expected to carry out the following tasks: (a) expand the political participation of different segments of population, (b) to direct the process of economic development to benefit all segments of society, and (c) to lay down rules for conflict resolution to lead to good governance. Accordingly, the second important objective of the development projects initiated was the redistribution of power to empower the common man and in particular weaker sections, who have so far never experienced power, including women. Democracy, as practised in western society, was seen as the only political system, to accomplish this change and in the process enhance the freedom of individual political action.

The process of development in a poor society begins by allocating enormous resources at the discretion of the state and the process of political development becomes a struggle with no-holds-barred to wrest the control of the state. As Rajni pointed out, the pristine formulation of state takes the form of a competitive play of interests in a free market. The characteristics of the poor society such as illiteracy, primordial loyalties of religion, caste and region, and above all concentration of economic resources make the war multidimensional in nature. The result is as Nandi (2000) pointed out, the state created to serve the society starts dominating it. A classical Third World syndrome is an opulent state amid teeming penury. The process of political development degenerates into a process of defining and redefining the rights of common man which no state or other institutions of society are able to deliver in actual practice. As Lerner (1958) pointed out way back in 1958 that the new states make haste in celebrating a revolution of expectations and possibilities, which only become a revolution of frustration. The process ends up generating tensions conflict and problems of law and order rather than empowering the common man.

The logic of change and openness is still very powerful. The new nations are under pressure to keep the pretense of democratic process going and the entire emphasis is on holding referendums and elections to legitimize governments. This process of keeping the civil rights intact brings about some changes. The grassroots consultations no matter how far spaced do result in some awareness of the nature of political power and its uses and abuses among a wider section of society. This awareness throws up a number of contenders and is capable of shift in power base. For example it can end the domination of higher caste and open up more space for other castes. The real power, however, continues to circulate among the economically powerful groups in different caste groups. The concern for the poor is kept in place by continuing the pretence of not violating cultural norms prevalent among different religious, caste or regional groups while making public policies. The original concern of redistribution of power is limited to incorporating elite from all segments of society.

The ruling elite identifies a domain outside the state institutions for infusing transparency and social justice. This is made possible through the activities and calculations of a proliferation of independent agents including philanthropists, doctors, hygienists, managers, planners, parents and social workers. The creation of the disciplinary institutions such as police and judiciary was accompanied by a variety of projects by lawyers, doctors, social workers and other experts, who claim to know how to direct business activity, family life and personal morality onto the path of virtue (Rose and Miller, 1992:181).

It is ironical that from overpopulation, poverty, the problem of illiteracy, health, housing, urban unrest, militancy, failures of productivity, to contemporary concerns with international competitiveness, the articulation of ruling elite has been concerned with the constant identification of the difficulties and failures of accomplishing the desired objectives. It is around these difficulties and failures that future programmes of development have been elaborated. Projects are not simply formulations of wishes or intentions, they lay claim to knowledge of the sphere or problem to be addressed – knowledge of the economy, or the state of health, education or poverty of the nation. These pronouncements are essential elements that seek to invoke and exercise legitimate and calculated power over the problems and people. The theories of the social sciences; economics, sociology, psychology, management and social work thus provide a kind of intellectual forum for elite to work out procedures for rendering the problem thinkable, taming its intractable reality by subjecting it to the disciplined analyses of thought. Theories and explanation play an essential part in reversing the relations of power between the aspiring ruler and those afflicted with problem, over which rule is to be exercised. Relations of reciprocity obtain between the social sciences and elite (ibid: 182). The social sciences thrive on the problems, the demand for solutions and on the glamour of theories, which have the plausibility of science and the promise of making the social amenable to technology. The representation of the governed is a highly technical process. A huge inquiry is needed to transform events and phenomena into information – births, illnesses and deaths, marriages and divorces, levels of income, health and literacy, forms of employment and want of employment. By means of inscription reality is made stable, mobile, comparable, combinable. It is rendered in a form in which it can be debated and diagnosed. Information is not the outcome of a neutral recording function; it is a way of devising techniques to make the domain in question susceptible to evaluation, calculation and intervention. The problematic of governance and development thus complement and justify each other. In searching for solutions of the problems of people of Divi Seema, the services of a number of experts such as economists, planning experts, engineers, health experts, educators, social workers, and NGOs were used. All of them became empowered except for the people who they were supposed to empower.

3

Social Development in India

Both Mahatma Gandhi and Jawahar Lal Nehru had a dream of their own about Indian society. Gandhi was happy with the simple life of a village like Rousseau. He, therefore, felt that transforming India into an industrial society would be pointless. Nehru, on the other hand, was dreaming of building a modern industrialized society in India. Since Nehru was in a position to experiment with his dream he went ahead and put his plan into action. Gandhi lost out since he did not have the power to put his dream into action. The controversy keeps resurfacing time and again and it is still a major question of how to provide the massive rural population a share in the development, but still the path to Gandhian development is closed. There cannot be any turning back now, though many critiques have questioned Nehru's wisdom, the quest for industrialization and westernization would continue.

In 1938, a national planning committee was formed with Jawahar Lal Nehru as its chairperson. Nehru felt that it was difficult to plan anything as they had very few facts at their disposal and neither the central government nor the states took any interest in the matter. This reflects the problems in the early days when not much was known about development per se or how to go about it in practice. Nehru did not realise that it takes more than the passion of a few to change the mindset of millions of people and their material environment. As Nehru ([1946] 1981), noted the original idea behind the formation of the committee was to further the process of industrialization as it was assumed to be central to all other problems. Though he referred to the difficulty of arriving at a consensus on matters of social policy and social organization, he went ahead with what he believed in. The major differences on policy were the freedom to business houses, and urbanization versus development of villages and cottage industries. Nehruvian model in India remained for a considerable time the core of economic planning with major emphasis on industrial development along with efforts for agricultural development to obtain self-sufficiency in food production. The Gandhian notion of village development and no industrialization did not find favour with the new elite. The efforts at 'modernization' of the Indian economy were formally launched with the beginning of the first plan in 1952. To be fair to Nehru, he did realise that there was a conflict between progress and stability (Nehru, [1946] 1981: 144). He assumed that despite economic progress the general principle of collective ownership of land and other resources would be possible, a spirit of co-operation would prevail. He was aware that the industrialization resulted in more unemployment and while capital accumulated at one end, poverty and unemployment increased at the other (ibid: 404). His account of differences with Gandhi is remarkable:

> "This fact of increasing mass poverty influenced Gandhi powerfully. It is true..... that there is a fundamental difference between his outlook on life generally and what might be called the modern outlook. He is not enamoured of ever-increasing standards of living and the growth of luxury, at the cost of spiritual and moral values. He does not favour the soft life; for him the straight way is the hard way, and the love of luxury leads to crookedness and loss of virtue. Above all he is shocked, at the vast gulf that stretches between the rich and the poor, in their ways of living, and their opportunities for growth.......".

He looked back with yearning to the days of the old autonomous and more or less self-contained village community where there had been an automatic balance between production, distribution and consumption; where political or economic power was spread out and not concentrated as it is today; where a kind of simple democracy prevailed; where the gulf between the rich and the poor was not so marked; where the evil of great cities were absent and people lived in contact with the life-giving soil and breathed the pure air of the open spaces (ibid:404). It sounds like a far away romantic dream. But the fact is that many millions believe in it even now and have rejected urbanism to stay in the familiar rural locale, though the half-baked education is making its impact now, by making the younger generation restless in the rural surroundings. Yet when they go to find a place in the urban society, they find themselves at a loss to handle the new societal pressures and become misfits. They become a part of the slum society, which is neither rural nor urban in character in the true sense of the term.

Nehru, however, believed that the state would be able to usher in a socialist era where everyone would be looked after irrespective of his/her caste, class or religious affiliation. He did not imagine that the economic growth would cut at the roots of his dream of socialism or a principled poverty free society. He perhaps was unaware that some people had expressed doubts about the outcome of state efforts as early as 1950s. Mukerjee (1951) wrote:

> "The modern philosophy of the secular state implies an exaggerated belief not merely in the all-sufficiency of economic goods, but also in the achievement or lapse of rightness in human relationships in the fields of economics and politics, of laws and institutions, rather than in the domain of religion" (i-ii).

He pointed out that equalization of the goods of life, oblivious of the relations of means and ends, lower and higher values, and understanding equality and freedom only from the economic and political view points was pointless. He never favoured the modernist approach, as he believed the task was to seek a renewal of, rather than a break with the past.

However, to be fair to Nehru there were other sociologists, economists and intellectuals in general, who welcomed the economic approach to development through industrialization and in particular the role of the state and the planning. Only some have expressed concern about the problem of "organization of values in the process of their evolution". D.P. Mukerji (1958) felt that enough attention has not been given by the planners to outlining clearly the nature of 'a new social order' and 'a new man', which in other words means that he believed in the possibility of reconstruction, though he thought more needs to be done. The 'modern' images, the luxury and affluence, the tall buildings, sleek cars, metal roads, the English-speaking elite, the sophistication of Oxford and Cambridge, Nehru has seen in the British society, were too powerful to allow him to opt for a dark and muddy though fresh and green villages in India. In fairness to Nehru it must be acknowledged that anyone, who either then or now would have opted to live in a village leaving the city life would have been termed an eccentric, as Verrier Elwin was described since he chose to live with the tribals (Elwin, 1998: 100). Though as Elwin commented, it is not eccentric to live in a beautiful place in the hills among some of the most charming people in the country, even though they may be ignorant and poor. It is only a different perspective from the one people generally look at things. The fact, however, remains that even the pre-colonial image of feudal agricultural society of India was not as romantic as it is made out to be. The oppressive feudal society was as coercive as the modern state in many ways and to find the kind of village virtues Gandhi has in mind one would have to go back to Rousseau's savage man. This in fact has been the central problem in viewing, the past, present and the future, the difficulty to separate the real from the ideal. There was a wide gulf between the grassroots perception and the elite perception of what constituted the good life and the means to construct it. In retrospect the choice of the political structure to a great extent determined the nature and response of the elite to accommodate the 'other'. The political structure gave the state the monopoly to define development in purely economic terms, but the democratic compulsions lead to the inclusion of access to education and health for all in the agenda of development.

In taking a look at the development process during the past fifty years it is not difficult to define what went wrong with it and consequently to offer any alternative suggestions. This process goes on to keep the project development going. It may be more relevant to capture the essence of what happened and what can happen. To put it simply we are as ill equipped today as we were in 1950s to construct the future. Any attempt to reconstruct the future, therefore, remains beset with problems.

The Size of the Problem

The population of India crossed the one billion mark on 11th May, 2000. The provisional population figure of India as on March 1, 1991 was 846 million. The vast population of the country, its ignorance and poverty, and a tendency to recreate at a very fast rate, created the biggest problem for the vision that Nehru had for transforming it into a 'modern' nation. Nehru and his team of planners were hopeful of extending the social services such as education and health to the millions who in the mid fifties has hardly any access to these. They had hoped that this would also help in controlling the growth rate of the population. However, their expectations failed as the efforts lead to a steep fall in the death rate but not accompanied by a similar fall in the birth rate. This simply resulted in the growth rate becoming higher instead of declining. Even the current efforts have not been able to fully check the growth rate since the level of socio-economic well-being which can lead to the spontaneous acceptance of the small family norm for the common masses remains a distant dream. The growth and decline of population have also remained uneven throughout the country, as has been the case with other socio-economic changes. The birth rate continues to be high in states, which are termed poor and backward, the birth rate even in better off states continues to be high in rural areas compared to urban areas. It continues to be high among the poor in urban areas compared to the well off. This simple equation has lead to an increase in the gulf between the rich and the poor and the rural and urban population.

Population and its Growth

The 1991 Census of India shows that in six most populous states, accounting for 59.7 per cent of the country's population – either the growth rate has increased or declined less than one percentage point in the 1981-91 compared to the previous decade. In seven states and four union territories, roughly contributing to one-third of the population of the country, the growth rate has increased during the decade 1981-91. In all other states and union territories, the growth rate has declined during the decade 1981-91. The birth rate in general has declined from 49.2 in 1901 to 29.5 in 1991, whereas the death rate has declined from 42.6 in 1901 to 9.8 in 1991 (IOAMR, 1998:11). The annual growth rate was 1.25 which rose to 2.14 in 1991. The decadal growth rate according to census 2001 during 1991-2001 is still 1.93.

Age Structure of the Population

The population of India is young, with nearly 36.5 per cent consisting of children below 14. Thus, two out of every five persons are below 14 years. However, the proportion of children below 14 years has fallen from a level of 42 per cent in the 1971 census to 36.5 per cent by 1991. In the context of socio-economic programmes, the special feature of age distribution of population is important. A young population imposes certain constraints in terms of investment decisions relating particularly to education, nutrition and child health. Also the young age structure itself favours rapid population growth unless special measures are taken.

	1971	*1997*	*2015*
Total population, millions	620.7	966.2	1211.7
Annual population growth rate % 1975-97	2.0	–	
Urban Population	*1975*	*1997*	
As % of total	21.3	27.4	
Dependency ratio, 1997	65.0	–	
Population aged 65 and above, 1997, as % of total	4.7	–	
Total fertility rate %	*1975*	*1997*	
	5.1	3.1	
Contraceptive prevalence rate %	–	41	

Source: Human Development Report, 1999.

		2001	*1991*	*1981*	*1971*
Population	(Mn.)	1027	846	683	548
Density	(per km^2)	324	273*	230*	177
Persons per household	(No.)		5.52*	5.55*	5.46
Urban as % of total	(%)		25.7	23.3	19.9
Birth rate	(per 1,000)		32.5	37.2	41.2
Death rate	(per 1,000)		11.4	15	19.0

Source: Statistical Outline of India, 1997-98 Tata Services Limited, Department of Economics and Statistics, Mumbai, 1997.

Note: Birth rate and death rate under 1991, 1981 and 1971 relate to 1981-90, 1971-80 and 1961-70 respectively; expectation of life at birth to 1991-92, 1971-80 and 1961-70. Workers are total of main and marginal.

Excluding Assam and J&K.

* Excluding Assam.

\# Excluding J&K.

The Political Development

India is considered the world's largest democracy. The system of electing a government through the use of ballet has worked fairly well during the past five decades, baring a short break in mid-seventies. The smooth working of the system has prevented many problems, whereas it created some others. The functioning of the democracy has ensured the smooth transition of power from one set of ruling elite to the other, within the constitutional framework. It has enhanced the credibility of the country to remain politically stable. The functioning of democracy has succeeded in generating public awareness about people's rights and obligations, and to direct this awareness to translate into a national identity. However, a closer look at the way the political system has undergone changes reveals some grave shortcomings. As Moon, who served as an ICS officer in India before independence felt that the democracy was introduced into a vast country of illiterate peasants, belonging to diverse races and religions, and held together only by geography and common subjection to British rule. In such a scenario the democratic system of government, has been and will continue to be a constant source of strife, disunity and disruption (Moon, 1998). The formation of democratic provincial governments, as a result of the constitutional reforms introduced in the 1935 Government of India Act, Moon indicated, has lead to corruption and the political interference with the bureaucracy. Gandhi had serious reservations about democracy and the modern state. Though his ideas changed somewhat over the years but he remained critical of the state. His ideal was greater power to people and minimum to the state. D.P. Mukerji (1958) has noted that though the efforts by the state to plan is a beneficent social force yet he feared that bureaucratic inefficiency, and corruption may lead to chaos. Tully (1998) noted that political corruption and the misuse of government machinery in every form has got worse over the years after independence. The history of last fifty years has shown that Gandhi from his spiritual perspective and Moon from his pragmatic understanding of humans were right in pointing out that the institutions the British established in India were alien and unsuited to the native genus of the country. The civil services and the police have expanded and have become perhaps the most well-entrenched institutions of corruption and exploitation of common people. Rajiv Gandhi as Prime Minister of India remarked that only 15 per cent of the money allocated for rural development actually reached the target population. There are so many court cases that the jails are full of people awaiting trials rather than those convicted. The court system has introduced an appetite for litigation, which has grown stronger, and a class of professionals, which thrive on the inefficiency of the system. Gandhi was aware of the need to adapt the foreign system to Indian conditions yet, even he could not rewrite these arrangements despite his power and political charisma.

The notion of democracy requires a politically conscious and empowered general public, capable of exercising its right judiciously. The coexistence of mass illiteracy and a highly manipulative elite, poverty and affluence, religious and the secular approaches to politics, has made the task of achieving a democratic mindset, extremely difficult. The continuance of a wide gulf between the rural and the urban masses have generated further problems of universalizing any value framework and building any consensus on objectives and strategies of national development. This has resulted in the use of primordial symbols and issues to invoke passion among the common masses to develop power bases for rival groups wanting to capture power. However, the problem of governance and the implications of implementing the development agenda with the help of international funding institutions, forces the ruling elite to dilute these symbols. The failure of the ruling elite to deliver the goods on both fronts lead to the withering away of the faith of the common man in the larger political parties. One party ruled in India for almost thirty years. The decline in the political party in power, Indian National Congress, in terms of its quality of leadership and its inability to develop intra-party democracy, in the largest democracy of the world, is a point worth taking note of in reviewing the possibility of development. The contradiction is often missed. The emergence of regional parties and the inability of any national party to acquire adequate political power at the national level, has lead to the problem of an unstable and weak centre. However, the pursuit of a development agenda on the terms of international financial institutions, requires a strong centre, capable of taking some unpleasant decisions. This has created a hiatus between the political and the economic compulsions of the ruling elite.

The future scenario in India therefore poses many difficulties as the events in Gujarat indicate. The political compulsions in view of the failure of programmes to deal with the more pressing economic issues in particular and other day-to-day needs such as water, health and effective education, are making politicians desperate to use religion, caste and regional ties to capture power. This would inevitably give rise to internal conflict and violence and would retard the process of political development. The political aspects of development are likely to pose more future problems and therefore, it is time that development experts make a note of these and take a fresh look at ways to deliver good governance, which is so crucial for economic growth.

The Economic Development

The Indian economic scenario provides a backdrop to the changes in India during the past half a century. Since independence, India has made significant progress in several areas of economic and human development, and the economy has diversified substantially. Food production has grown to provide adequate level of food security, though recent change in economic policy has made some scholars to question the claims of food security in India. The middle class has expanded and has benefited immensely from the economic development. The GDP has increased along with the technological expertise in the country. Infrastructure development has been considerable yet unable to meet the growing demand of the economy.

After about 40 years of planned development based on the dominance of government and public sector institutions and import substitution strategies, in 1991 India launched a number of structural adjustment programmes intended to improve economic performance. The programme sought to reduce the role of the state from many areas of economic activity. The first social development report produced by National Council of Applied Economic Research (NCAER) hoped that resources generated may be used for social expenditure. Though it is also possible that the state may disappear from social sector as well, since what the development report failed to acknowledge was the fact that the international monetary institutions were pressurizing India and other developing countries to cut down

Change in the Structure of Economy

Sectoral Share in GDP	*1980-81*	*1990-91*	*1995-96*
Agriculture, forestry, fishing, mining and quarrying	41.3	34.1	29.7
Manufacturing, electricity, gas, water supply and construction	22.9	26.6	27.7
Trade, transport, storage and communication	16.4	17.5	19.9
Financing, insurance, real state and business services	8.4	10.3	11.4
Community, social and personal services	11.0	11.6	11.3

Source: Man Power Profile India-1998, New Delhi: Institute for Applied Manpower Research, p. 337.

their expenses. Any cut in the government expenditure inevitably results in lower allocation for social sector. Public policy concerns for human development are always constrained by lack of adequate resources. The provision of basic needs requires huge resources and high quality of managerial skills. The task becomes all the more difficult when the population growth is high.

Economic Profile of Rural India

Even fifty years after independence, agriculture still remains the main source of livelihood of rural population, 60.23 per cent of the population still depends on agriculture (46.66% are self-employed in agriculture and allied activities and 13.57% are agriculture labourers). Non-agriculture provides livelihood to 39.77 per cent (9.91% are non-agricultural labourers and 14.15 are self employed in non-agriculture, 13.54% are salaried and 2.17 are others) of the population.

NSS estimate of rural Indian workforce (usual status) shows that share of agriculture in total rural workforce is declining, it declined from 85.6 per cent in 1972-73 to 78.2 per cent in 1993-97. Share of manufacturing, trade and services is widening in rural areas, share of these sectors increased from 12.0 per cent in 1972-73 to 17.2 per cent in 1993-94. However, casualization of rural labour is increasing, during the last two decades, share of casual labour in rural workers has increased from 25.4 per cent in 1972-73 to 35.6 per cent in 1993-94. The casual labour force is not able to find regular work throughout the year. Any kind of labour laws do not cover the casual labours. Even though some states may have some kind of minimum wages law it is seldom implemented in rural areas. The share of self-employed has declined from 65.3 per cent to 58.0 per cent during the period 1972-73 to 1993-94. The decline in self-employment may also be due to loss of land. The number of regular workers declined from 9.3 per cent to 6.4 per cent during the same period. Rural households generate 62.9 per cent of their household income from agriculture sector (55% from agriculture and allied activities and 7.9% from agriculture wages). Remaining 37.1 per cent of the rural household income is generated from non-agriculture sector, out of which 6.3 per cent from non-agriculture wages, 16.5 per cent from salaries and remaining 14.3 per cent from other sources. Since agriculture and allied activities are still principal source of income of more that 60 per cent of the population, it is worthwhile to look into the distribution of landholding and area operated by them.

According to the latest available agricultural census (1990-91), percentage of marginal holdings (area less than 1 hectare) in the country has increased from 57.8 per cent in 1985-86 to 59 per cent in 1990-91. At the same time percentage of small holdings (1 2 hectares) increased from 18.4 per cent to 19 per cent, whereas percentage of other holdings (more than 2 hectares) declined from 23.8 per cent to 22 per cent during the same period. Increase in the share of marginal and small holding led to an increase in their share of area operated by these two types of holdings. For marginal holdings, share of the area operated by them increased from 15.6 per cent to 17.3 per cent during the period 1985-86 to 1990-91. Average size of marginal holdings increased marginally from 0.39 hectare in 1985-86 to 0.40 hectare in 1990-91. Average size of all holdings declined from 1.69 hectares in 1985-86 to 1.57 hectares in 1990-91 (Pant and Patra, 1998). The majority of rural people have small or marginal land areas. The general conditions in the rural areas have not changed much. The conditions of the poor have in particular not shown any appreciable change.

Work Participation

According to India Human Development Report (1999), about 52 per cent of males and 18 per cent of females in rural India participate in some gainful economic activity, whereas the 1994 data provided by NSSO, the male participation was 55.3 per cent and female 15.5 per cent. The women not only get less wages, the specific work roles and conditions are socio-culturally determined. Women are commonly working in areas where men worked earlier, like stone breaking or carrying mud and bricks etc. The female work participation rate is lowest among Muslims at about 10 per cent followed by Hindus (17%), SCs (23%),

Christians (25%), and STs (28%). The female participation rate falls with rising income and ownership of assets like land. Large farmers tend to employ hired labour to replace females who work in the family. Female work participation rates are higher among poor households in lower income classes, poverty groups, and landless wage earners.

In an average household in rural India comprising 5.7 persons (3 males and 2.7 females), 2.1 persons are engaged in productive activities, that is, 1.6 males and 0.5 female. In other words, every one earner has to support 0.7 male and 1.1 female non-earning members within each average household in rural India. The dependency ratio is low among landless wage earners, both SCs and STs. This lower dependency ratio is largely due to a higher female work participation rate among these population groups (IHDR, 1999).

Employment

Productive work is not merely a means to the ultimate goal of economic well-being. It is a basic source of human dignity and self-respect. Although rapid economic growth is the surest and most sustainable source of increasing work opportunities, market forces alone cannot be relied upon to provide gainful work for all. This is particularly true in a labour-surplus economy like India. The congruence between the skill and spatial distribution of the labour force and the corresponding requirements of the economy may not be achieved through market-based mechanisms due to numerous distortions in the labour markets, information systems and infrastructural endowments that continue to persist in the country.

The growth process to generate employment have to concentrate on sectors, sub-sectors and technologies which are more labour intensive, in regions characterized by higher rates of unemployment and underemployment. The experience of the last decade has been that relatively rapid growth does generate employment opportunities, but this is not enough to achieve a hundred per cent employment. Nor economic growth results in adequate wage levels, which is directly linked to skill levels of the labour force. Average real wages for unskilled agricultural labour declined by 6.2 per cent in the year 1991-92, after an increase during the subsequent years, it again marginally declined in 1994-95 (GoI, 1997-98: 136). In Bihar, the decline in real wages of agricultural labour was 10.8 per cent, Maharashtra 2.8 per cent and in Uttar Pradesh 6.5 per cent in 1996-97 (ibid:141). The skill and geographical distribution of the emerging labour force reflect past trends in population growth and skill development, and cannot be changed significantly. Public intervention would be necessary to ensure better skills and organization of workers to safeguard against the decline in real wages. But, the efforts to ensure that adequate work opportunities are created, and that the labour force is able to access these opportunities, reflect that the battle is still to survive rather than think about a better tomorrow. The quest for a modern future remains illusory, particularly as state resources decline and the attitudes required to acquire higher skills or to get organized also do not exist.

The agricultural sector has historically played an extremely important role in providing employment in India, and is likely to continue to do so at least for the next decade or more. The skill profile of the emerging workforce is such that a large majority will have to continue to seek work opportunities in this sector. In order to create such opportunities, land and tenancy reforms are essential. The evidence strongly suggests that small farm agriculture, with secure land rights, is more productive than large farms and is more labour absorbing. The modernist can hope for active government intervention, both in implementation of existing laws and formulating new legislation for ensuring the tillers' rights, to create conditions of high labour absorption with adequate productive growth, but the reality does not support the assumption that this would happen. The Ninth Plan document, commenting on the tenancy reforms, admitted that very little progress has been made after the initial abolition of *zamindari* system and the transfer of title to owner-cultivators in the immediate post-independence period.

In fact, in the Eighth Plan, there was no progress in respect of conferment of rights on tenants and therefore the issue of tenancy reforms is still illusory (GoI, 1997:23). The hegemony of the landowning class remains firmly in place in the rural areas, extending to political hegemony in the state.

The minimum necessary condition for ensuring full employment is that the growth rate of creation of work opportunities must exceed the growth rate of the labour force, but so far it has not been possible to achieve this. Existing workers embody a certain structure of skills which may not be appropriate for the new work opportunities that may be created in the coming millennium. The market by itself may not be prepared to impart these skills to the displaced workers, since the preference will generally be for training the younger, new entrants in the labour force, whose potential life-time returns to the investment in human capital is likely to be significantly higher. It is necessary, therefore, to establish systems in the public domain for training and retraining or updating the skills of the labour force in line with the requirements of the economy, but as the experience from other countries, where economic reforms took place earlier show, this did not happen.

It is also necessary to shift the focus of employment strategies towards creating conditions whereby employment opportunities lead to significantly better living and working conditions of the people and to uphold the dignity of labour. In particular, the incidence of scavenging and child labour which arise out of acute poverty and prevailing social disabilities need to be eradicated keeping in mind the requirement of maintaining family incomes. Child labour is a big reality in India. In 1987-88, 21.3 per cent male and children in the age group of 5-14 were part of the workforce, which declined to 14.9 in 1993-94 (IOAMR, 1998: 218). However, India Human Development Report gave that 4.4 per cent male and 3.5 per cent female children are engaged in wage-earning activities on a regular basis. They number about 10 million in rural India. Participation of children, especially females, in gainful work falls as prosperity rises in terms of income, landholding, and also adult literacy.

It reflects the economic poverty of the millions of people and their inability to think about the future. The existing social environment is not conducive to deal with the problem. The western model of education uniformly applied in all areas, irrespective of their economic and cultural environment has resulted in the current apathy towards education. Many studies have documented the simple logic of the people that the current education only helps to alienate the younger generation from their present. A child having received some education does not want to work with his hands, at least not in the village. He also is unable to learn the traditional skills of crafts. He becomes a misfit in his present location. His future hangs in balance. Most of the children and their parents thus do not make the mistake and instead opt to work. The modernist hope that a family-centric strategy, sensitivity to the needs of the orphan or run-away, with rigorous implementation of the existing laws, would be able to effectively tackle this problem. The reality is, there is no such strategy. The ones that have been evolved and announced from the ramparts of the Red Fort in Delhi have not delivered the goods. Reason, lack of financial resources and a very inefficient and corrupt bureaucracy. But there is no dearth of further prescriptions and slogans to eliminate child labour. The private sector, which is the main source of work opportunities in the future, is expected to play an important role. It is obvious that private sector is not socially committed and therefore the initiative by the government is the only hope in skill building, since the bulk of the educational system in India is in the public domain.

Work participation among the elderly (over 60 years) is as high as 70 per cent for males in rural and 44.2 per cent in urban areas and 24.1 per cent for females in rural and 11.3 per cent in urban areas. Among the elderly, female work participation is lower in higher income groups, salaried, and professional groups in both rural and urban areas. The direct correlation of income level and the age at which you start work or age at which you withdraw from it is evident. The female work participation in rural areas particularly is a symbol of lower status and is stigmatized.

In view of the high incidence of unemployment and increasing casualization of labour, there is a need to enhance employment opportunities for the poor, particularly for those who are in seasonal occupations. The recent trend of lower labour participation rates among women is partly a reflection of the inadequacy of appropriate work opportunities. The modernists hope that a national Employment Assurance Scheme would deliver the goods. The reality is the efforts so far at employment generation, through many schemes, have been like a drop in the ocean, in view of the magnitude of the problem. Secondly, the effort only ensures the bare survival of the beneficiary, it cannot help in improving the access of people to better education, health or economic opportunities in future.

The diversification of economy away from agriculture, as measured by the sectoral pattern of employment, has been much slower than expected. The Second Plan has projected a decline in the workforce engaged in agricultural activities to about 60 per cent in 1976, i.e., by 10 percentage points over 20 year period, but the actual decline has been much slower. Even in 1972-73 agriculture and related sector provided employment to 74 per cent population which in 1993-94 declined to 63.9 per cent, representing a decline of 10 per cent (ibid:232). In terms of actual numbers, however, the total working force increased from 236.3 million in 1973-74 to 372.1 million in 1993-94 and therefore, the actual numbers dependent on agriculture would have increased. The share of the manufacturing sector in employment has continued to be low and accounts for 10.6 per cent of total employment in 1993-94, whereas the share of services was around 10.7 per cent (ibid:233).

The proportion of self-employed in employment has reduced but still it accounts for 56 per cent of those employed in 1992. The proportion of casual labour has increased from 19.7 per cent in 1972-73 to 28 per cent in 1992 among the male employees and from 30.7 per cent to 36.4 among the female employees. The regular salaried employees constituted only 16 per cent in the case of male employees and 6.8 per cent in the case of female employees.

Total labour force in 1997 was estimated to be 397.2 million. It is expected that 389.7 million persons were employed and 7.5 million were underemployed or unemployed. However, only 27.9 million were employed in the organized sector, either public or private which is around 7 per cent of the total labour force. Female workers constitute only 15.8 per cent of workers in the organized sector. The bulk of labour force continues to be in the unorganized sector and a large proportion of workforce is located in the rural areas in the agriculture sector. These millions normally do not possess any skills which are relevant for a modern industrial urban society.

Population, Labour Force, Employment and Unemployment

(in million)

Year	*Population*	*Labour Force*	*Employed*	*Unemployed*
1978	637.6	262.6	255.5	7.1
1983	725.8	289.1	283.2	5.9
1994	893.7	367.4	360.0	7.4
1997	949.9	397.2	389.7	7.5

Source: Economic Survey, 1997-98.

Unemployment during 1973-1994

There are different ways of defining unemployment. The general assumption of the economist is that generally few people could afford to be without any work for a long time. As a result unemployment is measured in terms of how many persons are unemployed on a day, for a week or the usual status which means for more than 162 days in a year. The NSSO collects data in respect of all modes of unemployment and the data indicates that in 1972-73, 4.8 per cent of the male labour force and 6 per cent of female labour force were usually unemployed which remained constant at 4.5 for males but registered an increase in case of females to 8.2. Since the population increased during the period the number of unemployed were much more than what was the case in 1972-73. Similarly, the daily unemployment figures were nearly 8 per cent for male and 13.7 for female in

1972-73 which declined to 6.7 for males and 10.5 for females, but in absolute terms the number registered an increase. According to NSSO data, the highest unemployment is to be found among 15-29 age group, which was 4.9 in 1977-78 and increased to 10.8 in 1993 (NSSO, 1995:81).

In India, over 40 million people were either unemployed or underemployed according to ninth plan official figures. This is equivalent to nearly four nations comparable to Australian population and ten that of New Zealand. The female workforce is comparatively small as the work participation rate is still low as compared to males. The situation would worsen as more females enter the labour force. According to NHDR, 2001, in 1999-2000, 2.3 per cent of total labour force was unemployed, this figure in 1983 was two per cent, indicating thereby an increase in unemployment in percentage terms and in absolute numbers as well as the total labour force has become much bigger.

Growth in Social Inequalities

Despite the development efforts of past fifty years, there are wide disparities between the rich and the poor, urban and rural sectors, male and female, lower caste and upper castes and between different states in India.

NSS estimates of rural Indian workforce (usual status) shows that share of agriculture in total rural workforce is declining, it declined from 85.6 per cent in 1972-73 to 78.2 per cent in 1993-94. Share of manufacturing, trade and services is widening in rural areas, share of these sectors increased from 12 per cent in 1972-73 to 17.2 per cent in 1993-94. However, casual nature of rural labour is increasing, during the last few decades, share of casual labour in rural workers has increased from 25.4 per cent in 1972-73 to 35.6 per cent in 1993-94. On the other hand, share of self-employed has declined from 65.3 per cent to 58.0 per cent during the period 1972-73 to 1993-94, share of regular workers declined from 9.3 per cent to 6.4 per cent during the same period. During the period 1987-88 to 1993-94 share of casual labour has increased by 2.7 per cent, mainly at the expense of regular workers (share of regular workers declined from 7.7%

to 6.4%). Rural household still generate 62.9 per cent of their household income from agriculture sector (55% from agriculture and allied activities and 7.9% from agriculture wages). Remaining 37.1 per cent of the rural household income is generated from non-agriculture sector, out of which 6.3 per cent from non-agriculture wages, 16.5 per cent from salaries and remaining 14.3 per cent from other sources. Since agriculture and allied activities is still the principal source of income of more than 60 per cent of the population, it is worthwhile to look into the distribution of landholdings and area operated by them.

According to the latest available agricultural census (1990-91), the percentage of marginal holdings (area less than one hectare) in the country has increased from 57.8 per cent in 1985-86 to 59 per cent in 1990-91. At the same time, the percentage of small holdings (1-2 hectares) increased from 18.4 per cent to 19 per cent, whereas percentage of other holdings (more than 2 hectare) declined from 23.8 per cent to 22 per cent during the same period. Increase in the share of marginal and small holdings led to an increase in their share of area operated by these two type of holdings. For marginal holdings, share of area operated by them increased from 13.4 per cent to 14.9 per cent and for small holdings share of the area operated by them increased from 15.6 per cent to 17.3 during the period 1985-86 to 1990-91. Average size of marginal holdings increased marginally from 0.39 hectare in 1985-86 to 0.40 hectare in 1990-91. Average size of all holdings declined from 1.69 hectares in 1985-86 to 1.57 hectares in 1990-91 (Pant and Patra, 1998).

Concentration of Income

	% Households	*% Population*	*% Income*
Rural	72.6	74.6	55.6
Urban	27.4	25.4	44.4
All India	100.0	100.0	100.0

Source: Pradhan, B.K., Roy, P.K., Saluja, M.R. and Venkatram, Shanta (1998), Income Expenditure and Social Sector Indicators of Households in Rural and Urban India. Paper presented in the NCAER-IDRC Workshop on Micro Impact of macro Adjustment Policies in India (MIMAP, India), 1998, NCAER, New Delhi.

The concentration of income is evident from the fact that 25.4 per cent population consumes 44.4 per cent national income. The amount of income spent on food is another indicator of the size of per capita income. The share of food item was higher in rural (56.2%) as compared to urban (39.9%). The share of cereals and pulses among food items was nearly twice (26%) in rural as compared to urban (14%). The concentration of income in few hands is a global trend rather than being exclusive to India as is evident from the income distribution of India, Pakistan and Bangladesh.

Distribution of Income

Country Gini Index	*Poorest 20%*	*II 20%*	*III 20%*	*IV 20%*	*Richest 20%*
India 29.7	9.2	13.0	16.8	21.7	39.3
Pakistan 31.2	9.4	13.0	16.0	20.3	41.2
Bangladesh 28.3	9.4	13.5	17.2	22.0	37.9

Source: WDR, 1999-2000: 238-9.

It is interesting to see that income distribution depicts a similar distribution across all classes with only minor differences in the share of the richest 20 per cent. It is not surprising therefore to find Gini Index showing marginal difference with 31.2 having highest inequality to 28.3 in Bangladesh as the lowest. The similarity across classes may reflect that the class structure before separation into independent countries have continued to be unaffected by the changing of national boundaries. In other words very little has changed during the past 50 years among the general location of the common people.

The mean household income for rural India is Rs. 25,653 per year, and a per capita income of Rs. 4,485. Over 58 per cent of all rural households fall into the less than Rs. 20,000 per annum income category with Rs. 6 per day to meet their minimum requirements. Only 4 per cent has an income above Rs. 86,000 per annum, which is 13 times higher than that of the poorest class.

Levels of income are closely related to ownership of land. The income of wage labourers is 58 per cent lower than that of salaried persons and professionals, and 77 per cent lower than that of big farmers. The income of households where both adult males and females are literate is 58 per cent higher than that of households with illiterate adults. Household and per capita income are low for the SCs and STs and Muslims (IHDR, 1999).

Ownership of Assets

About 63 per cent of rural households own land in India. Ownership of land is highest among Hindus (70%), followed by STs (69%), and lowest among SCs (47%), followed by Muslims (57%). Hindus also have the largest average landholding size of 5.1 acres while Muslims have 3.6 acres, SCs 2.8 acres and Christians 2 acres (IHDR, 1999).

Poverty

An estimated population of around 260 million persons is still below poverty line in India, which is 26.1 per cent of the total population in 1999-2000. The incidence of poverty is found to be much greater in rural (27.1%) than urban (23.6%). About 80 per cent of the total population below poverty line, lived in rural areas (Pradhan, et al., 1998). It is interesting to note that the actual number of poor below the poverty line was 321.60 million in 1973-74 and in 1993-94 it still was 320.37 million as per official sources, it declined to 260 million in 1999-2000 (Economic Survey, 2001-02). There are huge inter state variations as the poverty rate as lowest in Jammu & Kashmir (3.48%) while Orissa (47.15%) has the highest poverty, followed by Bihar (42.6%) in 1999-2000.

About 52 per cent of the total population living below poverty line belongs to the occupational category of wage earners and another 25 per cent from self-employed households engaged in farming. The incidence of poverty is much severe in wage earning households. In urban areas the incidence of poverty is found to be 61 per cent in households engaged in non-agricultural wage, followed by self-employed (non-farm) 38.7 per cent.

Percentage Distribution of Population below Poverty Line

Occupational groups	*Rural*	*Urban*	*All India*
Self-employed farming	24.7	0.8	25.5
Self-employed non-farming	2.7	6.3	9.0
Salary	5.3	5.4	10.7
Agricultural wage	35.0	1.5	36.5
Non-agricultural wage	10.8	4.9	15.7
Others	1.8	0.8	2.6
All groups	80.3	19.7	100.0

Source: Pradhan, B.K., Roy, P.K., Saluja, M.R. and Venkatram, Shanta (1998), Income Expenditure and Social Sector Indicators of Households in Rural and Urban India. Paper presented in the NCAER–IDRC Workshop on Micro Impact of Macro Adjustment Policies in India (MIMAP, India), 1998, NCAER, New Delhi.

Population below Poverty Line

	1999-2000	*1993-94*	*1987-88*	*1983-84*	*1977-78*	*1973-74*
Number of poor (million)						
Rural	193	244.03	231.80	251.96	264.24	261.29
Urban	67	76.34	75.17	70.94	64.65	60.31
Total	260	320.37	306.97	322.90	328.89	321.60
Poverty ratio (%)						
Rural	27.1	37.27	39.09	45.65	53.07	56.40
Urban	23.6	32.38	38.20	40.79	45.24	49.23
Total	26.1	35.97	38.86	44.48	51.32	54.93

Source: Statistical Outline of India, 1997-98, Tata Services Ltd., Department of Economics and Statistics, Mumbai, 1997, Economic Survey 2001-02.

Revised data based on the Expert Group headed by Dr. D. Lakdawala, Planning Commission, as accepted by the United Front government in 1997.

Social Development in India

As referred to earlier, social development is generally referred to as provision of social services to people in general, to increase their participation in economic development. In context of India, various indicators of social development, such as health and nutrition, education, women's development, etc., are discussed in the paragraphs to come.

Poverty at State Level, 1973-74 to 1999-2000

State	RU 73-74	RA 93-94	L 99-00	UR 73-74	BA 93-94	N 99-00	TO 73-74	TA 93-94	L 99-00
Andhra Pradesh	48.41	15.92	11.05	50.61	38.33	26.63	48.86	22.19	15.77
Arunachal Pradesh	52.67	45.01	40.04	36.92	7.73	7.47	51.93	39.35	33.47
Assam							51.21	40.86	36.09
Bihar	62.99	58.21	44.30	52.96	34.50	32.91	61.91	54.96	42.60
Goa	46.85	5.34	1.35	37.69	27.03	7.52	44.26	14.92	4.40
Gujarat	46.35	22.18	13.17	52.57	27.89	15.59	48.15	24.21	14.07
Haryana	34.23	28.02	8.27	40.18	16.38	9.99	35.36	25.05	8.74
Himachal Pradesh	27.42	30.34	7.94	13.17	9.18	4.63	26.39	28.44	7.63
J&K	45.51	30.34	3.97	21.32	9.18	1.98	40.83	25.17	3.48
Karnataka	55.14	29.88	17.38	52.53	40.14	25.25	54.47	33.16	20.04
Kerala	59.19	25.76	9.38	62.74	24.55	20.27	59.79	25.43	12.72
Madhya Pradesh	62.66	40.64	37.06	57.65	48.38	38.44	61.78	42.52	37.43
Maharashtra	57.71	37.93	23.72	43.87	35.15	26.81	53.24	36.86	25.02
Manipur	52.67	45.01	40.04	36.92	7.73	7.47	49.96	33.78	28.54
Meghalaya	—	—	—	—	—	—	50.20	37.92	33.87
Mizoram	—	—	—	—	—	—	50.32	25.66	19.47
Nagaland	—	—	—	—	—	—	50.81	37.92	32.67
Orissa	67.28	49.72	48.01	55.62	41.64	42.83	66.18	48.56	47.15
Punjab	28.21	11.95	6.35	27.96	11.35	5.75	28.15	11.77	6.16
Rajasthan	44.76	26.46	13.74	52.13	30.49	19.85	46.14	27.41	15.28

Contd...

State	RU 73-74	RA 93-94	L 99-00	UR 73-74	BA 93-94	N 99-00	TO 73-74	TA 93-94	L 99-00
Sikkim	—	—	—	—	—	—	50.86	41.43	36.55
Tamil Nadu	57.43	32.48	20.55	49.40	39.77	22.11	54.94	35.03	21.12
Tripura	—	—	—	—	—	—	51.0	39.01	34.44
Uttar Pradesh	56.53	42.28	31.22	60.09	35.39	30.89	57.07	40.85	31.15
West Bengal	73.16	40.80	31.85	34.67	22.41	14.86	63.43	35.66	27.02
A&N Islands	—	—	—	—	—	—	55.56	34.47	20.99
Chandigarh	27.96	11.35	5.75	27.96	11.35	5.75	27.96	11.35	5.75
Dadra	46.85	51.95	17.57	37.69	39.93	13.52	46.55	50.84	17.14
Daman	N A	5.34	1.35	N A	27.03	7.52	N A	15.80	4.44
Delhi	24.44	1.90	0.40	52.23	16.03	9.42	49.61	14.69	8.23
Lakshadweep	59.19	25.76	9.38	62.74	24.55	20.27	59.68	25.04	15.60
Pondicherry	—	—	—	—	—	—	53.82	37.40	21.67
India	**56.44**	**37.27**	**27.09**	**49.01**	**32.36**	**23.62**	**54.88**	**35.97**	**26.10**

Source: Economic Survey of India, 2001-02, p. 239.

Note: Poverty ratio of Assam is used for Sikkim, Arunachal Pradesh, Meghalaya, Mizoram, Manipur, Nagaland and Tripura. (But it still does not explain how the combined poverty figures could be different in these states while rural urban figures are same. Similarly the note says that poverty ratio of Tamil Nadu is used for Pondicherry and A&N Islands, but the combined figures are different.) The statement is true only in case of Chandigarh, where the urban figures of Punjab has been given for both rural and urban Chandigarh. Similar statement about Goa is also not true as the figures are different, while the statement about Kerala and Lakshadweep figures is correct which are same.

Health and Nutrition

The total number of government hospitals in the country in 1993 was 4,579 with 3,85,216 beds and number of private hospitals was 9,113 with 2,10,987 beds. The number of primary health centres supposed to serve 30,000 rural population in plain areas and 20,000 population in hilly areas in 1997 were 22,010 covering an average population of 28,564 persons (MPI, 1998: 160-68).

In terms of health care parameters and service utilization, ANC is widespread in Kerala and Tamil Nadu whereas only one-third of mothers receive this service in Rajasthan, Madhya Pradesh and Bihar. Not more than one-fourth of mothers receive post-natal care in rural India. Untrained health personnel in rural India conduct about 60 per cent of total births, especially in Bihar, Orissa and Rajasthan (more than four-fifths of all births). Overall, government health care facilities are utilized more frequently than private clinics in almost all states and also across all population groups in India.

Likewise, about 37 per cent of children aged 0-4 years suffer from second-degree malnourishment or 'stunting'. About 29 per cent of children aged 5-12 are stunted. Boys have marginally higher rates of stunting. Stunting does not appear to be related to income, landholding, occupation and social groups. About 5 per cent of children aged 0-14 years suffer from wasting. Boys have higher levels of wasting than girls.

Less than 6 per cent, or about 41 million people suffer from major morbidity in rural India. The incidence of hypertension is 589 per lakh person and tuberculosis 423 per lakh population. Crude birth rate (CBR) is high among the poorest households and among Muslims and lowest among Christians. Crude death rate (CDR) is high among landless labourers and shows an association with household income.

Education

Over the past 45 years the country has been making efforts to achieve the goal of universal primary education and adult literacy. Education is free for both sexes in all the government and local board schools at least up to Class VIII. Many of the states provide free education up to Class X. Some states provide free education even up to Class XII. This trend is likely to continue despite the trend of a decline in the state resources.

Literacy levels are lowest in Rajasthan, Bihar, Uttar Pradesh, and Madhya Pradesh and high in Kerala, the north-eastern states, Tamil Nadu, Maharashtra, Gujarat and West Bengal. Rajasthan has the highest gender differential among states. The literacy rates show an increase with rise in income but this is not true in case of female literacy levels. Landless wage earners, SCs and STs have low levels of literacy (IHDR, 1999). About 17 per cent of adult males and 9 per cent of adult females complete middle school in rural India.

There has been considerable increase in the number of educational institutions of all types. Over the last five decades, the number of primary schools more than doubled from 2.1 lakh in 1950-51 to 5.9 lakh in 1995-96. The increase in number of middle schools was more significant from about 13.5 thousand to 171.2 thousand.

Teachers

Besides provision of schools, availability of adequate number of qualified and trained teachers is also important from the viewpoint of education of children. The total number of teachers increased from about 5 lakh in 1950-51 to 17.9 lakh in 1996-97 at the primary level. At the upper primary level the increase was from about 86 thousand to 11.96 lakh during the same period. Despite the increase in the number of teaching force, more than a quarter of primary schools continued to be single teacher schools in 1996. This trend is likely to continue.

Further, about 90 per cent of teachers at the primary level and roughly the same proportion at the upper primary level were trained teachers. Great state-wise variations can, however, be observed in the percentage of trained teachers to the total teachers. Most of the eastern states had more than 50 per cent of their teachers in the untrained category. Even in Assam and West Bengal about one-third of the teachers were found to be untrained. The trend is likely to continue.

Pupil-teacher ratio at the all-India level was 42 and 37 in 1990-91 at the primary and upper primary level respectively. There are large interstate variations. Pupil-teacher ratio ranged from 15 in Sikkim to 53 in Andhra Pradesh at the primary level. At the upper primary level Mizoram and Manipur with 14 had the best ratio whereas Karnataka had the worst ratio of 54. The pupil-teacher ratio is likely to register a decline in the coming years as the enrolment will increase but the number of teachers may not keep pace with growing enrolments.

Enrolment Ratios

While provision of infrastructure is a necessary condition, it does not ensure utilization of available facilities by the children. Enrolment ratio is widely used as an indicator of assessing educational status of children. There has been spectacular increase in the number of children enrolled at elementary level. In 1950-51, the enrolment in classes I to V was only 19.2 million which increased to 110.4 million by 1996-97. The enrolment in classes VI to VIII had also increased from 3.1 million to 41 million during the same period. However, it shows the large drop-outs of children at the primary level it self. Considering the quality of education in rural areas in particular despite all this, even attaining the target of universal literacy is still far away. And also the fact that half-baked education can also lead to problems. Gross enrolment ratio (GER) for the age group 6-11 was 104.3 per cent in 1995-96, it was 114.5 per cent for boys and 93.3 per cent for girls. GER for the age-group 11-14 was 79.5 per cent for boys and 54.9 per cent for girls respectively.

Female Education

The education of female children continues to lag behind at the primary and secondary level of schooling. The participation of girls in school education has been increasing at all stages of education. At the primary level, the share of girls in total enrolment increased from 5.4 million in 1950-51 to 47.9 million in 1996-97. At the upper primary level, the same increased from 0.5 to 16.3 million during the same period. The percentages, however, remained below fifty per cent at all the stages. As long as the proportion of girls enrolment does not reach 50 per cent, the disparities in access to education owing to gender difference would continue to persist in the coming years as well.

At the national level only 54.9 per cent males and 38.5 per cent females were attending school in the 6-10 years age-group (corresponding to the usual age group of 6-11 years). Almost 4.6 crore children were out of school in 1981 as against 60 lakh given by the enrolment statistics. In rural areas, as expected, the proportion of boys and girls attending schools was lower as compared to urban areas. There were wide inter-state variations in the proportion of children attending schools in different states such as Bihar, Madhya Pradesh, Rajasthan, Uttar Pradesh, with only one-third of their children in 6-14 age group attending schools. The situation in these states is much worse in 6-11 age group. The disparity shows that as one moves from outer circle to inner tracks, the magnitude of the problem becomes more pronounced. The inner circle and track represents the core of the problem of educational development.

Retention Rates

The main reason for the inability to achieve the goal of universal elementary education (UEE) is the poor retention capacity of the education system. Retention rates, however, continue to be very low in the north-eastern states of Arunachal Pradesh, Meghalaya, Mizoram, Nagaland and in the western part of India, that is Rajasthan. These were also low in Andhra Pradesh, Assam, Sikkim and West Bengal. All the union territories had retention rates higher than the national level. The female retention rates are very low compared to male retention rates. Among the states, Goa and Kerala had very high retention rates, both at the primary and middle level. For achieving universal coverage of children, retention rates from class I to class V will need to be increased to almost 100 per cent. The first India Human Resource Development Report brought out by National Council of Applied Economic Research (NCAER) in 1999 reported that the average discontinuation rate is about 6 per cent for rural India. Contrary to general belief, drop-outs are negligible (about 1%) among children aged 6-9 years; they increase to 2.1 per cent among 6-11 year olds and to 13 per cent among 12 year olds (IHDR, 1999). About 68 per cent of all children go to government schools while another 22 per cent attend government-aided schools. While 11 per cent of boys go to private schools, only 8 per cent of girls do so. The proportion of children seeking education in private schools has increased from 2 per cent in 1986 to about 10 per cent in 1994 (IHDR, 1999).

Qualitative Aspects

For ensuring quality of educational progress, the institutions need to be provided with certain essential facilities like buildings, furniture, playgrounds, laboratories, libraries and certain amenities like drinking water and toilets. There has been a considerable improvement in the availability of various facilities over the past two decades or so. In 1996, 72.8 per cent of primary schools were housed in *pucca* buildings or partially built buildings as against 59.9 per cent in 1978. There were only 13.5 per cent of schools without any type of building. At the upper primary level the situation was still better as 87.8 per cent of the schools had *pucca* buildings and only less than 5 per cent of the schools were without any type of building. Deficiencies however continue in respect of availability of classrooms, playgrounds, educational equipment, libraries and laboratories. Very few schools had urinal and lavatory facilities especially for girls. Twenty-six per cent schools still do not have a usable blackboard, fifty two per cent do not have a play ground and 12 per cent are still single teacher schools (Probe, 1999: 39). The fact is that even in some small towns where new colonies have developed on account of growing population, government primary schools are not available within one kilometre.

Resources for Education

A quick glance at the trend in public expenditure on education shows that the expenditure on education as a proportion of GDP has increased over the years from 1.2 per cent in 1950-51 to 3.63 per cent in 1995-96. The share of elementary education also increased from 0.48 per cent of GNP in 1950-51 to 1.63 per cent in 1995-96. Despite the rise in expenditure as a proportion of GNP it is still much below the actual requirements of the system and the general target of 6 per cent as specified in NPE, 1986. Total plan outlay on education has been declining gradually. Much of the growth in expenditure on elementary education, has been aborted by an increase in prices, and a rapid increase in population, particularly students. In real prices, the increase in expenditure on elementary education has been quite modest.

The data on per capita expenditure on education show that there are wide disparities among the states.

Cost of Schooling

The IHDR, 1999 reported that total household expenditure on elementary schooling is Rs. 378 per student per year. The cost of schooling is Rs. 300 per child in government schools, Rs. 380 per child in aided schools, and Rs. 735 per child in private schools. To impart elementary education to all children in India at the prevailing level of quality, involves an expenditure of Rs. 2,36,348 million which is equal to about 3.3 per cent of GDP. The current expenditure is only 1.7 per cent of GDP (IHDR, 1999). Total expenditure to impart universal elementary education was estimated to be Rs. 2,49,690 million. In addition mid-day meals would cost an additional Rs. 61,500 million, and to provide bare minimum infrastructure, about 19,70,000 classrooms, an additional Rs. 49,250 million (IHDR, 1999).

Higher Education

The objectives of higher education were three-fold – to provide trained manpower, generation of knowledge and social change to modernize the attitude of the people to bring about changes in the social institutions, to increase the participation of weaker sections in particular, in economic development to ensure gender justice and redistribution of economic resources. The emphasis in the coming years would shift to the first two and the objective of social change would be relegated to the background with the marginalization of the state. The higher education that even now is out of the reach of the common man it would become more elitist in character in future. The current state of higher education is marked by a trend of decay in general. In most of the states the institution of higher education are gradually decaying as the resources of the state are drying up. There is a very vast gap between the central and state institutes of higher education. This is leading to a concentration of intellectual resources in few centres only and the institutes in the periphery are unable to retain both intellectually bright faculty and the students. In the coming years the trend will become more market driven as the content, and the mechanisms of delivery and the recipient all will become market oriented.

The increase in education expenditure which was 2.26 of the GDP in 1968 rose to 3.63 in 1996, though the percentage in the total budgetary allocation declined somewhat, reflects the importance attached to the sector. Yet, in terms of meeting, the needs of a growing and young population the resources fall short of the current need. The recent efforts at curbing the governmental expenditure may either lead to a further decline in allocation or the allocations may remain stagnant. It is clear that in future decades too, higher education which is considered the gateway to economic prosperity and change in social attitudes, would remain outside the reach of the majority.

Women's Development

A very large part of the thinking, writing and efforts to change the status of women is confined to a narrow stratum of urban, educated middle class women. Vast differences distinguish the lives of women in different parts of the country and within different caste class, religious and ethnic groups. It is very difficult to make generalizations and put together comprehensive descriptions of the life and struggles of Indian women (Kishwar and Vanita, 1984). The heavy work burden, several unwanted pregnancies at short intervals, still births, miscarriages, infant deaths, lack of sufficient food are responsible for the very poor health of most Indian women. As one woman activist from rural Rajasthan put it, in the village hierarchy a woman's life is in many ways valued at less than an animal's. The logic is simple, it takes money to replace an animal, whereas to replace a woman is not only easy but under certain circumstances even remunerative (ibid: 6).

A significant symptom of the increasing devaluation of women is the spread and increase of dowry. Despite decades of propaganda by political parties, socially conscious groups and women's organizations, dowry has spread to groups where either it had relatively small presence or was completely absent. It has spread in groups where there was a bride price (ibid: 14). Similarly while the women remain oppressed and severely restricted in their freedom, a strong tradition of according them respect as mothers in the family also coexist. Since the family is the only source of social and emotional support available to most women in India, it occupies a very central place in their lives and they pour all their energy into working for its well-being.

The seclusion of women from technology and economic skills have lead to the development rooted in science and technology affecting them adversely. The women are being pushed further and further into destitution. Even low-level improvements in farm technology has lead to seclusion of women from economic tasks. It is interesting to note that women still are not supposed to touch the plough or drive a tractor or operate any kind of machinery. In many areas she is still not supposed to ride a bicycle.

Sex Ratio

The sex-ratio is a potent indicator of how gender free a society is. Generally the sex ratio should indicate a balance between male and female population and its increase or decline. However, it is interesting to note that the gap is increasing with development efforts to improve health and the child mortality rates. It was 972 females per thousand males in 1901 which has declined to 927 in 1991. The decline has been more or less steady over the decades, except for a marginal increase between 1941 and 1951, between 1971 and 1981 when it rose to 934 from 930. It declined to 927 in 1991 and rose marginally in 2001 to reach 933.

The adverse sex-ratio for females and its decline since 1901 is attributed mainly to higher mortality among females, as compared to males, in all age groups right from childhood through child-bearing ages. Limited access to the health infrastructure contributing to high maternal mortality and relative deprivation of the female child from nutrition, health and medical care have also been identified as some of the other contributory factors.

The sex-ratio should have improved from 946 in 1951 on account of development efforts, but in 2001 the sex-ratio is still 933 barely improving from 927 in 1991. But this is only part of the truth, most relatively better off states in India have a poor sex ratio. In Delhi, the sex ratio was 827 in 1991, it declined to 821 in 2001, similarly in Punjab it declined from 882 to 874, Haryana from 865 to 861 and Chandigarh from 790 to 773. The adverse sex ratio for women needs to be seen against other indicators of falling death rates for both men and women, higher child survival rates and the improvement of life expectancy, which is more significant for women than for men. The improvement in health care in India should have contributed to a more favourable sex ratio.

The age-specific death rates for female population declined for all age groups. Despite significant decline in the mortality in overall population and simultaneous improvement in life expectancy at birth, there is still relatively quite a high proportion of deaths taking place among children of 0-4 years. The 0-4 mortality has been higher for female children during the eighties. Age-specific death rates also declined for males in almost all age groups but the decline in the case of females was greater. During 1979-81, female death rates were higher than male death rates for the younger age groups up to 30-34, whereas for the groups above 35 years a reverse trend is noticed. Due to the greater decline in female mortality during the decade, by 1989-91, female death rates were higher than male death rates only up to the age group 25-29 and beyond the age of 30, female deaths were lower. Further, the gap between male and female deaths at younger ages up to 35-39 years is narrow while for ages beyond 40 years, the gap widened because of lower female death rates.

Age at Marriage

By the age of 25-29 years, more than 90 per cent of women were married in 1992. About 30 per cent females got married while they were still in their teens (i.e., 15-19 years).

Mean Age at Marriage (in Years)

Year	*Female*	*Male*
1951	15.6	19.9
1961	15.5	21.3
1971	17.2	22.4
1981	18.3	23.3
1991	19.5	NA

Source: Sample Registration Systems (SRS) – Fertility and Mortality Indicator 1991, Registrar General and Census Commissioner, New Delhi, India.

The mean age at marriage for females which was around 13 years at the beginning of the century rose to 19.5 years by 1991.

The Child Marriage Restraint Act, 1976 raised the minimum age at marriage of girls to 18 years from 15 years and for boys to 21 years. This was intended to prevent child marriages, early marriage of girls and consequent early pregnancies and thereby curtail fertility at young ages and birth of premature babies. It was also expected to lead to higher education and higher work participation rates for women.

Fertility

The age-specific fertility rates declined for women in all age-groups between 1981 and 1991, but not uniformly. The decline was small for the peak fertility ages 20-29. The reduction in fertility rate was significant for the age-groups above 30. The reduction in fertility in the 30 plus age-group were substantial for rural areas between 1981 and 1991. This shrinking of the age span of fertility among urban women especially after 35 plus years facilitated their joining other productive activities. Total fertility rate declined from 4.5 births in 1981 to 3.6 in 1991. The maternal and child health services remain only on paper in many tribal and rural areas. The percentage of child births attended by trained personnel is only one third of all births.

Employment

Employment of women is an index of their economic status in society, specially with reference to equality. According to the census data, the work participation rate (i.e., the proportion of employed or total workers to population) of females steadily rose from 14.22 per cent in 1971 to 19.67 in 1981 and to 22.27 in 1991. The rise in work participation of rural females has been even steeper from 15.92 in 1971 to 26.79 in 1991. The rise in work participation of urban females over the last two decades is somewhat less impressive. During the 1991 Census, conscious efforts were made to count women workers more completely and remove their invisibility. This could be one of the reasons for the increase reflected in the work participation rates between 1981 and 1991.

Out of the 22.27 per cent female work participation in 1991, main workers contributed 16.03 per cent and marginal workers 6.24 per cent. While participation of main workers increased between 1981 and 1991 both in rural and urban areas, marginal work participation increased only in rural areas but remained unchanged in urban areas at around 1 per cent. It is significant to point out that women constituted 90 per cent of the total marginal workers. Regional variations are wide – the female total work participation rate ranging from as high as 34 per cent to as low as 4 per cent among the major states.

The distinction of female main workers by industrial categories shows a change in the pattern of activity of females between 1981 and 1991. Cultivators among main workers account for 34 per cent workers and agricultural labourers 45 per cent. In the household manufacturing industry, the percentage of female main workers has decreased from 4.6 per cent in 1981 to 3.5 per cent in 1991 in rural areas whereas the corresponding decrease in urban areas is from 10.4 per cent to 7.5 per cent. Another significant change is in the increase in percentage of main workers in 'other services' from 6.9 per cent to 8.3 per cent in rural areas and the corresponding change in urban areas from 37 per cent to 40 per cent.

Women's employment in the organized sector has increased from 1.9 million in 1971 to 4 million in 1993, constituting 14.6 per cent of the total employment of 27.18 million. Of these 2.7 million women, i.e., about 62 per cent were employed in the public sector and 1.6 million, i.e., 38 per cent in the private sector. As compared to women in the organized sector, the representation of men is almost six times more. About 56 per cent of women's employment in the organized sector is in community, social and personal services, 16 per cent each in transport, storage and communication and financing, insurance, real estate and banking services. Of the total employment of women, the organized sector employment forms only 4 per cent, whereas, for men, organized sector employment constitutes 10 per cent of total employment.

A matter of great concern is the unemployment rates for female workers in recent years. The rate of unemployment is more significant for urban females at 4.7 per cent compared to 0.3 per cent for rural females. In 1994, the number of women on the live register of the Employment Exchanges in the country was 80.90 lakh.

Several factors account for this situation. Among these are absence of appropriate skills. Women also tend to get easily displaced by new technologies and are either pushed out or pushed down when job requirements call for skilled and trained persons. With the introduction of new macro-economic policies, women may further be pushed into low-paying jobs or unemployment.

The SEWA Report (1989) underlined the critical contribution of the marginalized poor women in both rural and urban areas, to the growth of the formal economy. The situation of women in the informal sector, including self-employed and wage labour, paid and unpaid workers, as well as contractual employees was studied by the Commission. Among the significant findings, based on observations and discussions with governmental and non-governmental organizations and social activists, was that one-third of all households were solely supported by women and in another third, over 50 per cent of the earnings were contributed by women. Further, 94 per cent of all women were found to be working in the unorganized sector such as agriculture, dairy, animal husbandry and fisheries. One of the key factors underlying the exploitation of women workers was lack of organization in the informal sector. Based on detailed analysis of such findings, many valuable recommendations were submitted in the report. These included, recognition of women's work as home makers, as social/economic producers, enlarging the definition of women workers in all subsequent data collection efforts to embrace all paid and unpaid work performed at the home and outside, setting up of an exclusive credit body for poor and self-employed women and linking all training programmes to employment with the objective of increasing the remuneration and improving the living conditions of poor women.

State Efforts at Women's Development

The Constitution of India not only grants equality to women but also expects the state to adopt measures of positive discrimination in favour of women for doing away with the cumulative socio-economic, educational and political disadvantages faced by them. The state efforts are best reflected in the five-year plans. The approach to women's development in the First Five-Year plan was not clear. Women were seen as a part of the general social reality which was being addressed, as poor, illiterate and generally in need of health services. Significantly issues identified by the sub-committee on women ('Women in a planned economy' 1941) were not considered. In the Second Five-Year Plan (1956-61) efforts were geared to organize *'Mahila Mandals'* (women's groups) at grassroots levels to ensure better implementation of welfare schemes, like education, health, especially maternal and child health etc. The subsequent plans (1961-74) continued in the same direction. To address the major problem of poverty, illiteracy, non-enrolment, drop-out, etc., that affected the large majority of girls and women, the issue of population control acquired increasing priority. With all these efforts, the education, maternity services and child health did not make any headway.

In the Fifth Plan (1974-78), it is argued that there was a shift in the approach from 'welfare' to 'development' as the scope of social welfare was enlarged. The women's developmental needs were seen as multi dimensional, cutting across economic, social and political sectors. In practice nothing significant happened.

The Sixth Plan admitted the failure in its efforts to remove the gender disparity and injustice in both social and economic life. Including women within the chapter on employment and manpower and rural developments, this plan made a departure from earlier plans where women had been mentioned only in the chapters on social services. Strengthening of voluntary organization of women at the grassroots, originally attempted during the Second Plan, was advocated for creating a proper climate for change. The quota for women in employment, education and decision-making bodies is the latest effort in ensuring gender justice. Despite the Seventh Plan document's refusal to adopt the quota approach, a 30 per cent quota for women in all anti-poverty programmes in the rural areas was provided. The implementation however commenced in the Eighth Five-Year Plan. The Government of India prepared a National Perspective Plan (NPP) for Women. The Eighth Plan (1992-97) promised to ensure that the benefits of development from different sectors do not bypass women. The flow of benefits to women in the three core sectors of education, health and employment was to be monitored and the general belief was that the approach has now moved from development to empowerment.

How does development planning relate to women? A recent survey by the Indira Gandhi Institute in Mumbai records a dismal picture in the last fifty years (Dev, 1997). Women barring a few in the middle and upper strata of the society remain deprived in work opportunities, in access to markets, in ownership of productive resources, in education, science and technology, in all those things that makes it possible for a human being to experience freedom and participate in and enjoy the fruits of economic development. The old policy as it was did not do any good either for the poor or women though it did achieve some improvements here and there and made a lot of noise about its good intentions. The new economic policy has merely dropped all pretentions about equality either between classes or between genders. Tension between democracy and development rather economic development is evident in the formulation of policy, in setting developmental priorities and in controlling the outcomes of biases in development (Krishnaraj, 1998).

The opinions on what these efforts have delivered differ and vary from little to great change in the status of women. The truth however is indicated by the title of a book, modern myths and locked minds. The myths of what development efforts have achieved or will achieve notwithstanding the mindset in India continues to be highly male oriented. All ideals and institutions in society converge on one thesis to control the women and her product. The women are still looked at as a commodity to serve the needs of a male society. Domestic violence is a normal feature of a woman's existence. While the data on domestic violence against the women are limited, two recent studies in India, suggests its widespread prevalence. One of the studies of family health survey reported 56 per cent women themselves justify beating of women to control them (*Times of India*, 18 November 2000). Another study reported that 75 per cent men of lower castes and 22 per cent of upper castes admitted beating their wives (Mahajan, 1990). The problem is that focus group discussions brings out the fact that women accept domestic violence as an undisputed aspect of marriage (Jejeebhoy, 1998: 856).

The western-dominated concept of development generally poses more problems for women, as cultural preferences remain rooted in a different ideology from that of an individual-oriented secular ideology. She hardly knows, accepts or wants what is called the true freedom of body and mind. The male dominated society has over the years evolved a structure of value preferences, which allows freedom to males but restricts freedom of women. It accepts polygamy but rejects polyandry, tolerates a higher caste male marrying a low caste woman but reacts violently if a higher caste woman marries a low caste. Ironically, these arrangements have become a part of social psyche. The individuals who deviate from these, themselves are unable to come to peace with themselves on account of social trauma it generates, despite fully believing in the justness of their act. Any attempt of change in these arrangements meets the fate of Bhanwari Bai (Ramchandran, 2000). Partnership with women activists, researchers and NGOs is withdrawn by the state, if it threatens the existing gender arrangements. Commenting on movements fighting the injustice of the state Khaparde (1998) felt that these movements have failed in protecting women from bad development policies, as they have not addressed issues specifically faced by women on account of the patriarchal structure of the state and society. Here again is an example of the gap between ideal and the real remaining firmly in place despite years of efforts.

Sharma (1989) reviews the impact and efficiency of the

development interventions in employment generation critically. The household approach in target group oriented planning has come in for severe criticism in anti-poverty programmes. The loan/subsidy distributed to beneficiaries under IRDP, covered only 7 per cent women with a heavy emphasis on animal husbandry and stitching and tailoring. The problems of fuel, fodder and water availability in certain areas, distribution of milch cattle under the anti-poverty programme, has added to the burden of poor women.

The concept of integrating women's issues in public policies ignores existing class and gender inequalities. A mere compensatory approach does not 'empower' women (policy documents contain such ideological emphasis) as there is no redistribution of economic resources and opportunities. There is little prospect of state supported or state-mediated redistribution of sources by gender. Women's right to inherit, own and control property are determined primarily by the social values and norms and the mechanisms of intra-household decision-making and distribution. Economic theory seems to have little to offer in understanding these forces (Mukund, 1999).

In her study in Andhra Pradesh, Mies (1986) has noted that Andhra Pradesh Women's Cooperative Finance Corporation (APWCFC) schemes do not aim at improving the economic position of rural women in their major productive occupation as agriculture labourers or cultivators. Questions such as minimum wages or equal wages for women and men are not within the purview of the objectives of the programme. The basic production relations in the villages, the unequal structure of land relations, the fact that the wage income of neither men nor women is sufficient to cover the production costs of an agricultural labourer family, are not considered. India's agricultural extension system largely bypasses 48 per cent of the nation's self-employed farmers – the ones who are women. (According to the 13th round of the NSS in 1983, 48 per cent of those who were self-employed as cultivators or unpaid family labourers in agriculture were women). The men dominate in membership of India's 58,885 village-level dairy cooperative societies (DCSs), even though female family members do most of the dairy production work. Although there are now 1,086 all-women DCSs in India, gender-wise data on membership for the remaining 57,799 are not available. Women constitute less than 3 per cent of total DCS board members. The reality of women's life remains largely untouched by the changes taking place around her.

A Newspaper Image of India

As the editorial in one of the dailies recently commented, a new form of 'two-nation theory' is taking shape in India, the final outcome of which could prove even more traumatic than the consequences of the formulation espoused by religious parochialism. The current two-nation theory is represented by the two sharply divergent Indias emerging today. One is the India of a creaking, floundering leviathan state marked by gross inefficiency, corruption, callous irresponsibility and a 'shirk culture' of rights without responsibilities that has become the birthright of the government employees at all levels including universities. In that India, a migrant worker is cheated of her livelihood by an unscrupulous contractor or a policeman, in other words either the market or the state, aided and abetted by the ruling elite. The other, radically different and dynamic India, that of private enterprise has all the resources, the will to succeed, even a culture to work hard but no morals. The editorial in the usual mode of creating a utopia has proffered a magical formula that the state must learn to harness technology for governance to bridge the gap. When Rajiv Gandhi had started the information technology revolution in India by emphasizing the use of computers in early 1980s, I had a dream that we will discover a computer which would help us make the millions of illiterates literate, now we expect it, not only to make them literate but change their mindset for us. The formulation has one serious problem, it forgets that there is a computer inside every individual which we have not been able to decipher yet and our attempts to programme the same has failed miserably so far. More so if we try to make it market friendly, it becomes anti-social in the process. The thought of the day in the same paper quoted Paine, the sublime and the ridiculous are so nearly related that it is difficult to class them separately (Times of India, 20 January 2000). The problem of sublime has become so acute that the judiciary is talking about a code of ethics for itself.

Commenting on the power theft, Das (2000) reported that out of the hundred units of electricity that is generated in the country, 15 are lost in transmission, 20 units are stolen, farmers get 20 units either free or highly subsidized. Contrary to what is generally believed, it is not the poor who steal. The well off population steals 70 per cent of the power. A colony of Indian Administrative Service officers in Lucknow has allegedly not paid for electricity in 20 years. He suggested privatization of electricity boards to tackle the problem. Gupta (2000), in another report suggested, it takes 9-11 persons to produce one MW of power in Delhi by Delhi Vidyut Board as compared to one to two persons in National Thermal Power Corporation and 0.2 to 0.5 in foreign countries. Transmission and distribution losses touched 51 per cent in 1998-99. Deficit stood at Rs.1,007 crore in 1998-99 which has been projected at Rs.7,000 million in 1999-2000. Gupta noted that we run the world's most successful protection racket in the name of governance. Home Minister, Law Minister and Chief Justice of India among others have asserted that people's confidence in the justice administration system which includes criminal justice system is fast eroding (ibid: 24 January 2000). Affluence and extreme level of poverty co-exist thanks to an obsession with industrialization and the neglect of the agriculture sector (Mungekar, 1999).

Sakina Khan (2000) noted that over the years the government's financial commitment to health care has diminished greatly. The government has never spent more than 1.8 per cent of the GDP on health the current figures are just 1.2 per cent of GDP. TB in India still kills one person every minute and there are more than 1,000 deaths every day. She reported that about four million adults are estimated to be infected with HIV in India. The Indian government has abdicated its responsibility towards people by openly favouring privatization of health care. What they said about Henry Kissinger is true for all kinds of governments in India – he wanted to become the architect of US Foreign Policy, but ended up a plumber, just plugging perpetual crises and leaks (Jain, 2000). Every one claims to be the new architect of India's development but ends up plugging the leaks, that too without much success. But the path of hope is the truth of God and hope is a Christian virtue.

A television correspondent went to a village in central India and asked who the Prime Minister of India was. Several names were mentioned (including that of a son of a former Prime Minister who had died long ago in an air crash), except that of the current Prime Minister. As the commentator later noted, in this village literally in the heart of India, the nation-state operates in absent minded slow motion, if it does at all. For millions of people the boundaries of nation remain coterminus with the boundaries of their village. The local identities are far more important and real. It is a common thing to be born and live a life devoid of any understanding or meaning of the world unfolding around them some distance away. They still manage to live, when there is a drought or a flood or a cyclone or an earthquake. What they usually remember is that they had seen better times and once upon a time it was not so hard to survive. They remember having lots of trees around or that the water table was not so low and more important there was peace. The market does not rule the man in the village, although in appearance he is part of the village economy. The wages he pays or receives, the prices of goods he buys in the local *'haat'*, are governed by custom (Chakravarty, 2000). The old ties and hierarchies are very much there and followed. The caste hierarchies, the old rules of sexual segregation and strict enforcement of these rules are all real. This reality has its own dynamics and relative autonomy from the nation-state, although the exploitative organs of state in the form of police and other officials keep taking their share from their meagre income.

The urban reality has several layers of identities. There are those millions who live on the street including children on the one end of the continuum. Then there are those who could be counted as members of an upwardly mobile society, the number running into millions and millions in between, some still hoping for a better tomorrow, some having given up. Yet the mindsets are not very different. Over 95 per cent marriages are made in heaven and arranged by parents. The females are born to serve and love serving by consent even with degrees in women's studies, sociology and law, not necessarily in that order though. Having a male child is the wish of the millennium and having too many won't disturb anybody's peace of mind except perhaps their neighbours. Neither their present nor their future seems to bother them. Life goes on smoothly even during power cuts and when the taps run dry in temperatures exceeding 40°C. What more could one expect from a nation-state which is only 50 years old? Amidst all this there is no paucity of people from different professions who keep the dream of a 'better' tomorrow alive.

Environment degradation has emerged as a major issue particularly in the media. The government is as usual unable to do much about it, so the judiciary took it upon itself to put the matters right. However, as Gupta (2000) reported despite the strict vigil by the Supreme Court, the measures taken by polluting industries remain far from adequate. The state again failed to withdraw the polluting vehicles from the roads in Delhi and was seeking an extension of the deadline which the court refused to oblige, yet polluting vehicles are still on roads as a newspaper report suggests. It may sound harsh but it is true that people no longer feel safe in the hands of the police, was the admission made by home secretary, Kamal Pande while addressing the batch of officer trainees to join the police at Hyderabad (*Times of India*, 22 January 2000). He suggested major changes in the police system which he described as "oppressive, unfriendly, incompetent and outmoded".

Conclusion

The trend thus depicts that the growth process can at best be described as stagnating. This stagnation is bound to result in the deterioration in quality and access of common people to any means for participation in the mainstream economy. The common man in the country would receive an average of 6-10 years of education. The globalization of economy would require a much higher level of skills for being able to participate in the growth of the mainstream economy. A large number of people would thus be marginalized as they would not have the requisite economic skills. The gap between rich and the poor would widen further. At the same time, the current acceptance of the respective status and a marginal position in society would become problematic, as the people are more aware of their new identity as a member of a democratic state and the concept of human rights in a democratic state. Ironically, the expansion of education and awareness would lead to greater problems of governance as the state tries to balance its political and economic constituencies. The conflicts within the country are likely to increase further.

It is clear that continuing on our present path of accelerating development at the cost of environmental degradation would severely compromise the ability of present and future generations to meet their needs. The rate of fertility decline, and thus the eventual size of Indian population, would only be marginal as there are wide variations in different parts of the country. The conditions in some of the areas which support fertility decline are not likely to improve in case of many states at least in the near future. However, if access to health facilities do not increase, which is likely, the death rate may climb as the infant mortality rate in some areas have indicated. The general state of social services is likely to decline as the conflicts within the country grow and the power of the state to govern in view of rapidly growing corruption and social fragmentation decline. Rapidly growing population has already created land, water, and fuel shortages. In many of the poorest regions of the country, it is clear that increasing population density has contributed to severe and accelerating degradation of the very resources that these growing populations depend on for survival. To meet expanding needs, environmental devastation would be ignored; the productivity of existing resources would be stretched further so as to benefit more people. Increases in GNP and food production are slower than population growth; as a result per capita levels of food production and supply would decline. Ironically, the resulting persistence of poverty would perpetuate high fertility rates, as the poor depend on large families for survival.

The general impression is that despite development efforts in the past half a century, a large segment of population remains either acutely poor or on the margin of acute poverty, though improvement is noticed in literacy levels, per capita income and in life expectancy at birth etc. It is sociologically more important to assess whether the society has become more 'modern' in India. Modernity assumes that local ties and parochial perspectives give way to universal commitments and cosmopolitan attitudes. Work should be based on choice not birth; and identity be chosen and achieved, not ascribed and affirmed. Humanity is given prominence than race and that government cease to be a manifestation of powers out of the reach of ordinary men (see Rudolph and Rudolph, 1967: 3-4). Theoretically considered a mere utopia, such changes are not likely to happen in the Indian society in the near future. Educational progress, was and still is, conceived as the main strategy of achieving 'modernity'. There has been a considerable improvement in the availability of education facilities, yet the education has not lead to the desired change in social institutions such as family and marriage. The education imparted in schools, devoid of even toilet facilities for girls not only in rural but urban areas, with poorly paid, poorly trained and frustrated teachers have made the students more uncertain about themselves, though the earlier self-perception of being nobody has undergone a change. They now consider themselves as victims of a conspiracy, and the explanation is either rooted in caste, region or religion, depending upon the political elite they put their faith in. The general despondency about their present and future, is often taking recourse to violence. The saving grace is that this change in self-perception is limited to males only, as female self-image remains largely unchanged. Modernity of the European variety remains a far off and undesirable dream.

It is not surprising therefore, that in India millions of people have hardly ever paid any attention to anything else other than the need to survive. The national intellectual discourse for change has thus been, limited to a minority, on behalf of the majority. The majority thus remains marginalized from the main stream of economic and social development process. Change in social sector, is not keeping pace with the material changes. As somebody commented, we are trying to achieve in India, in a matter of decades, what Europe achieved in two centuries, at the cost of the whole world.

4

Social Development in Pakistan

The term 'Pakistan' was coined in the third decade of the 20th century by Rehmat Ali, a student of Cambridge University (Munir, 1979) when he advocated reorganization of certain states in India to form an exclusive Muslim state. Pakistan was defined territorially during the last days of British Raj and as Samad (1995) noted it was by no sense a product of long-term historical developments. The motives for creation of Pakistan are still debated vigorously both in India and Pakistan. However, there is enough evidence to show that the idea of creation of a separate homeland for Muslims was a product of the thinking of political elite, who felt that their own future in a democracy based on numbers, was rather bleak. What implications it had for the common masses was not even debated in any great detail as not much was known about the issues common people faced in any case. The provincial elections in 1937 clearly indicated that Muslim political unity was a myth. Muslims politically and socially were heterogeneous in character, had different interests and aspirations, and most of them were not interested in presenting a unified front at the all-India level. The creation of a separate state consisting of culturally very divergent groups and the subsequent tensions within the newly formed state on the one hand and with its neighbour India, particularly relating to issues arising out of territorial boundary, pushed the development agenda in the background. A great deal of resource was spent on managing law and order within the country and on military expenditure. The internal tension lead to the eastern part of the country, then known as East Pakistan, seceding to become Bangladesh, after yet another bloody battle, again as a result of the conflict between political elite rather than common people. The process of creation of three independent states out of India continues to create problems for development in all the three countries. Pakistan has in a sense gone from one crisis to another and has seldom been in a position to achieve the smooth functioning of democracy. The crises were a creation of the elite, wanting to consolidate their hold on power. Different scholars have advanced several explanations of happenings in Pakistan over the years, but as is the case with other third world countries, these are what one can call, different perspectives of history. The central fact is that there is a large gap between the perceived objectives of an idea and what comes out as a concrete reality. It is one thing to hope that the attitude of the people would change in the desired direction but it is difficult to achieve it in practice. The idea of a nation committed to an ideology or a religious doctrine has seldom been achieved in practice, as perceptions of the dream differ along with the passion to convert the dream into a reality. The interpretations of the dream or doctrine also differ among the elite as the game of power hegemony unfolds. This in itself explains the difficulty of having a theoretical base of planned social change.

Social analysis of a country poses more problems, as individual scholars generally lack resources to cover all dimensions of social reality. The only course open for a national analysis is to rely on the secondary sources. Secondary sources seldom provide adequate insights about the causative factors. The purpose in the present study is to indicate that so far neither the causes are fully known about various issues relating to development, in different countries nor any strategy to deal with these. We have therefore confined ourselves, to try and describe the social, economic and political situation, by selecting some indicators, depending on the availability of sufficient data and compare them with other countries in the region rather than attempting a cause effect analysis. It is difficult to say for example why the poverty is so widespread and how it can be tackled than how widespread it is in comparison to India or Bangladesh.

Even this description poses some problems since the methodologies used to measure poverty and the definition of poverty may vary. What can be done to ensure a certain level of economic well-being for all is still more difficult to deal with. A great deal of diversity exists among poor. Trying to change people's thinking and attitude about anything is almost beyond theory so far as the events in these countries have amply proved. Feudal mindset in Pakistan is still rampant, that too both in the rural and urban areas as is the case in India as well, despite the economic progress accompanied by education of some kind. Development in that sense remains a rather vague term in the light of different kind of changes which make it difficult to assess the social environment as either positive or negative.

The founder of Pakistan, M.A. Jinnah realized fairly soon that all was not well in the country he has founded and that the fact of creating an international border with the majority following a particular religion, has not been enough to built a nation. There were wide ranging differences among the political elite regarding power sharing between centre and the state, the place of religion, the official language of the country and so on. The relations between different segments of population, the language, the role religion should play in the life of the new nation, and how it should govern itself, all these issues were far from settled. It was however clear that the religion did not help in reducing the conflicts among people, and has failed to unite people and guide them towards their so-called Islamic destiny. Jinnah had to remind them:

> "If you change your past and work in a spirit that every one of you, no matter to what sect he belongs, no matter what relations he had with you in the past, no matter what is his colour, caste or creed, is first, second and last a citizen of this State with equal rights, privileges and obligations, there will be no end to the progress you will make".
>
> (Munir, 1979).

By progress Jinnah meant that Pakistan would become economically prosperous and civilized. That every person in

Pakistan would have a reasonable income level, access to health and education and all other goods and services. He obviously was hoping that people would be hard working, honest and law abiding in the process. People in Pakistan would become civil and love their neighbours and the motherland. As Burki (1993) aptly puts it, he was seeking to create a paradise on earth. What is significant is that his dream was very similar to the dream of Nehru in India and the reason for that is not far to seek. Both had learnt to dream in United Kingdom. Both however, had very little idea about the middle class functionaries with a philosophy of their own and the fact that economic progress and the spirit of love thy neighbour, is a contradiction in terms.

A feudalistic aristocracy and a group of rich professionals and merchants (Gardezi and Rashid, 1983) dominated the leadership, which headed the new nation, and the bureaucracy was trained in Britain. It was not surprising that the state embarked upon a process of economic development in line with the thinking in the west. The state emphasized foreign trade based on the exporting of raw materials and industrialization geared to the production of consumer goods. Through out the 1950s, defence expenditure accounted for over 50 per cent of total government expenditure, however till 1955 the government produced surplus budgets (ibid). The first international credit agreement was signed with USA in 1948, and in 1950 Pakistan joined the International Monitory Fund (IMF) marking the beginning of a long client relationship with the western powers. This process was further strengthened with the training of bureaucrats and social scientists in USA.

The Pakistan administration guided by Adam Smith lifted the direct controls to ensure full play of market forces. During the period 1958-71 economists trained in the west formulated policies encouraging the economic growth, which only lead to further escalation of inequality within the country. As the chief architect of the economic growth Haq pointed out:

"It is well to recognise that economic growth is a brutal, sordid process....the essence of it lies in making the labourer produce more than he is allowed to consume for his immediate needs.... It would be wrong to dub the consequent emergence of surplus as exploitation: it is justification of economic growth." (Haq, 1963)

Pakistan, like India, followed a centralized planning approach to address the problem of economic development. As the Seventh Five-Year Plan document 1988-93 with a long-term perspective plan till 2003 stated:

"Over the course of the last four decades economic development in Pakistan has been directed by a pragmatic effort in securing initial, national survival and subsequently, attending to the task of providing basic social necessities, however the process only indirectly addressed the higher social and political objectives.

Now that the economic foundations are firmly established, it is time to be more sensitive to the larger social vision. Presently we are very far from the realization of that vision, largely because of difficulties in arriving at a consensual view of common objectives between a strong modernizing elite and the relatively poorer, traditional mass of common people."

There are two important aspects to this disparity between national growth in production and the inability to satisfy the real aspiration of people. First, the majority have not shared equitably in the benefits of economic growth. Poverty and economic prosperity have coexisted. Second, economic planning has not addressed existing social and political realities: social mobility remains limited; privilege often triumphs over merit; intellectual questioning is penalised rather than rewarded; and a consensus on fundamental values has failed to emerge (Government of Pakistan, 1987: 15).

It is interesting to note the use of the term 'modernizing' for the elite and the term 'traditional' for the poor masses earlier. This reflects the belief that 'modernization' whatever the term meant was a necessary condition for change from a poor status to an elite status. The later explanation, however, attributed poverty to lack of equitable sharing, and the inability of the economic planning to address the social and political realities. The similarity of the outcome, with what we find in India, is obvious despite the fact that, Pakistan has a much smaller population than India. It followed a more open door policy of economic development than India, it got more financial support from the Muslim countries, in terms of employment for its workers of various categories and consequently subsequent remittances. While all this was on the positive side, democracy was never firmly in place and it had long periods of military rule. The internal strife is still very high with recurring violent conflicts and a return to the military rule after a short span of democratic rule.

The so-called strategies for rectifying the situation in future are – full employment, national integration to reduce conflicts, rural uplift, social improvement programmes of women and youth, a target approach and technological innovation (ibid: 15-16). The idea of turning the rural into an urban population remains firmly in place, with little awareness of how to accomplish the task. The dream of creating a Pakistan offering a middle class life to all is often repeated by the elite, though now fooling nobody, as neither the effort has been sincere nor the economic models functional. The feudal mindset is firmly in place and ironically has a strong support at the grassroots for the continuation of the same, a trait which is found in a more democratic India as well.

Agriculture is the main stay of Pakistan's economy accounting for over 23 per cent of gross domestic product (GDP), employing about 50 per cent of the labour force, and providing livelihood to 70 per cent of the rural population. The average growth rate was around 3.3 per cent per year (ibid: 162).

Pakistan's initial economic success as Burki noted was achieved due to generous aid from abroad and remittances from Pakistanis employed in the oil producing states, besides development of an industrial base in the country. He noted that despite this economic success there was extraordinary pessimism about the future of the country. There is a general sense of fatigue (Burki, 1993: 1). He attributed this to a tendency to feel with greater intensity the pain and discomfort of the moment. He stated the truth without realizing it. The human tendency to feel the pain is transformed in the process of economic progress. The pain becomes more individualized and the 'other' becomes the cause of it. The distance between the individual and collectivity increases but in case of Pakistan it happened largely in case of males as females were kept outside the main stream of development, to preserve their capacity of suffering the pain on behalf of their male counterpart. The tendency to have women to shield the men and to surrender to them in their moments of despair is the most cherished possession in this part of the world. However, as Burki (ibid) and Bean (1993) noted that this negated the economic progress as the fertility rate continued to be around 3 per cent.

Population Growth in Pakistan

Pakistan's population was 33.7 million in 1950 and it has become 132 million in 1998. The Human Development Report, 1999, estimated Pakistan's population in 1997 as 144 million. In other words it has added a hundred million people approximately, three times its population, during the last five decades of its development efforts. The annual population growth rate has been well over 3 per cent during the period and has shown only a marginal decline in recent years (HDR, 1999). As per World Development Report, 1999-2000, it was 4.6 per annum during 1980-90 and has now come down to 2.8 during 1990-98. The total fertility rate was 7 in 1975, which has come down to 4.8 in 1997. The contraception prevalence rate was 17 per cent during 1990-98. The population in the age-group of 15-64 years was estimated to be 44 millions in 1980, which has grown to 71 million in 1998. The percentage of population above 65 was estimated to be around 2.6 per cent of the total in 1997.

Year	*Population (million)*	*Growth rate (%)*
1951	33.7	—
1961	42.9	2.3
1971	65.2	3.7
1981	84.2	3.1
1991	110	3.1
1997	144 (132)	3.0

Source: VII Five-Year Plan, Planning Commission, Government of Pakistan, Human Development Report, 1999.

In 1975, the urban population was 26.4 per cent of the total, which has increased to 36 per cent in 1998.

Economic Development

Labour Force

The total labour force was around 29 million in 1980, out of the population of 44 million in the age-group of 15-64, which increased to 49 million as the 15-64 age-group population increased to 71 million. The percentage of females in the labour force has increased from 23 per cent in 1980 to 28 per cent in 1998. The percentage of children in the age-group 10-14 in the labour force declined to 17 in 1998 from 23 per cent in 1980.

The economic survey of Pakistan 1997-98 noted, that based on its estimates of a population of 139 million, and its growth rate of 2.7 per cent and participation rate of 27.46 per cent, the total labour force was 38.18 million and it was growing at the rate of 2.63 per cent. The unemployment was expected to be around 5.37 per cent during 1997-98.

Size of Economy

The gross national product was 63.2 billion US dollars in 1998 with an average annual growth rate of 5 per cent, whereas the GNP per capita was 480 US $. The annual growth rate of per capita income was 2.5 per cent in 1997-98. The GNP in PPP$ was 204.9 billion and the per capita income was 1,560 PPP$.

The Gini Index, reflecting the inequality of income between the rich and poor, was 31.2 in 1996. The poorest 10 per cent consumed 4.1 per cent of the total income, whereas the highest 10 per cent consumed 27.7 per cent. The share of the 2nd, 3rd, and 4th, 20 per cent from the bottom was 13, 16 and 20.3 per cent respectively, whereas the highest 20 per cent consumed 41.2 per cent (WDR, 1999-2000). The share of the top 20 per cent was 36.5 per cent in 1963-64, whereas the share of the lowest 20 per cent was 5.8 per cent which has now increased to 9.1 per cent in 1996 (ibid:239).

Poverty

The population below the national poverty line on the basis of a survey conducted in 1991 was estimated to be 36.9 in the rural areas and 28 per cent in the urban areas. In all, 34 per cent population was assessed to be living below the poverty line. However, the population having less than a PPP dollar a day was calculated merely to be around 11.6 per cent, and two PPP dollars a day at 57 per cent. Pakistan, like India, in the mid of the twentieth century, was largely an agrarian economy. Majority of the people was simple in character. The majority worked as farmers or as labourers on the farms. They had simple needs and had very few resources or economic assets. In the modern economic sense they were termed as poor. One of the objectives of the development process in Pakistan was to alleviate this poverty. In 1960 the total population of Pakistan was around 43 million and 73 per cent or nearly 31 million people were poor. In 1991 the total population of the country has become 110 million and 51 per cent or 56 million people were still poor. In other words in forty years of development the country has added 15 million poor. If we take the current figures of 34 per cent as the proportion of poor, out of a total population of 144 million, the total number of poor would still work out to be around 48 million. The number of poor is difficult to estimate correctly in such large populations and high illiteracy rates. The different definitions and methods of poverty measurements further add to the problem.

Poverty in Historical Perspective

Year	*Poverty Line (per capita per month)*	*Poverty (%) Headcount*
1969-70	42.8	73.4
1979	129	51.8
1984-85	213.6	48.9
1991	373.7	51.4
World Bank, 1991	NA	34.0

Headcount ratio, defined as the percentage of population whose actual consumption expenditure falls short of the reference poverty line, was constituted from the published data of households income and their share in population across different income groups.

Although Burki (1993) felt that Pakistan has done away with absolute poverty to a great extent, according to his estimates only about 20 per cent or 20 million were absolutely poor in Pakistan, but others feel differently. The economic survey of Pakistan 1997-98 noted that poverty increased in Pakistan in the early nineties after registering a decline from a high of 46.5 per cent in 1969-70. It noted that structural adjustment programmes and macro-economic stabilization measures have imposed heavy burden on the poor. The expenditure on safety net programmes was 0.2 per cent of the GDP. The amount collected through *Zakat* and help from *Baitul Mal* were also insufficient to help the poor (GoP, 1998: IX).

However, the problem is neither of economic poverty nor of numbers, it is about the way the people in general feel about their life and their future at any given point of time. And people were feeling despondent in early nineties and they are still feeling the same at the turn of the century. Further, the economic progress has not brought the progress that Jinnah had in mind. Even after more than five decades the different segments in Pakistan, Mohajirs, Boluchis, Sindhis, Punjabis and the Pakhtuns remain separate units (Haydar, 1993). The frustration among the Mohajirs lead to the creation of Mohajir Qaumi Movement and they are still treated as 'other' by the local Sindhis who believe themselves to be the sons of the soil. The crossing of the border is not on, not even if you believe in the same god simply because god and land ownership contradict each other. The struggle to come to terms with one or the other goes on and is further complicated by projects of modernity.

Structural Changes in Pakistan's Economy

Pakistan's economy in 1947 and for several years after its birth was predominantly agricultural as the sector contributed nearly two-thirds of its gross domestic product (GDP). The agriculture still is the single largest contributor of the GDP in Pakistan, though has registered a significant decline from 53.2 in 1950. Manufacturing has almost doubled its share but otherwise the change in all other sectors has not been very spectacular. A large segment of the population is still dependent on agriculture for earning its livelihood. Burki (1993) feels that the agriculture has become modernized during the five decades of development and is participating in the world trade. Pakistan has developed an industrial base, which is diverse in character, and possesses a certain level of technological sophistication according to Burki.

Sectors	*1949-50*	*1996-97*
Agriculture	53.2	24.2
Manufacturing	7.8	17.9
Mining and quarrying	0.2	0.5
Construction	1.4	3.9
Electricity and gas	0.2	4.1
Trade	11.9	16.3
Transport and communications	5.0	9.9
Banking and insurance	0.4	2.6
Housing	5.1	5.7
Public administration and Def.	7.0	6.4
Services	7.7	8.5

Source: Quraishi, Sarfaraz Khan (1997), The Pakistan Development Review, 36(4) Part I, p. 323.

The statistics on income distribution on the other hand indicate that there was no significant change in the distribution of income, except that whereas in 1963, 2.8 per cent households had an income less than Rs. 50, it declined to 1 per cent in 1969. The percentage of households having an income of 50-100 also declined from 17 per cent in 1963 to 12 per cent in 1969. In 1963, there were only 0.9 per cent households having an income of over Rs. 900, in 1969 only 0.8 per cent had an income over Rs. 1000. The bulk of the population 79.8 in 1963 and 83.4 in 1969 had an income of Rs. 50-300.

Income Shares of Various Groups

(percentages)

Year	*Lowest 20%*	*Middle 60%*	*Highest 20%*	*Ratio of highest to lowest 20%*
1963-64	6.4	48.3	45.3	7.1
1971-72	7.9	49.1	43.0	5.4
1984-85	7.3	47.7	45.0	6.2
1992-93	6.2	45.6	48.2	7.8
1993-94	9.2	47.7	45.0	6.2

Source: Federal Bureau of Statistics, Pakistan Economic Survey, 1997-98.

The poorest 20 per cent had a share of 6.4 per cent in 1963 and it was 6.2 in 1992-3, whereas the share of highest 20 per cent was 45.3 in 1963, which increased to 48.2 per cent in 1992-93. In 1993-94, the poorest 20 per cent registered an increase of nearly 3 per cent and the highest 20 per cent registered a decline of 3 per cent. Qureshi in his study noted the share of poorest 20 per cent to be 5.7 per cent in 1991, as compared to the share of highest 20 per cent to be around 49.2 per cent. The World Bank figures in 1996 noted the share of poorest 20 per cent as 9.4 and the highest at 41.2. The economic survey in Pakistan gave the share of rural poorest 20 per cent as 10.6 compared to the highest 20 per cent in rural areas, as 34.6 per cent, the Gini coefficient was 0.35. In contrast the Gini coefficient in urban areas was 0.40 since the share of the lowest 20 per cent in urban areas was 9.4 compared to the share of the highest 20 per cent of 40.9 per cent (PES, 1997-98).

The growth of household income has been higher in urban areas in Pakistan, which is the general trend in most developing countries in the region. The growth appears to be substantial in terms of volume but it should be seen in the context of its purchasing power and nature of consumption to understand the true meaning of this growth and its consequences in promoting human happiness.

Monthly Average Household Rural/Urban Income (Rs. per month)

Year	*Pakistan*	*Urban*	*Rural*
1963-64	203	236	193
1971-72	265	361	234
1984-85	1774	2390	153
1993-94	3915	5571	3248
Compound growth rate	10.37	11.11	9.87

Source: Government of Pakistan (1998), Economic Survey, 1997-98: 44.

Social Development in Bangladesh

Social Services in Pakistan

The provision of social services for the common man is far from adequate. Pakistan ranks 127 in the Human Development Index (HDR, 2001) with adult literacy of 44 per cent, access of potable water and sanitation to only 88 and 61 per cent of population respectively. However, as compared to HDR, 2000, when it was classified as a country with medium development level it has now been classified as a low developed country by HDR, 2001. Similarly, the participation rate at primary level is 70 per cent and almost 50 per cent of the students drop-out by the fifth grade. Moreover, not only health facilities are inadequate, the quality of services is also very poor. The public sector expenditure in Pakistan on education and health is very low.

A number of schemes have been implemented to provide social services to the poorer sections of the society in the past. They include, among others, Rural Works Programme, Integrated Rural Development Programme, People's Works Programme, Five Points Programme and Tameer-e-Watan Programme. However, these programmes have not been very successful due to various problems associated with implementation. The most recent and a very ambitious initiative is the Social Action Programme which aims at increasing the literacy rate to 70 per cent by the end of the century. Besides, the programme aims at improving the quality and standard of education by improving teachers' training, revision of curriculum and providing better learning environment. It also emphasizes on the basic health facilities, population welfare, and rural development and women development.

A study by the World Bank in 1995 suggested that private voluntary income transfers were helping in meeting the needs of the poor. At the state level, the system of *Zakah*, *Ushr* and *Baitul Maal*, Islamic institutions for helping the poor, have been instituted to transfer the income to the poorer sections of the society. The *Zakat* fund provides a monthly rehabilitation grant as a one-time transfer. However, the impact of these measures has been relatively limited as it caters to a small number of beneficiaries compared to the wide spread poverty. The revenue collection is very limited by way of *Zakah*.

Baltul Maal was established in 1992 and two schemes funded through this are, the food subsidy scheme and the individual financial assistance scheme. A person who does not receive *Zakah* and has an income of less than Rs. 1,500 can receive the grant from *Baitul Maal*.

Education

The adult literacy rate in Pakistan was 21 per cent in 1970 and has increased to 45 per cent for population aged 15 years and above in 1999 (HDR, 2001:142). Nearly half the male population became capable of reading and writing as compared to 25.4 per cent women who acquired the same skills during the same year. Similarly, only one in four girls (28%) was going to school as compared to one out of two boys, 58 per cent (HDR, 1999: 140). It is interesting to note that the demand for education has been low in Pakistan, as the common man shied away from it and it compensated the weak state response (Jalil, 1993:78). In Pakistan, in 1948-49, the participation rate at primary level age-group 5-9 was about 19.8 per cent. It was 63.5 in 1993 (79.5 for boys and 45.7 for girls). At secondary education level, the gross national enrolment rate for Pakistan during 1989 was 20 per cent, with a high drop-out rate.

Government Expenditure on Education

In Pakistan, the state was spending nearly 3 per cent of the GNP on educating people in the country in 1996, compared to 2 per cent in 1980, as per the data provided by the World Bank Report of 1999-2000. Nearly 66 per cent of this expenditure was for promoting primary and secondary education and 13.6 per cent for promoting higher education. Pakistan economic survey gave the figures for public sector outlay on education during 1995-96 as 2.4 per cent, 2.5 in 1996-97 and 2.25 in 1997-98, which again reflects the problem of accurate data on the one hand and the declining trend in expenditure on education, despite the fact that the survey itself admitted that the illiteracy rate of 40 per cent was one of the lowest in the world. Jalil (ibid) has noted that historically Pakistan has accorded a low priority to education. During 1958-69, education was given a back seat both in terms of effort and relative importance since the government was mainly concerned with promoting economic growth. Subsequently, more attention was given to promoting education but with little impact. During 1983-88, the expenditure was 2.02 per cent of the GNP from an earlier average of 1.5. The international institutions promoting development have been insisting on raising the level of expenditure to 6 per cent of the GNP. In the education policy announced in 1992 for the next ten-year period, the primary education was allocated an amount of 51.34 billion compared to 38.99 for secondary and 10.16 for university and 9.44 billion for technical and vocational education (ibid).

Participation Rate

Jalil (ibid) noted that participation rate at primary level age-group 5-9 was about 19.5 per cent in 1948-49, which increased to 63.5 per cent in 1988. However, the participation revealed a gender gap of 33.8 per cent between the participation of boys and girls, and the urban participation rate was higher than the rural participation rate by 19.2 per cent. Girls in rural areas were in particular lagging behind their urban counterparts, as their participation was 60 per cent lower than the urban girls. At secondary level the gross enrolment in Pakistan in 1989 was 20 per cent. The participation rate in 1997-98 was given as 77 per cent for primary level, 49 for middle level and 34 for class IX and X level. Compared to other levels, the tertiary level expanded during the past 40 years from the base in 1948. The college level enrolment increased by 30 times and university level enrolment by 98 times compared to primary 12 times and secondary 16 times. But, in all, only 4.6 per cent of the relevant age-group 18-23 years has access to higher education. Jalil (ibid) made a significant point that the demand for education among the general population was rather weak as pointed out earlier.

Salient features of new education policy make interesting reading. Ninety per cent children in the age-group 5-9 would be enrolled at the primary level by 2003. The level of government expenditure on education would be increased from the current 2.2 per cent of GNP to 4 per cent. One of the objectives of educational policy is given as making education purposeful and job-oriented. Religious education has been made compulsory from class I to VIII. The Quranic principles and Islamic practices has been made an integral part of the curricula, to integrate the message of the Holy Quran, in the process of education. The future generation of Pakistan is thus expected to be true practising Muslims, who would be able to face the challenges of the twenty-first century and the next millennium with courage confidence, wisdom and tolerance. This reflects the dilemma of development and modernization, as there is a strong urge to safeguard the culture and religion and the modern school education attempts to open up issues such as higher economic orientation, greater freedom for women and more individual freedom, which directly contradict some religious values and practices. Debate about the implications of modern education, has occupied the Muslim mind, even before Pakistan was born, It was resolved by allowing freedom to males to modernize themselves, within the framework of Islam, while keeping the females away from the school, and its modernizing influence to the extent possible. The fact also remains, that the current education, particularly at the school level, does not generate any skills among the learners. Even the language skills acquired are far from satisfactory. There is no wonder that the common man who is far more logical, does not feel the need for it.

Percentage of School-Going Children in Pakistan 1955-79

Year	*Male*	*Female*	*Total*
1955–56	34.4	6.5	21.1
1978–79	68.0	32.7	51.2

Source: Dilawar Ali Khan (1970), Planning for the Poor in Pakistan, in R.P. Misra (ed.), *Humanizing Development*, UNDP.

In recent times, eminent development economists including Amartaya Sen, have been emphasizing the importance of promoting education for accelerating the pace of development. However, continued low enrolment ratio and nearly 50 per cent population remaining illiterate scores the point that people in general are not interested in the 'education' being offered. The Human Development Report, 1998 noted that the education was largely irrelevant to the needs of the people. People in rural areas who are generally engaged in agricultural activities for earning a living have felt that 'school education' creates difficulties for them at several levels. For example, the educated boys would prefer employment rather than working in the field or carrying out other agriculture related activities. They would prefer to migrate to urban areas and their cultural preferences for food or clothes may change. The education generally expands the need but it may or may not expand the resources. Lack of success in finding suitable employment or poor wages may generate frustration and relationship problems.

Female children are in particular not sent to school since the parent do not want them to interact with their male counter parts or work outside the house. The people, in general, in Pakistan, as in India and Bangladesh, view maintaining close vigil on their daughters, to preserve their sexual morality and the family ties. The concept of freedom is, therefore, almost non-existent for females. These arrangements are laid down by cultural preferences, in conformity with religious laws, and supervised by females at the family and community level informally. The school education is generally seen as disturbing these arrangements. The logic for such arrangements is, the greater emphasis on the well-being of the family and the community. In other words, the 'self' is allocated very little space in the construction of the social relationships, in the case of females, within the family and the community. The 'school education' can and does effect this construction, which has far reaching implications, both for the individual and the society. The result of the transformations which the 'school education' is capable of introducing in society, can be viewed from several perspectives. But, in the cultural milieu of Pakistan, the transformations have generated a lot of apprehensions, particularly for the common man. The western values of individual freedom and new gender roles are unacceptable, as they are unable to cope with these, at both, the individual and the family level. Individual freedom results in diluting the emotional content of family relationships, which is the core of these relationships in the eastern societies. As a natural consequence, school education has not been the immediate priority of the common man, if it has not been rejected altogether.

Health

The people in Pakistan are now expected to live longer than they were some three decades earlier. However, the life expectancy at birth, which was 49.2 in 1970 and 64.4 in 1998, has declined to 59.6 in 1999 (HDR, 2000 and 2001). The life expectancy index has come down to 58 from 66. It is difficult to explain this sudden decline except that perhaps all of a sudden the health facilities have declined or the data available has been differently interpreted. The number of children dying before reaching their first birthday has come down from 118 per thousand in 1970, to 95 in 1997, and 84 in 1999, showing further improvement and those dying before their 5th birthday has come down to 112 from 181 in 1970 (HDR, 2001). The percentage of people not expected to survive their 60th birthday has come down to 27 per cent of the total population from nearly 50 per cent in 1970. The incidence of TB is given as 3.1 per 1,00,000 population in 1997 and as 60 per 1,00,000 in 1998. There is no explanation available for the sudden increase. The population with disabilities is 4.9 per 1,00,000 population. Nearly 52 doctors and 32 nurses are available to 1,00,000 population, provided you have the resources to use their services. The number of people having access to safe drinking water has increased from 38 in 1982 to 88 in 1999 and people living in more sanitary condition are 61 per cent as compared to 16 in 1982. Nearly 340 women die during their pregnancies in a population of 1,00,000. However, the government spent only 0.8 per cent of the GDP on public health in 1997 which was better than what it spent (0.3%) in 1960.

Pakistan Economic Survey (1997-98) noted that health facilities are extremely below the desired level. The existing network of medical services in the public sector consists of 865 hospitals, 4,523 dispensaries, 5,121 basic health units 853 rural health centres and 262 tuberculosis centres. In 1997, there was one doctor for 1,724 persons, one nurse for 5,460 persons and one bed for 1,504 persons. The expenditure on health services was a healthy 0.72 per cent of the GNP and in per capita terms it works out to be Rs. 142 per annum.

The net result of some of the gains in the health sector appears to be a higher growth rate of the population and people living longer than they were earlier. For many poor households it means feeding more people for a longer period of time. The women in these poor households have more children on their hands. These children are unable to or do not want to go to the school. Some of them work in a natural way alongside their parents but others are forced to earn a living in more hazardous circumstances. In general, one way of looking at more children surviving is to see them suffering for decades to survive, instead of dying before their first or fifth birthday. Once they survive, they have hardly any freedom to decide, the kind of life they would like to live.

Housing

The estimated housing shortage in 1987 was around 3 million units of which 1.4 million was in urban areas. Nearly 25 per cent urban population lived in slums. The housing conditions were deteriorating further as the occupancy per housing unit increased from 5.4 in 1973 to 6.7 in 1980. The average number of persons per room increased from 2.7 to 3.5. Only 5 per cent houses in rural areas were built with bricks. Only 38 per cent population, 22 per cent in case of rural areas, had access to safe drinking water in 1980. Only 36 per cent had access to electricity (PSA, 1987).

Development of Women

Development of women is perhaps the weakest in Pakistan compared with India and Bangladesh. The rural Pakistan like India is as feudal in character as it was when the development efforts commenced in 1950s. Social policy with reference to women in Pakistan has changed with the frequent change of governments. Differences in ideological orientations of the governments particularly how they construct women in the social order and her consequent status and role, account for these shifts. The image of women plays a significant role in the construction of societies in the economically less developed countries, with a large segment of population still rural in character. The symbolic representation of women is done first to define its own cultural identity, then to redefine its tradition to indicate a movement towards westernization also referred to as modernization. Pakistan, India and Bangladesh all have gone through the process of such symbolization without being very sure of what they wanted. They have accepted the universal logic of reform in the existing status of women but are unable to accept the logic of gender equality. The first significant change occurred in Pakistan, in the form of Muslim Family Law Ordinance in 1961, during the military rule of Ayub Khan, regarded as the first attempt to provide protection to women by regulating divorce and polygamy. It provided for registration of all marriages and eliminates divorce solely by repudiation (*talaq*). The written permission of wife (wives) is to be obtained and brought before an arbitration council, for permission to remarry. To what extent it can be enforced on the ground is another matter, but it was a step in the direction of reform. During the Bhutto regime women were allowed to participate in politics and trade union activities, being a more empowering attitude towards women, but, Zia-ul Haq, the military ruler, relegated women to *chadar* and *chardiwari*. He went to the extent of wanting to have separate schools for girls including universities. It is surprising that the first woman Prime Minister Benazir Bhutto did little to change this attitude. While the legal rights of Muslim women are guaranteed by Quran, the customs and attitudes in South Asia have generally not adhered to these in practice (Rawjee, 1989).

While in India the spread of education and access to mass communication has made minor inroads, the mindset in Pakistan, with the growth of religious orthodoxy, remains unjust towards women, as pointed out by official status of women report on women's status in Pakistan. As Rawjee (ibid) pointed out, the laws and ordinances tried to push women back into the confines of the proverbial *chadar* and *chardiwari*. Some studies, however, indicate that in rural areas, laws for curbing the freedom of women are not taken note of by common people, as they are neither aware of these laws, nor the concept of *chadar* and *chardiwari* are helpful to them. In the normal life, women have to move outside the home to work, on the farm or to look after the cattle. Only the rich farmers are imposing practice of *purdah* on their women. The urban women, like their counterparts in India and Bangladesh, are gradually becoming economically active and better off in terms of education and access to health facilities, yet they do not have the kind of mobility and independence, one expects among educated women. The women are still considered inferior to male and to be kept under control. This notion was particularly reinforced during the government under Zia ul Haq (1977-88) as stated earlier (Weiss, 1994). The dominant belief is that the woman is created to serve the family, a sentiment dominant in India and Bangladesh as well. Female children are in particular not sent to school since the parent do not want them to interact with their male counter parts or work outside the house. The women in particular are not free to choose their spouse. The parents want to exercise this right in conformity with the social norms and to marry her as per their own convenience. The prime consideration is the notion of social approval. The logic is that the marriage is between families and not between individuals. The people, therefore, in general in Pakistan view maintaining close vigil on their daughters to preserve their sexual morality and the family ties, a trend found in India and Bangladesh as well.

A study (Ali, 1995) in assessing the status of women in Pukhtun society noted that a Pukhtun woman has a layered identity, which is Muslim, Pukhtun and national in character. But, in actual practice, her life is governed more by social norms of Pukhtun society rather than by religious or civil laws. The woman is not free under the *'riwaj'* (social customs). She is considered the property of her male agnates to be bartered away at a suitable brideprice known as *'sar paisey'*. The amount is generally used by male kins. The male kins of the deceased husband of the widow would negotiate the remarriage. Pukhtun women are by and large excluded from inheritance in general and landed property in particular, a practice common in rural India, though the Islamic law provides for a share for daughter, wife and mother. If a man dies without any male heirs leaving only daughters, the property is taken over by the male relatives of the deceased. In 1986, an official report on women's condition in the country stated that:

> "Rural women tend to have an extremely low status self image. They believe themselves to have been born inferior, they curse themselves for being deficient and they glorify the males in their lives. Their fathers are often tyrants, their brothers selfish, their husbands uncaring in their attitudes towards their women, and yet they dwell in a state of resignation, accepting the myth of male superiority as an important part of their perceptions...thus the average rural woman of Pakistan is born in near slavery, leads a life of drudgery and dies invariably in oblivion. This grim condition is not a fantasy but the stark reality of nearly 30 million Pakistani citizens...." (Pakistan Commission, 1986:29-31)

Most Pakistani women live under extremely poor physical conditions as the sex ratio indicates. It was 91 females to 100 males in 1986 (Weiss, 1994: 415). Ironically, despite a much better record of female literacy and overall improvement in women's development, the condition of rural women in India and Bangladesh is no different.

A study of illiterate women (Muhammed, 1998) cites data about illiteracy quoting a UNESCO report (1985) and a demographic survey conducted in Pakistan in 1988-92. The survey reported 7 per cent female literacy in rural areas whereas the national female literacy level was around 20 per cent. In the tribal belt of Pakistan, the rural female literacy was less than 5 per cent. Weiss (1994) cited literacy rate in Pakistan being 8.6 in 1951, 6.7 in 1961, 11.6 in 1972, 16 in 1981 and 21.3 in 1991-92. According to Bhatti, 96.5 per cent rural Pakistani women, aged twenty-five and above, were illiterate (Bhatti, 1988: 44). Pakistan's low female literacy rates are comparable to some of the poorest countries in the world, whereas Pakistan in 1990s was likely to be included in the category of middle income group before it started to decline to the frustration of the World Bank economists.

According to HDR, 1999, the female literacy in Pakistan is one of the lowest in the region at 24.4 per cent, whereas even in Bangladesh it is 26.1 per cent. The combined first, second and third level gross enrolment ratio of school-going age children remain lowest at 28 per cent in Pakistan, compared to 30 per cent, in Bangladesh and 47 per cent (1991 census) and now above 50 per cent, in India.

Despite the growth of the health infrastructure and the realization that Pakistan's population is growing at a faster rate than their neighbours, the efforts at fertility control have not been very successful, nor it has lead to an improvement in the status of health of the common woman. As Sweetser (1993) noted, full comprehension of the health and health care issues facing women in Pakistan requires an understanding of the way women are viewed. The western scholars often miss the significance of Islamic viewpoint in population growth and that the role the women occupy in social life. Wide class differences separate a very small number of well off, educated women in urban centres from the vast majority who have little or no education, virtually no independent mobility and extremely limited control over property or productive resources. Despite these class differences, the women throughout the country have widely shared notions about the nature and capacities of women. According to popular belief, if women acquired the tools required for life outside the household like men, they would cease to be women (ibid). The women's participation in economic and social activities outside the home is considered a big threat to the moral fabric of the society in Pakistan. Social norms for women are primarily defined with reference to their bodies. Ability to become pregnant with a male child along with the ability to prove the source of pregnancy is the most cherished activity expected of a women. Women's access to health care is very limited due to family norms, besides economic constraints (ibid:57). A study in 1976 reported that though 76 per cent women were aware about family planning, 54 per cent did not approve it.

There is a belief about employment of women that only poor families send their women to work. However, Rawjee (1989) noted that despite social opposition a large number of urban women are taking up employment. She felt that the growth of industrial and service sector has opened up more avenues for the employment of women. A large number of women worked in the unregistered, undefined informal sector as piece rate workers. Most women accept lower wages than men. In most instances, a woman's income usually makes the difference between barely surviving and providing basic necessities such as education for the children. As a textile women worker pointed out that all her income is spent on her family and children, she has no savings. Sexual harassment at work is common and even educated women are not immune from the malady. A study (Abbasi, 1980) found that women's work participation rate in the rural areas of Sindh was around 44.7 per cent. Shaheed and Mumtaz (1990), in their study, found that culturally it is still considered desirable that women should not work for wages as it jeopardizes the 'honour' of the male and raises issues about the chastity of women. Yet, in their study they found that a majority of rural women contribute to the family income either as part time or full time workers. Work for poor women add to her misery by increasing her working hours. It does not help her in getting a better deal, since the mindset of men remain unchanged in treating her as a secondary citizen. A study of women (Baqai, 1976), however, has noted that women felt that education and employment leads to an improvement in the status of woman. It helps in marriage at a higher age and a low fertility rate. But this may be true for a small section of urban educated class, the bulk of women in rural areas and in informal sector in the urban areas are characterized by low education, no technical skills, and low incomes. Another study (UNICEF, 1993) found undernourished and overworked women in Sindh province, with a 16 hours plus work-day. No wonder, 700 women out of 1,00,000 die while trying to reproduce and 70 per cent mothers deliver at home.

The contraceptive prevalence rate was low though the awareness rate was pretty high. This indicates that information alone is not enough to bring a change in the practices.

Political Development

Pakistan faced more tensions in its political development like Bangladesh as compared with India. As noted earlier the idea of Pakistan was a myth in the sense that at no point the entire Muslim population in India was politically culturally or socially united. Secondly, the bureaucracy and the military inherited by Pakistan were structurally very different from India. And, finally, the centre-state relations in India did not pose the kind of problem Pakistan faced. The cultural diversity posed more problems and finally resulted in secession of Eastern Pakistan. But what is more important for us is to note that the key of political development, that is, the sovereignty must rest with people and the state and its institutions must serve the common people in a transparent and just manner did not happen. From the very beginning the Muslim politics was dominated by the aristocratic families which has continued in the present day Pakistan, while the base has shifted in Indian politics making it more broad based.

The death of the founder of Pakistan, Jinnah in 1948, barely a year after the new nation had come into being created a political vacuum, which severally affected the political development in Pakistan. It could not evolve even a broad consensus on what kind of government would best serve the national interest. As a result Pakistan so far has had a series of constitutions (1956, 1962 and 1973) and perhaps many more to follow. It also could not make up its mind whether it wanted a secular state or a theocratic state. It has continued to experiment with dictatorship as a desired mode of governance with brief spells of electoral democracy.

Summing up the political development in Pakistan, Korson (1993) noted that amendments to 1973 constitution made the governance of Pakistan look like a three legged stool – one leg being the prime minister and the other two being the president and the chief of army staff. This reflects the constitutional dilemma of Pakistan and its inability to evolve a stable democratic system like that in India. However, the real problem in political development of a newly independent state like Pakistan is the process of political development and the manner in which other developments, such as social and economic development, provide inputs to the political development. It would appear that lack of development of modern education alone contributed a great deal to the growing influence of religion in Pakistan, but the non performance of economic system and the continued hold of the land owning class and the business houses supported the Islamization process in Pakistan. Some other related issues are the process of political development and the development of institutions. Development of political parties and its functioning and leadership reflect the importance of the process. Political leadership requires many skills and people who undergo a process of political work over the years become adept in these skills. Formal training institutions to train people in the skills of democratic political leadership have yet to emerge in many new nations including Pakistan. Pakistan has failed to develop a democratic society, simply because the elite had no faith in masses and never wanted them to participate fully in decision-making. The most notable feature of political development in Pakistan has been the decision to concentrate all powers in the hand of earlier the governor general and later the president. It was a ploy by the bureaucracy to dilute the power of the politicians. The military acting independently under the control of the chief of army staff has also added to the demise of democracy in Pakistan. It is not surprising that in Pakistan no social movement capable of mobilizing public opinion cutting across the cultural and ethnic boundaries could emerge. As a consequence no national level leadership emerged which could provide stability and substance to the democracy in the country. The widespread corruption among the political elite in particular and other levels of state functionaries, in all new nations have also contributed greatly to the non-performance of democracy. Still it is surprising that many think that so long the elections are held the democracy is alive. Not many look beyond the surface to assess the capability and opportunity for freedom of choice at the grassroots. Anyone seriously interested in the real political participation of people, in deciding issues impacting their life, would be grossly pessimistic about the future political developments in Pakistan.

The reports in the media in Pakistan highlight some interesting facts, which provide a good commentary on the current state of affairs. A news commenting on tribal affair noted that tribal area straddles the Pak-Afghan border for about 1,200 km. The area, rich in minerals and forestry, is inhabited by hard working, agile people, predominantly Pathans, who are ethnically Afghans with close interests in the affairs of Afghanistan. It was in 1950, that the tribal areas were given representation in the National Assembly. Being a federally administered area, it is not represented in any provincial assembly. The tribesman were not allowed the right to vote till 1997, as the right to vote was limited to only few thousand Maliks only (Mahsud, 1999).

Jafri (1999) noted that during the recent past, four 'elected' parliamentary governments, headed in turn by Benazir Bhutto and Nawaz Sharief, have been audaciously evading a categorical imperative of the Constitution by suppressing the local tier of government. This he felt is contrary to the spirit as well as letter of the Constitution. In the post-Zia phase of Pakistan, two prominent political rivals had been virtually at daggers drawn. However, with all that hostility, they remained indistinguishable in their political pursuits. Both were afraid of the voice of the people. Both evaded the obligation to enfranchise the people. Both relied almost entirely on increasingly corrupted political strategies and deliberately corrupted government services. Both failed to restore local self-government, a right the British colonial administration had conceded almost half a century before relinquishing the South Asian part of their empire.

Ahmed (1999) noted that a parliamentary form of government is not suitable for Pakistan, for local governance, because responsibility becomes obscured. He felt that there should be a local government for every group of 50,000 voters. He suggested five executives to manage education, health, police, public works and utilities and finance. In addition 50 representatives to be appointed to maintain liaison, and to communicate public demands and expectations.

The law and order seems to be deteriorating, as there are daily reports of robberies, violent clashes among different political and religious factions. The tendency for violence in place of dialogue is yet another indicator of low political development.

To sum up, one may ask has Pakistan emerged as a stable democracy. The answer is a simple no. The very concept of democracy even the way it seems to be functioning in India is a distant dream in Pakistan. In India, at least in recent times, the judiciary has emerged as a major force along with media to assert its influence on the government. In Pakistan both media and judiciary have failed to safeguard even the basic constitutional provisions. The constitution itself has under gone several revisions in line with the convenience of each successive government. The democratic attitudes among the common man to debate and decide issues based on a system of dialogue seems to be in its infancy as is the case in India and Bangladesh. Pakistan seems to be struggling to come to terms with the notion of secularism as well and still does not know what role the religion should play in governance.

Pakistan continues to be plagued by a controversy regarding the precise role of religion with politics, an issue which resurfaced in India after nearly three decades of having adopted a very secular constitution. The demand for the partition of Indian territory into two nation-states was based upon the notion that Muslims and Hindus constituted two distinct nations. This communal division implied a theologically determined divergence of social structure. Muslims could refer to a holistic conception of society outlined in the Quran. Jinnah's rhetoric often conformed to this vision: *"Islam is our guide and complete code of life"*, yet he was a leading advocate for separation of religion and politics and firmly believed that constitution of Pakistan and the civil society should be secular in character. Maududi (1960) pointed the contradiction inherent in such dualism. He argued, if the intention was a secular Pakistan, then what was wrong with a united India. There are obvious contradictions in the term 'secular Muslim state', and the same is the case with a 'secular Hindu state'. Pakistan has created a catch twenty-two situation for itself. In order to survive, the politician played the religious card and now the religion has a much stronger appeal for masses than was the case in 1947. Yet, Pakistan's close association with Americans, who earlier helped them in creating religious groups including Taliban to contain the threat of communism, now want the ruling junta in Pakistan to suppress religious groups. The gap between elite and the masses is growing and the religion still continues to be a potent weapon for any opposition group to use against the ruling party or group.

The protection of elite interests required the creation of a separate state, though not a theocracy, to begin with, but others used the religious card in Pakistan to capture power. Modernity advocated by economic development is consciously rejected despite economic development. The dominant ideologues and rulers of Pakistan after 1947 charted a course of action, which had no relation to the historical aspirations of a people, who had borne the oppression of exploitative class relations under centuries of pre-colonial and colonial modes of production (Gardezi and Rashid, 1983: 4). The bulk of Pakistan's population consisting of peasants and labour remains at the periphery of growth and economic development. As the country enters the twenty-first century, military rule is in place and the return to democracy remains a big question mark.

Modernization in Pakistan

Modernization theory views economic development as a part

of the larger process of social and cultural change. Modernization is seen as a process for a total 'transformation, of a '*traditional*' society, from the technology to social organization in line with the advanced, economically prosperous and politically stable nations of the western world. The preference for urbanization is closely associated with modernization. It assumes the superiority of urban social organization and for that matter, western urbanism over the rural life style. The rural-urban differences have been examined by using a number of frameworks, but there is a common theme which underlies these studies. It is the dichotomous mode of viewing rural areas as a repository of '*folk*' culture and regarding cities, as the seat of what Redfield called '*urban*' culture. It assumes cross-cultural typologies of social system characteristics and, a linear model of evolution from folk-local traditions to urban-western ways of life.

The test question is whether the urban communities acquire the characteristics associated with modernization such as a change in their reproductive health behaviour or an individual outlook in comparison to the rural communities. Further, whether this is solely a function of urbanization associated with better education, health and economic development or is it associated with religious/cultural belief and practices. The modernization theory does not offer any suggestions, with respect to the level of education, health, and economic development, to impact upon the religious and cultural beliefs and practices, either in negating or reinforcing these.

The quest for greater consumption of resources, to live at a higher level of need satisfaction, the very logic of development, breeds discontent with the present, since in a fast growing population scenario, the resource generation is not able to keep pace with needs. In simple terms, in order to achieve the target of higher need satisfaction, the growth of population has to be checked, so that the pace of generation of resources is higher than that of the population growth. It is obvious that in absence of population growth slowing down, the resource generation would fail to increase the need satisfaction level of the people. The 'development' process in Pakistan as in other countries of Asia, with large populations and a high rate of population growth tried to achieve the same, without much success, as is evident from the continued high growth rate of the population. The 'development' experts in particular relating to demographic trend have advocated for the following changes to curb the population growth in Pakistan:

(a) Greater investment in health.
(b) Education with emphasis on female education.
(c) Delaying the age of marriage.
(d) Spacing between children.
(e) Generating acceptance of small family norms.

The complexity of achieving the goal of fertility reduction becomes obvious in view of the current realities in respect of all the indicators. There has to be a simultaneous progress on all these fronts to achieve any significant change in the fertility pattern. Changes in the above-indicated areas require a change in the mindset of people. The western educated experts have all along assumed that spread of 'modern education' coupled with economic well-being would bring about the desired change in the attitude and values of people. The level of education and level of economic well-being that would deliver the goods have not been very specifically indicated by the experts. The other obvious problem is that on both of these indicators the general population of Pakistan is way behind. The female education is one of the lowest, compared with other countries in Asia. As Population Institute at the East West Centre noted most couples in Pakistan desire large families and there are many cultural and religious objections to contraception (Bean, 1993:25). The development experts highlight the fact that medical system appears to be poorly structured. In Pakistan, there is approximately one nurse for every five doctors, in comparison to a ratio of 2.8 per doctor in other industrializing countries and 4.2 nurses in industrialized countries. The emphasis in Pakistan was in producing more doctors at the expense of other types of health workers (ibid:28). However, the fact remains that availability of more doctors or nurses would not be able to change the attitude of people towards fertility behaviour per se. Another study cites the problem of poor accessibility of services, poor quality of services, ineffective management and administration and the lack of political and administrative support at all levels (Rukanuddin, 1990). The inability of any programme of development to address itself to so many variables is obvious. Fertility behaviour is a product of a series of values, which are inter linked and part of a specific cultural orientation. The modernists in their eagerness to extend their logic ignore the simple fact, that the process of assimilation moves unevenly among different strata of the society. Industrial development succeeds in impacting upon a number of social values but still fails to change others. The population of Pakistan uses soaps, tooth pastes and watch television programmes but fails to accept the western value of individual freedom – in particular female freedom. The feudal attitude to control everything predominates. Even women are reluctant to accept the true concept of freedom despite the worst forms of patriarchal controls and exploitation. The dilemma of individual vs collective well-being is however, a complex matter. Is there a conflict between the two or the two can be reconciled, are some basic issues in feminist theory.

As Sweetser (1993) noted, full comprehension of the health and health care issues facing women in Pakistan requires an understanding of the way women are viewed. The significance of Islamic precepts in population growth perceptions and the role the women occupy in social life. Wide class differences separate a very small number of well off, educated women in urban centres from the vast majority who have little or no education, virtually no independent mobility and extremely limited control over property or productive resources. Despite these class differences, the women throughout the country have widely shared notions about the nature and capacities of women.

It is therefore not surprising, as Zaidi (1999) noted, the high growth performance of nearly 6 per cent per annum for more than forty years is a fact alongside a very dismal state of the achievements in the social sector in Pakistan. Human resource development remained weak throughout since 1947. Social development signifying access to social services such as education, health and employment, etc., remained low on account of non-participation of women and the feudal hang over. Other reasons identified for low level of social development are, lack of transparency in the financial sector, huge debts and lack of decentralization (Ranis and Stewart (1997). The central problem is that so far no economic or technological innovation has succeeded in changing human behaviour in the desired direction. Constituting an ideal society remains a myth. Planned social change and the mirages of development would continue to inspire both the elite and the masses though for different reasons.

5

Social Development in Bangladesh

Bangladesh is one of the poorest countries in the world. Having emerged as an independent nation in 1971, it has been trying to attain both political and economic stability during the first three decades of its existence. It has undergone like Pakistan, spells of military rule and democratic governance from time to time. The quest for 'development' remains the central concern globally. Though the underlying objective of development policies remains the fulfilment of human needs, but the basic thrust of development project was economic in nature. The choice of an appropriate policy remains a widely debated issue in Bangladesh, with a number of political parties presenting a wide range of prescriptions to bring about economic prosperity. There is hardly any clarity as to how it can be done, despite many success stories being suggested as the model in international debates on rural poverty in particular, based on experiences in Bangladesh. The general thrust of the political and intellectual elite of Bangladesh remains giving primacy to economic development in line with the prescriptions being provided by international financial institutions. Discourse on development is carried on at several levels and at times reflects an emotional understanding of issues rather than any ideological orientation. A Bangladeshi intellectual and contemporary writer, Selina Hossain, commenting on western perspective, for example, commented:

> "I do not believe we are poor; we have been kept poor and this word 'poverty' has been thrust upon us. We have an incredible richness in our literary traditions – a tradition of a thousand years....

> Our poet Bharat Chandra wrote, *'May our children flourish in milk and rice'; that is the world I long for"* (Haneefa, 1998).

It is an excellent commentary on the different versions of dreams and the wide gap that exist in grassroots reality and 'modern' utopia. Majority of women in Bangladesh generally gets married early. The primary role for a woman continues to be that of a housewife in her current milieu. The process of economic development classifies her as dependent and plans to exploit her labour for production rather than reproduction. It in fact expects her to give up her reproductive role altogether in the society.

The joy of holding her child in her hand and constructing the entire life world around him/her does not fit well with the 'modern' perspective as it adds to the dependency ratio. The idea of living at a low level of subsistence and a shorter life span is considered outmoded and 'primitive'. Such practices can no longer be tolerated as it hampers economic growth, the central concern of 'modern' development. The process of social construction of 'development' is a complex one and is capable of evoking passions. The common man is still far from capable of exerting his influence in any significant way, therefore, the elite must step in, to construct their dreams for them. The elite obliges them by projecting its dreams in the name of nationalist interest but is not very sure of the process of translating the dream into a reality. It however, remains a routine exercise generally entrusted to the state. In recent times on international public demand, some space for development has been allocated to the NGOs. The ruling political party constructs the issues and its solutions, to frame the national agenda. Since the political elite themselves is contesting the available space for domination, the number game and energies of common man is used to fight the battle on behalf of their chosen mentors. Religious and other primordial issues become centre stage as they evoke real passion. The real issues of economic poverty and strategies for alleviation of the same are too complex an issue for the common man. But, somehow, they know, better than anybody else, that a solution to mass poverty of the kind found in particular in the third world, has not so far been found. The political process tries to generate a false hope and only succeeds in generating conflicts.

Historians would offer different explanations, the dream of creating a 'Golden World,' intolerance of ruling elite of Pakistan, cultural conflict, difficulties of a distant land with a hostile neighbour and so on which lead to the separation of Bangladesh from Pakistan. The fact, however, is that the quest for dominance and power is intrinsic to human nature. It is now given a more respectable term 'national development'. Power to rule is justified in the name of creating a better tomorrow for the millions. It is also described, sociologically speaking, as the social responsibility of the state to exercise social control. Bangladesh as an 'independent' dream is smallest in South Asia, surrounded by India with the total land area being 1,47,570 square kilometres and had a population of 66.7 million in 1971, which has grown to 126 million in 1998 and is likely to become 162.7 in 2015. The male population was 57.3 million compared to 54.1 million females with the overall sex ratio being 106 according to official statistics based on 1991 census released in 1996 (Government of Bangladesh, 1996). The total population was given as 111.4 million which is the figure based on 1991 census, the total population in 1996 was estimated to be 131.2 million with 72.6 million males and 58.5 million females and a sex ratio of 124. The annual population growth rate was 2.2 per cent whereas total fertility rate was 3.1 per cent in 1997. The dependency ratio is 69.9. Nearly 3.2 per cent of the total population was estimated to be over 65 years of age, in 1997 (HDR, 1999: 199). Nearly 19.4 per cent population was living in urban area in 1975, which grew to 30.8 in 1997. The average household size was given as 5.6 as per 1991 (adjusted) figures given in the Bangladesh Statistical Pocketbook, 1996.

High population growth like in India and Pakistan is directly related to the declining mortality rate and little or no change in the fertility rate. The onset of declining mortality was evident during the period 1921-47, as the crude death rate declined from

47.3 in 1911-21 to 37.8 in 1931-41. The same trend continued up to the mid-sixties whereas the fertility rate decline did not commence till the mid-seventies. The population of Bangladesh as a result grew from 33.3 million in 1921 to 111.4 in 1991. Therefore, what is seen as human development as per western development indicators became the worst curse for the developing countries. It is significant to note that during the colonial period the growth rate remain low because of the absence of public health services. It was the post-colonial period in the mid-fifties, when public health was suggested as an important strategy of development and they still do, which resulted in the population explosion. The simple reason being, the expectation that improved health facilities or other inputs such as education and economic development would change people's attitude towards family size, age at marriage, women's role and status, greater self-discipline and commitment to so called 'modern' values did not materialize.

The urban population grew mainly after the 1960s in Bangladesh. It crossed the 20 per cent mark in 1991.

Period	*Population (million)*	*%*	*Growth Rate*
1901	0.70	2.43	—
1911	0.81	2.55	1.39
1921	0.88	2.64	0.85
1931	1.07	3.02	2.0
1941	1.54	3.66	3.59
1951	1.82	4.33	1.69
1961	2.64	5.19	3.75
1974	6.27	8.78	6.62
1981	13.22	15.18	10.63
1991	22.45	20.15	5.43

Source: Experiences with Economic Reform, 1995: 302.

The Human Development Report has revised its methodology in its 1999 report. The overall human development ranking of Bangladesh was 147 in 1995, it declined to 150 in 1997. In other words, only 24 countries out of a total of 174 had a worse record of human development than Bangladesh in 1997.

In other words majority of the population has remained unaffected by economic and political transformations in the country.

Economic Development

Bangladesh like India and Pakistan is predominantly an agrarian economy. It is now getting converted into a service sector economy, as the share of agriculture has declined to 30 per cent from 51 per cent in 1974, compared to the 60.4 per cent contributed by services of various kind including construction. Manufacturing contributed a small share of less than 10 per cent. However, agriculture remains the biggest source of livelihood, as 55 per cent of the labour force is located in the agricultural sector.

The majority of the population still depends on agriculture and related activities for their livelihood. The growth of the service sector in the economy reflects that people are generally dependent on employment and do not posses any means of production. Some studies have pointed out that the growth of service sector, a large segment of which remains informal in character, leads to a decline in wages and other benefits to the labour class. The poor and illiterate self-employed also operate illegally and hence are subject to exploitation by different state agents. The general living standard of those who are in the service sector remains poor. The per capita income may increase but this may not necessarily mean an improvement in the condition of the poorest people.

	1991-92	*1995-96*
National income at market price (in million Taka)	518432.0	625133.0
Population (in million)	111.3	122.1
GDP (per capita)	4732.0	5260.0
Annual growth of GDP (per capita)	2.1	3.4
Annual growth of GDP	4.2	5.3

Source: Bangladesh Statistical Year Book, 1996: 272.

The total GNP was around $44 billion in 1998 and the annual growth rate during 1997-98 was 5 per cent. The per capita GNP was $350. The GNP in PPP dollars terms was around 137.7 million and per capita GNP was 1,100 (WDR, 1999-2000: 230). The real GDP per capita in PPP $ was 1,382 in 1995 which declined to 1,050 in 1997 (HDR, 1998: 149, 1999: 136). The economic growth rate was 4.4 per cent per annum during 1975-95.

Development Strategy

The development design of Bangladesh was scripted long before the nation was born. By the time the new nation officially known as Gano Prajatantri Bangladesh (Peoples Republic of Bangladesh) took shape, India and Pakistan had made up their mind about the kind of future they wanted to create. The strategies for achieving the same were also spelt out in broad terms, since nobody really knew, how the grand objectives of achieving wealth and physical facilities comparable with the western society could be achieved. After its separation from Pakistan, the new government headed by Awami League opted for a multi-party parliamentary form of government, which was supposed to be secular in character. The economy was expected to be socialist in character. In other words the rich business class was not supposed to have complete freedom and was to be guided by the state. This was the initial dream, on which in practice, there was no consensus, among the major actors in the Bangladesh society. Even within the ruling elite there was a deep dissention over secularism, the system of government and the strategy of economic development (Chakravarty, 1994: 10).

The ensuing political conflict resulted in drastic changes in the Constitution and form of government. The significant point to note is that political differences were settled by using extra-constitutional methods and recourse to violence is quite frequent and wide spread. The multi-party parliamentary system gave way to single party presidential system through a violent take over. The economy became more liberal in character. The freedom of press and citizens were curtailed (ibid: 11). It culminated in the brutal assassination of the then President along with his family. The faction opposed to secularism and socialism came to power briefly to be replaced by military rule which lasted a long time.

The military rulers opted for Islamic thrust in the governance of the society. The economy was opened up to follow a capitalist orientation. Close links with the developed world, in particular US, were established. The budget allocation for the defence went up from 600 million Taka in 1973-74 to 2,524 million Taka in 1980-81 (ibid: 12). Presidential system of governance was again changed to parliamentary system in 1991. Political situation has continued to be fluid but the economy seems to be developing on capitalist lines. Though the rate of growth varied it has not been able to achieve the desired result of providing the common man any substantial gain. In fact, the real wages seem to have registered a decline.

The general view is that economic progress of Bangladesh has been negated by continued growth of the population, its vulnerability to natural disasters and poor production capacity both in agriculture and non-agriculture sectors (Hossain and Rahman, 1997: 811). In reality, so far no economic prescription has been found to raise the level of economic production beyond the natural rate of growth at 4-5 per cent per annum. More importantly controlling the population growth and channeling the human behaviour in desired direction requires controlling the minds of the millions. In scientific terms it remains an unachievable target. The hope that any strategy would succeed either in doing away with the economic poverty or controlling the greed of the people appears to be fragile optimism. Yet, the pursuit of economic development and 'modernization' continues. If we take the poverty percentage to be 70 per cent in 1972, and 50 per cent now, the population of poor has increased from nearly 50 million in 1972 to 61 million in 1997. If the poverty percentage goes down to 30 per cent there would still be around 50 million poor in 2015. The dream of providing more economic resources to people through any strategy of economic growth is likely to remain unfulfilled even in the next millennium.

Trend in rural poverty in Bangladesh has been studied in sufficient detail to lead to some broad characteristics since independence. People generally are reluctant to migrate to urban areas resulting in low migration rates. There appears to be some improvement in rural living standards though the poverty levels in general have remained unchanged from 1960 (Amin, 1997:218). Amin, in her study, found that the female headed households were poorer than the male headed households and that they get less opportunities for their economic development (ibid: 230). It is interesting to note her conclusion. She concludes that data from her study indicates that women contribute more than the males in coping with poverty, yet they are not accorded any significant status in the family since they do not earn cash.

Planned Development

An attempt at planned development was made in Bangladesh as it was done in other neighbouring countries, on the advice of various friendly western donors of various variety, including the international financial institutions. The frequent political upheavals resulted in abrupt changes in thrust and design, however, the idea of planned development remained firmly in place.

State Development Expenditure

(in million Taka)

	1991-92	*%*	*1995-96*	*%*
Agriculture	5115	8.3	6148	6.7
Rural development	3709	6.2	3772	4.1
Flood control and water resources	7678	12.6	10123	10.4
Industry	4211	7.0	4926	5.1
Power resources	15488	25.8	19347	20.0
Transport	12912	21.5	25925	26.0
Communication	2240	3.8	9493	9.9
Education and training	1521	2.7	8500	8.9
Health	1147	1.9	3467	3.8
Population control	2787	4.5	1937	2.1
Housing	2936	4.9	827	0.8
Others	496	0.8	2065	2.3
Total	60240	100.0	96530	100.0

Source: Bangladesh Statistical Year Book, 1996: 281.

Government development expenditure has largely been incurred on developing the infrastructure as more than 50 per cent was spent on power generation, transport and communication during both 1991-92 and 1995-96. The social services, education, health and housing together accounted for nearly ten per cent of the expenditure during 1991-92. The overall allocation to this sector went up by nearly 2 per cent but the bulk of this nearly 9 per cent was spent on education and training whereas housing received the lowest, less than one per cent in 1995-96. Rural development including agriculture received nearly 15 per cent in 1991-92 which declined to 10.8 in 1995-96. Since recurring floods are a major problem in Bangladesh, it is not surprising that nearly 12 per cent of the expenditure was allocated for flood control measures in 1991-92 but it also declined in 1995-96. Only 7 per cent resources were spent on industrial development in 1991-92 which further declined to 5 per cent in 1995-96. The size of government expenditure which was nearly 60.2 million Taka in 1991-92 increased to 96.5 million Taka in 1995-96. The thrust of state development seems to be following a simple pattern of developing the infrastructure base, by streamlining power generation, developing transport and communication network, flood control and some attention to human resource development. This mode of development produces different kinds of outcomes depending upon how efficient the bureaucratic machinery is, and the mix of market and state in managing power and transport. However, the allocations in the social service sector are not able to create the infrastructure needed to cater for the needs of the entire population and the quality of services offered remain a big question mark. The elite never uses the government school facilities which are far inferior to the ones offered by private sector.

Labour Force

Labour force of the country was 64 million out of a total population of 125.6 million in 1998, the women constituted 42 per cent of the labour force and children in the age-group of 10-14 years, 29 per cent (WDR, 1999-2000: 234). In other words, 19 million children in the age-group of 10-14 are working. The number of child labourers was estimated at 16.9 million in 1961, 21.9 in 1974, 25.9 in 1981 and 28.5 million in 1984 (Hye, 1993). Child labour below 10 years of age was estimated to be around 0.63 million in 1983-84 by Labour Force Survey in Bangladesh. The agriculture provided the main source of employment, as it accounted for 65 per cent of the workers in 1995, whereas it was 84 per cent in 1970. The industrial workforce went up from 7 per cent in 1970 to 16 per cent in 1995, whereas services had a share of 10 per cent in 1970 which went up to 18 per cent in 1995. The real annual earnings of employees declined by 3 per cent during 1970-80 and by 0.7 per cent during 1980-92 (HDR, 1998: 165). The shift in employment from agriculture to non-agricultural activities is very slow. Further, this shift may not necessarily bring about any significant change in the overall socio-economic condition of the poor. The data on wages, health, housing and education of the new entrants or in general of the working class is generally not available.

According to Hossain and Rehman (1997), the economically active population increased by 2.1 per cent per year during 1987-95. The labour force participation rate was 49 per cent in 1995. The low participation rate is due to a high dependency rate as a large segment of the population consists of people below 14 years of age, high rate of unemployment and lower male to female participation rate in Bangladesh. The sector wise labour force indicated that agriculture continues to be the major source of economic participation, as 55.3 per cent of the population was engaged in agriculture in 1995. The figure for agriculture was 65.5 in 1988. The wage labourers were 16.8 per cent within the agriculture sector. The service sector accounted for 20.5 per cent of the labour force in 1995 compared to 16.2 per cent in 1988 (Hossain and Rehman, 1997:822).

The female work participation rate was very low till 1981 as per the data provided by (Hye, 1993). The work participation rate in general continued to be very low and also remained stagnant around 31-34 per cent of the total population. However, the Bangladesh Bureau of Statistics (BBS) provides a different picture for the years 1991-96.

There is a discrepancy in the definition of labour force in the data. In the case of BBS, all persons above 10 years of age are included in the labour force. In case of Hye, the fact that figures for male and female differ very widely it cannot refer to all persons above the age of 10 years, since in that case the figures cannot differ beyond a point considering the overall male, female ratio in the overall population. It means that data by Hye about the percentage of labour force is in fact referring to persons employed full time as a percentage of the total population, while BBS data of activity rate is based on the percentage of employed persons out of the civilian labour force. In that case Hye is giving figures of active labour force as a percentage of total female population. I have worked out the numbers in millions in bracket in the data provided by Hye to make the comparison easier. However, the BBS data suggest a much higher female participation than what is suggested by Hye. It is interesting to note that according to the data by Hye the female labour force increases from 6.5 million in 1901 to 25 million in 1961 but declines to 14.5 million in 1981. According to BBS data it remains stagnant around 20 million during 1989-96. Refined activity rate in case of both sexes declined from 74.7 in 1989 to 64.8 in 1995-96, during the same period as per BBS data indicating an increase in unemployment.

Official statistical data further clarifies that housewives were not included in the labour force and their number as such was declining in Bangladesh, while the number of child labourers was on the increase, though its overall share in the labour force has marginally declined.

Population Not Included in Labour Force

Million	*1989*	*1990-91*	*1995-96*
Housewives	18.2	9.6	12.0
Other inactives	1.9	12.8	18.4
Children 0-9 yrs	37.3	35.5	35.4

Source: Bangladesh Statistical Pocketbook, 1996: 155.

Child Labour (5-14 yrs)

Year	*1989*	*1990-91*	*1995-96*
Number (million)	6.1	5.8	6.6
Per cent of civilian labour force	12.2	11.3	11.6

Source: Bangladesh Statistical Pocketbook, 1996: 155.

Inequality: Landownership and Income

The major source of inequality appears to be the distribution of land, as the bottom 40 per cent has merely 1.9 per cent of the total land. Its share in the total income declined to 15.7 in 1995 compared to 18.7 in 1988. The top 10 per cent of the population owned 50.6 per cent of the total land area and its share in the total income increased from 26.2 per cent in 1988 to 31.6 per cent in 1995 (see table below). The WDR, 1999-2000 gave the share of lowest 10 per cent as 4.1 and the top 10 per cent as 23.7 based on a survey in 1992. One of the major causes of persistent poverty and inequality is the landownership pattern in Bangladesh, India and Pakistan. Whereas some measures have been taken in India with some success at bringing about a change

Income Distribution

	Share % of	*Land*	*Share % of*	*Income*
	1987	*1995*	*1987-88*	*1994-95*
Bottom 40%	2.1	1.9	18.7	15.7
Middle 40%	29.6	27.9	39.3	35.8
Ninth Decile	21.0	19.6	15.8	16.9
Top 10%	47.2	50.6	26.2	31.6
Top 5 %	30.0	34.6	16.0	19.9
Gini ratio	0.67	0.69	0.35	0.42

Source: Hossain and Rahman, 1997: 819.

Survey Year	*Gini Index*	*Lowest 10%*	*Lowest 20%*	*Second 20%*	*Third 20%*	*Fourth 20%*	*Highest 20%*	*Highest 10%*
1992	28.3	4.1	9.4	13.5	17.2	22.0	37.9	23.7

Source: World Development Report, 1999-2000:238

in land ownership pattern all such measures in Bangladesh and Pakistan have been largely insignificant. In India also, the change has not benefited the poor and the lower castes.

The data by Hossain and Rehman (1997) indicate that the disparity between the rich and poor is increasing both in terms of land ownership and in income as the Gini ratio seem to indicate (0 represents perfect equality). The World Bank data based on a survey in 1992 gives the Gini Index as 28.3.

Prices and Wages 1990-95 (Base 1973-74=100)

	1990-91	*1994-95*
Whole sale price index	511	592
Agriculture products	568	665
Industrial product	419	473
Wage rate index real	162	192

Source: Bangladesh Statistical Year Book, 1996: 293.

The fact that prices of agricultural products have registered the maximum increase during the period 1990-95. In other words, it means that the food has become costlier and is likely to affect the common man most. The real wage has however nearly doubled in the past thirty years. However, it is not clear which sector has been covered in calculating the real wages. Generally, the wages in the informal sector rise slowly as compared to the organized sector.

Poverty

Nearly half the population (48%) was estimated to be below the national poverty line during 1989-94. Hossain and Rehman (ibid) have collected data about poverty based on two poverty lines one they term as indicating moderate poverty and the other extreme poverty. Almost one in every three person was extremely poor in Bangladesh and one in two were moderately poor according to their estimates. However, they noted that the poverty percentage has marginally declined from 57.5 to 51.5 but since the population has increased the absolute number of poor would have increased in both type of cases.

Change in the Incidence of Poverty, 1987-1995

	1987-88	*1994-95*
Poverty line (Taka/person/year)		
Moderate poverty	4150	6287
Extreme poverty	2480	3560
Headcount index (% of households)		
Extreme Poverty	31.7	29.9
Moderate poverty	57.5	51.7
Poverty gap index (%)	21.7	19.2

Source: Hossain and Rahman, 1997: 820.

The official figures of poverty based on poverty line indicate that nearly 47.2 per cent population was living in poverty. There was only marginal difference in rural and urban poverty reflecting the mass scale nature of poverty. The poverty line was at about the same level in the 1980s and 1990s as in the early 1960s (Amin, 1997: 217). The vast majority of the poor continue to live in rural areas.

Hossain and Rahman (1997) suggest land reforms as the strategy to alleviate poverty although they realize that land reforms are difficult to implement. They further note that it is difficult to reach the poor households with public rural development services (ibid: 831). They suggest strengthening agricultural research and extension system, but do not specify how this would help the poor. Amin (1997) is more optimistic and noted that though life styles have remained traditional and at the subsistence level, fertility and mortality rates are declining, disaster relief system and food policies would be able to prevent mass scale famines. According to her, contraceptive use has crossed 50 per cent mark in some areas and access to safe drinking water has increased.

Social Development in Bangladesh

Social Expenditure

The public expenditure on education as percentage of GNP was 1.9 in 1985 which increased to 2.9 in 1996. Whereas on health the same was 1.2 per cent of GDP in 1995 (HDR, 1999: 190). The current emphasis on reducing the government expenditure and reducing the budgetary deficit by international financial institutions suggest that the expenditure is not likely to register a radical increase in future. Other areas of government expenditure have been on development of infrastructure such as roads, electricity, improving sanitation and availability of safe drinking water. In Bangladesh, flood control measures have been an important area for government expenditure.

If we compare the data of government expenditure in different sector given earlier with the data as the allocation to different sector here assuming that the earlier data refer to the actual expenditure during the years under review, it indicates that actual expenditure is smaller than allocations made. In other words, the bureaucracy is not able to carry out the development tasks assigned to it. Though the social sector allocation is shown as 34 per cent in 1991-92 increased to 36.4 per cent in 1995-96, only education and health are two areas for which allocations have been indicated and they have largely been stagnant around 7 per cent in terms of allocation, but the expenditure tells a different story. The expenditure on health was only 3.8 per cent in 1995-96. However, no details are available for nearly 20 per cent of allocation listed as other.

Education

Bangladesh like other countries in South Asia had not felt the need for school education in view of the prevailing socio-economic milieu. The country therefore has not thought of developing any system of imparting 'modern' education for its common people. The adult literacy rate defined in terms of modern education skills was 25 in 1970 which became 38.9 in

1997. The emphasis there is on measuring skills which are valued by the modern economy and society. Literacy, in that sense then becomes an important indicator of economic development but education is a broader concept and should not be confused with literacy. The combined school ratio was 35 in 1997, 30 for females as compared to 40 for males. In other words, more boys were likely to go to school than girls. Schooling is helpful in acquiring education but is not a necessary condition. Present day schools are known more for imparting literacy skills than education.

The data indicate that the educational infrastructure is slowly expanding in Bangladesh. It is important to note the discrepancy in number of primary and secondary schools. It indicates that all those enrolling for primary education are not expected to carry on to the secondary stage. In India, a recent report made a difference in calculating pupil teacher ratio and child teacher ratio. The latter include the out of school children and indicates the readiness of the system for universal elementary education. The pupil teacher ratio was 50 and child teacher ratio 68 in villages studied (Probe, 1999). The number of universities and colleges also indicate that only a small section is able to reach the stage. The presence of private universities indicate that privatization of education has already commenced in Bangladesh, while it is heading that way in India.

The student teacher ratio at the primary level is very high indicating the shortage of teachers. The fact that it has reached 1: 36 at the university level indicates that the quality of higher education would be inadequate. The operating expenses indicate that the education remain by and large out of the reach of common people. The average cost of schooling a child at the primary level in India was estimated at 1996-97 prices in 1986-87 by National Sample Survey to be Rs. 212, by Probe in 1996 at 318 and by National Council of Applied Economic Research (NCAER), New Delhi in 1994 at elementary level to be 478 (ibid: 19). The same would be true for Bangladesh.

Drop-out Rate in Primary Schools, 1995

	Class I	Class II	Class III	Class IV	Class V
1990	19.3	12.0	15.6	15.8	11.0
1992	18.7	8.1	13.6	6.9	7.9
1993	21.8	19.3	17.0	15.8	13.2
1994	15.2	15.3	11.6	4.6	6.2

The figures show a lot of fluctuation in the drop-out rate in Bangladesh. But even the last figure while signifying an improvement indicates that in actual practice out of 100 children enrolled in class I only 26 will reach Class V. The reason, however, may not be poverty alone; it also indicates irrelevance of school education for a sizable percentage of the population.

Health

The indicators for showing development in the health sector is usually depicted by increases in life expectancy, immunization coverage, availability of doctors and nurses, better nutrition etc. The availability of safe drinking water, sanitary conditions of living and distribution of disabilities are other ways of looking at the health situation. Out of all the indicators of health increase in life expectancy at birth has been very spectacular. In 25 years, 14 years have been added in every person's life. This has largely come about on account of control of large-scale epidemics and increase in immunization coverage particularly for children and lactating mothers. Its result has been obvious. More children and mothers survive. Like its counterparts in India and Pakistan it has resulted in a steep rise in population growth rate. The life expectancy at birth was 44.2 in 1970, 56.9 in 1995 which increased to 58.1 in 1997. This is despite the fact that even now very few mothers have access to proper medical care both in rural and urban areas. Only a very small per cent of women are attended by doctors or nurses. Majority is still looked after by a midwife.

There has been an expansion of health services in Bangladesh since 1992. It now has 906 government and 280 private hospitals. The total bed strength is around 34,393 thousands. Bangladesh health system consists of big hospitals and medical colleges located in cities, followed by district hospitals.

Percentage Distribution of Mothers and Type of Help during Birth

	National	*Rural*	*Urban*
Doctor	7.6	3.7	12.7
Nurse	5.8	3.2	12.7
Family welfare visitor	1.3	1.5	1.0
Trained midwife	21.2	21.0	18.6
Untrained midwife	25.0	25.9	23.0
Relatives	26.9	29.9	20.7
Neighbours	11.0	13.5	6.4
Others	0.6	0.7	0.6
Do not know	0.6	0.6	0.8

Source: Bangladesh Statistical Pocketbook, 1996: 341.

Upazila health complexes, health and family planning centres provide primary health care to people. However, in 1990, half of all deaths were of babies or children under 12, the situation in Pakistan was still worse with the median age of death being seven years, compared to India, 37 years, China 64 years and Sri Lanka 73 years (Grieve, 1995: 114). Bangladesh Rural Advancement Committee (BRAC) conducted a study of health services in Bangladesh in 1990. The study found that the health workers lacked motivation and were demoralised. There was no supervisory mechanism in place. The situation was further complicated by the lack of coordination between health and family planning wing of the government. The study concluded that the purpose of ensuring active community surveillance of communicable diseases, sanitation, personal hygiene, nutrition, maternal and child health, etc., through a domiciliary health service system has not been met. Most of the rural people were not aware of government services. The participation of people in the health management was remote (BRAC, 1990: 130).

However, the common people had very little to gain from this expansion as the availability of drugs and personnel in these hospitals remain questionable (Centre for Policy Dialogue, 1995). The statistics on health services reveal very little by way of condition of common man and his access to health services. Lack of access to safe drinking water, sanitation and nutrition in itself make him susceptible to a lot of health problems.

The immunization coverage seems to have covered a lot of ground but it is difficult to believe such large coverage in view of the massive illiteracy and poverty in Bangladesh. The difference between the coverage of the first and the third dose is usually very large in case of illiterate populations. The high percentage of disability figures also raise doubts about the claims of immunization coverage. Nearly a quarter of the population suffers from visual and nearly one out of five from hearing impairment, whereas nearly 15 per cent suffer from physical disability in Bangladesh.

Broadly speaking in 1973 there were three main problems related to health, viz., population, malnutrition and communicable diseases. In addition, there was a marked disparity among the health services in the rural and urban areas. There has been only marginal change in these areas. The major success has been achieved in immunization and achieving reduction in maternal mortality rate and infant child mortality rate. These measures have lead to an increase in the population.

The suggestion for improving health system, in particular the reach of the common people, reflect the emergence of the new global economic policy. The possibility of cost sharing or shifting the burden to the people themselves is the general thrust. Grieve (1995) felt that it would be beneficial to lessen the dependence of the local institutions on the central resources and they should be encouraged to raise funds locally. He quoted World Bank studies to say that poor people were willing to pay. The future of health services in view of the state withdrawal remains a big question mark in Bangladesh.

Nutrition Status

The calorie intake seems to have increased in both rural and urban areas since 81-82 as also the daily protein intake in rural areas. However, the calorie intake is just the bare minimum required to stay above the poverty level.

The nutritional status as per the Gomez classification reveals that it keeps fluctuating as the rate of normal status increased from 3.49 in 1975-76 to 10 per cent in 1981-82 according to INFS data but declined to 5.30 in 1985-86 according to BBS data. The severe malnutrition however declined from 25.81 in 1975-76 to 9.60 in 1985-86, the moderate figures remain stagnant at around 52 per cent and the mild increased from 17.68 to 33.10 per cent during the period.

It was found that the women cutting across all age-groups were getting far less nutrition than males.

Development of Women

One of the goals of development addressed by western model of economic development has been bringing about a radical change in the status of women. The usual strategy adopted in many developing countries has been to promote education of women with a view to increase their economic participation. It is generally expected that economic participation of women would give her more freedom, bring about a change in her traditional roles within the household and provide her an opportunity to be able to exert her right to participate in decision making process in general. The cultural values grounded in religion and social customs have generally opposed these changes. Many studies have pointed out that though the poverty may force women to work, even outside home, but as the economic situation of the family improves there is a tendency particularly among lower middle and middle classes to withdraw women from full time work.

Women face a dilemma as they try to break free from the traditional role of remaining inside the four walls and step out to work. The family forces them to work and yet they face criticism from the community. Such a woman, who works alongside other males, is said to have become a bad woman, as the, religious discourse remains highly male dominated. On the other hand, the outside world has become so anti-Islam and their attempts to completely restructure the identities of these women, make them uncomfortable, as they still prefer their own cultural roots. However, the common women seldom get a chance to think about philosophical issues of religious identity and outsiders. They have enough on their hands to worry about more real and demanding situations which continue to threaten their survival.

Even where women work they have not been allowed to participate in other important affairs of life. The ideology of female seclusion is strong and dominates the work behaviour of both rich and poor (Amin, 1997: 213). The seclusion of women continues despite poverty. The lower migration rates and continued practice of *purdah* are indicators of strong presence of traditional practices rooted in the cultural values of local people. The recent increase in women's wage employment is seen as a process of negotiation between cultural values and demand for economic growth (Feldman, 1992). The continued practice of women's seclusion, however, can be interpreted as a rejection of the western thesis of women's development. People are willing to concede some space as it concerns economic development, but are very firm not to concede any space in the area of social change, particularly when it concerns women. The western discourse of women development is also not prepared to concede any space to indigenous gender arrangement, as it believes in total individual freedom. Right to construct the self and believe in it remains a big question mark. As has been noted the studies on women's status often deliberated on these issues, yet in delineating strategies for women's development they seem to have ignored these realities, as they could not transcend their own class biases.

To quote Prof. Raunaq Jahan (1975):

> "Since the leadership of the women's organization is in the hands of urban, educated middle class women, the 'women's issues' which gained prominence in the last three decades were education and legal reforms. The women's organizations failed to perceive that legal reforms and establishment of girls schools will only benefit a

small number of middle class women because only they will have the resources to take advantage of the legal reforms and school facilities."

The low level of participation of women in welfare programmes, have formed the subject of many seminars and studies. The fact remains that little success has been achieved in motivating women to change their life styles. It is not surprising, given the cultural orientation of the women in Bangladesh, to find that women prefer the four walls of their homes, rather than to venture outside, for a working status. They would choose to remain subservient, in order to survive, rather than demanding an equal status within the household. The rural social milieu remains more firmly traditional and different from the western discourse. Culture in general and religion in particular, has a very strong hold on the psyche of the individual in India, Pakistan and Bangladesh. Severe acts of violence directed against women still have a very wide public support in all these countries.

The first description of village women in rural Bangladesh is Tahrunnissa Abdullah's, *Village Women as I Saw Them*, written in 1965-66. She pointed out that *purdah* and strict division of labour between the sexes was highly valued. The women work included cooking, child care, cleaning, care of animals and post harvest operations. Marriage was a must. The divorce was prevalent in lower classes only. Only girls between 7-12 went to school. The general story in 2000 in rural Bangladesh is not very different. Another study of rural women in 1975 found that nearly 20 per cent women over 16 years were widows (Ellickson, 1975). Yet another study of rural women found that in three-fourths of the households, help from neighbours is very widely prevalent. Women help each other in tasks which they cannot do alone, e.g., rice processing. Giving and receiving help was more common among the poor (Gudrun, 1981). The study reported that the women devoted nearly 53 per cent of their time to household and family related work and 43 per cent to agriculture related work. Another important finding was that women from rich families devoted more time to cooking than the women in poor households.

According to census data, 43 per cent women have agriculture as their primary occupation and 12 per cent as secondary occupation, the highest percentage being in the landless and small farm households (Safilios-Rothchild and Mahmud, 1989). The study showed a high participation rate of women in homestead production. The report noted the vital role of women in food security. Another study by Halim and Ali (1986) noted that most decisions on crops, hiring of labour, selling and buying, as well as taking loans were taken jointly by females and males. A study by Begum and Greeley (1987) reveals a considerable reduction in female wage labour demand following the introduction of power mills. The study revealed that 73 per cent of the farmers who started using the mills, used to employ female wage labours, and together they accounted for 66 per cent of all employers of female wage labour. Greeley (1987) noted that in 1980 milling cost was Taka 6.4 per maund compared to Taka 9 per maund with the use of female labour. The data show that not only were rural female displaced by power mills their wages also declined from Taka 5 a day to Taka 3 a day. Ahmed (1982) noted that about two-thirds of the rural poorest employed by the producer farmers in husking were converted from contract labour to permanent labour for more than three months. This change meant a decrease in remuneration and increase in working hours, as the so-called permanent labour is forced to work double the working hours than that of the contract labour. According to 1974 Census, 2.5 per cent rural adult women were in the labour force and in 1981 the figure was 2.7 per cent. This is due to the fact that economically active population is defined as those who are either employed or looking for work. Most rural women working on their own farms are excluded from the labour force and listed as housewives (Westergaard, 1993: 437). A series of studies on time use among the rural population reveals quite a different picture. Adnan (1988) who recomputed Bangladesh Bureau of Statistics data, by adding to the conventionally defined labour force, all those involved in household work, noted that women in Bangladesh accounted for 48 per cent of all persons employed in productive work, in 1974, and 50 per cent in 1983-84.

Farouk's study (1975) showed that women spent longer hours than men in productive work. However, for both men and women, the hours spent in productive work differ from region to region. For women average hours spent in productive work varies between 10 and 13.6 hours daily, for men between 9 hours to 10.8 hours daily. Ahsan et al (1986) also documented the long working hours of women. The study noted that the time spent on direct and indirect economic activity by women is highest among the landless, 11.3 hours a day throughout the year. In large farm households the women were spending nearly 10.5 hours a day in economic activities.

Traditionally in Bangladesh only widows and divorced women worked as wage labourers and the common view is that wage-earning women come from families with no male earners, however the studies refute this notion (Greeley, 1987; Rahman, 1986; Nur, 1988). However, 86 per cent of the income earning women belonged to poor segment of the population having an income of less than 1000 Taka a month and only 14 per cent came from the middle income group having an income of 1000-4000 Taka per month (Nur, 1988). Out of the total 33 per cent were married, 24 per cent unmarried and 43 per cent widowed, divorced or separated. A Bangladesh Institute of Development Studies (BIDS, 1988) provides data about female employment in rural industries. The study reports that whereas male wages registered an increase of 12 per cent during the period from 1980-87, the wages of women and children declined by 17 per cent during the period. The availability of work also declined due to more women and child labour entering the labour force.

Islam (1979), in her essay, "Social Norms, Institutions and Status of Women", felt that though the women are assigned an important role of wife and mother they are not treated with dignity and are not given the independence and authority which these roles deserve. However, the question of status per se remains unclear. The debates on the theme have focused on three themes: (a) women's access to and control over resources, (b) decision-making, and (c) implications of *purdah* norms on *off-bari* work and consequently their status.

The control over land as a resource is a simple indicator of differences between men and women. According to Muslim Law, in Bangladesh, the father's land is divided among the children in such a way that all sons get an equal share and daughters get half that of the sons. A widow is entitled to one eighth of the deceased husband's property and if there are no children the share is to be one fourth. But generally the women neither claim their right nor are given any land. In a survey of 1,221 households only 15 women were found to be owning land (Jehangir, 1986; Westergaard, 1983).

The findings differ on the decision-making role of the women. Westergaard (1983) felt that the women had limited role to play in production related matters, but other studies point out a higher participation rate of women in decisions regarding economic matters.

The studies on *purdah* and work reflect a defensive approach of justifying cultural norms and at the same time making out a case for woman's work off the *bari* (home) variety. White (1992), on the other hand, argues that the gender issues reflects the wider political context, and the women's issues cannot be considered without taking into account the general poverty and inequality. The author points out that the women do not distinguish the personal from household advantage, and they have a strong notion of linking their personal interest with the household interest. This clearly brings out the central difference between the western view of women's development based on an individual freedom perspective and the Bangladesh's own vision of women's development.

Studies have reported a desire on the part of women to educate their daughters even in rural and slum areas, but the female enrolment continues to be low and drop-outs enormous. Studies including the census data reveal that there is a phenomenal decline in the percentage of females at the post higher secondary level. The studies of drop-outs, besides highlighting the economic reasons have identified the irrelevance of present education particularly for girls, also as a major cause along with other factors. The studies have also pointed out that a general apathy leading to low motivational level both among parents and children result in the female drop-out. This can be explained on the basis of the low importance accorded to women's domestic roles.

The overemphasis of feminist movement on an independent career for females and consequent women's education and employment by implication has undermined the importance of role that women play within the home. It in a way has legitimized the male dominance by accepting the importance of economic over other roles. The feminist movement originating in west as a response to the industrialization and urbanization that societies in the west were able to achieve, hardly hold any relevance to the Third World societies. The majority of women still live in rural areas. Even urban women are not culturally looking forward to an independent identity of their own. They are more concerned with their family. The relationship with spouse, children and parents dominate their life. The studies of women in the west have shown that women's employment lead to an increase in marital conflict. Bradburn and Orden (1968) pointed out that there is less happiness in marriage if the wife participates in the labour market out of necessity than if she participates by choice. There is a decline in sociability for wives.

Some of the dilemmas faced by dual career families have been classified as follows. Which are particularly relevant to women in third world societies:

(a) Dilemmas arising from sheer overload of work.
(b) Dilemmas arising from strongly conflicting ideas and directions about what is considered right and proper in a given behaviour.
(c) Dilemmas arising from conflicts within one-self about whether one is a good person (good human being, good wife

and mother, good woman) in leading a certain type of existence.

(d) Dilemmas arising from the conflicts between roles that may vary at different points in the lifecycle.

The major causes of these dilemmas are identified as lack of adequate attitudinal change on the part of husband and other family members, and general societal expectations and lack of adequate support facilities for women to share their domestic workload, beside other factors. The cultural differences in shaping the self-image of both men and women and consequently perceiving their role in and outside the family have not been highlighted.

Gore (1968) has reported in his study that a woman's lower status in the family is related to her exclusion from economic activity. He based this observation in a comparative study of upper caste and lower caste families in which it was found that lower caste women usually participate in gainful activities whereas upper caste women are excluded from economic activities. Such assertions have been questioned by other studies which have emphasized the fact that working status of poor women have failed to enhance her status. The concept of status based on greater freedom also raises certain doubts. Greater freedom by way of mobility outside the house can be taken as one of the indicators of women's status, however, other factors such as a shift in power relations within a family is a more potent indicator of change. The cycle of change in a woman's life poses more problems in studying her status. The status she enjoys as a daughter is different from the status of daughter-in-law. Similarly, her status undergoes a significant change, when she assumes the role of a mother. Even during her role as a mother, her status may show some change when her children are grown up and set up their own families. Madan (1976) has pointed out that economic participation of women may not improve her position in the family in all cases. It is the prestige of a woman's work and its economic value in relation to her husband's work, much more than the presence of an income that is crucial to her status at home. It would however be erroneous to conclude that the status of working women is worse than their counterpart at home. The fact, however, remains that women's employment alone cannot elevate their status as is generally believed by western model of women's development. The right of women to gainful employment should be considered a fundamental right.

Unless necessary conditions are created as pointed out by many studies, the working status of women would continue to impose more strain on women rather than ensuring a better life for them, particularly for the poor women, who constitute the vast majority in the developing countries (Kapoor, 1970). The question of providing women with better-paid higher status jobs is by no means an easy task. Neither it can be discussed or debated ignoring the prevailing and ever increasing income disparities between various strata of society and the concept and strategies of social development. Amin also noted that the growth in urban areas has been unsatisfactory and the necessary infrastructure in the urban areas is still inadequate.

A related problem of women's employment outside the home has been the question of the freedom over their bodies. In Bangladesh, religion still is a dominant force. The individual freedom associated with higher education and employment of women, in the west, is generally looked at with great apprehension by the people. A change in that direction is considered as a decline in social aspect of the society, as it is likely to affect the institutions of marriage and family.

Bangladesh, with a predominantly Muslim illiterate population, faces a crucial dilemma in pursuing change. As Kaviraj (2000) noted in the context of India, the durability of the basic morphology of social arrangements of the village community is remarkable. The elements in these arrangements often changed, but their relations did not. Some studies of social relations in rural India would disagree with Kaviraj, since they feel that a different elite has replaced the feudal oppressive structure in the post-independence era of democratic elections. However, perhaps it has also not helped in restructuring or modifying the gender relations in particular. The state has remained marginal to the fundamental process of every day life of society. The intense every day repressions of social order could not be directly attributed to the state structures. These are to be seen as the impersonal functioning of the structures itself, sanctioned by religion. The state cannot rectify these, because it has no control over the source of its creation, that is religion. The idea of state assuming responsibility to reform the 'social' was introduced during the colonial rule in India. The nation state assuming power later, accepted it by default, as it has used the promise of reform as a plea to dislodge the colonial rulers. The subsequent regimes have been using religion in Bangladesh, as a tool, to dislodge each other. The state's capacity to reform the 'social' constructed by religion has diminished rather than increased during the past decades in Bangladesh.

The issue of reform is looked at with a different perspective by some who feel that there is a big gap between what Islam teaches and how Muslims treat their women (Engineer, 1997). The argument is that some religious practices are distorted versions of what the actual spirit of the prescription is. Referring to two recent judgments in Bangladesh, Engineer noted that the past-oriented Muslim men not only legitimize their resistance to change in terms of Quranic pronouncements but also justify their action by using invented logic. It is interesting to note that some Muslim countries have reformed their laws relating to marriage and divorce, whereas in some there is no change, including India, Pakistan and Bangladesh. In India, in recent times, a lot of heat was generated around the issue of whether the law of the land can overrule the personal law of Muslims. The bone of contention was the maintenance of a divorced woman. Muslim stand was that the Islamic law does not provide for any maintenance obligation for the husband beyond the period of *iddat*.[1] A Supreme Court decision, however, has granted maintenance to a divorced Muslim woman beyond the stipulated period of *iddat*.

The two judgments of High Court in Bangladesh, were in

respect of maintenance of widows and polygamy. The first have been recorded in a law journal whereas the other has been reported in a Bangladesh newspaper. The first judgment concluded that the two provisions, i.e., for *iddat* and for maintenance are two different things and have been dealt within two separate verses and should not be mixed with each other. The maintenance period therefore should not be necessarily confined to the period of *iddat*. The learned judges finally conclude:

> "Considering all aspects, we finally hold that a person after divorcing his wife is bound to maintain her on a reasonable scale beyond the period of iddat for an indefinite period, that is to say, till she loses the status of a divorcee by remarrying another person."

In the second judgment, the details of which are not available the court has observed that Islam has not approved polygamy and therefore family law should be suitably amended. These judgements reflect a tendency to rethink and look at the religious practices in the true spirit of the Quranic text. This, however, indicates the gap between ideal and the real, which is generally found in case of religious prescriptions and practices everywhere. It has generated immense controversies among religious scholars themselves, to define what is the true spirit and what is a distorted version of the same. The studies indicate that change in religious practices has been difficult to achieve and the state efforts have been in the negative direction generally in case of Bangladesh.

Political Development

Political development in Bangladesh poses similar problems as in Pakistan, although in recent times the change of governments have been rather smooth and democracy seems to be taking roots gradually. But ironically it is the democratic system of election, which is posing problems of governance. The issue of keeping religion and politics separate and not invoking religious symbols to generate public hysteria is proving difficult in absence of any other means to influence the mindset of common people. The people in Bangladesh unlike India and Pakistan, except for a very small minority, belong to a single cultural stock, having in common, most notably, the language and social customs and practices. The economic problem in Bangladesh, is located around class orientation and rural/urban location. The western orientation of the urban elite and the religious and customary orientation of the masses are a common feature of India, Pakistan and Bangladesh. As Gupta (1994) noted the urge for upward mobility in the middle class, sets it loose and away from cultural roots. He noted the possibility of orthodox Islam coming into clash with westernization of the elite. But, the central problem is rooted in the democratic system of election. The political parties are forced to use religious sentiments to capture power since no other symbol is capable of generating instant mass hysteria. The ruling elite comprising of political leaders, bureaucracy, armed forces and judiciary is far from being objective and principled in character. The general population largely illiterate and economically poor, majority of them located in rural areas, continue to hope to be redeemed by a benevolent state. On the one hand, they are under pressure to check population growth, allow more freedom to women to work outside home and to become generally more materially achievement oriented and on the other to conform to the Islamic practices. All this generates more confusion and the recurring conflicts to capture power adds to this confusion. The differences among the political elite are more personal than ideological, it also helps in greater involvement of religion in politics.

The Jamat-i-Islami movement, for example, calls upon its followers to generate a willingness to wage *jihad* (war) in defence of Islam and its honour. As Maududi, the founder of the movement, noted that the main objective in his political philosophy was to keep alive in Muslims a sense of their separate identity and to prevent their assimilation within their own local culture. The Jamat has evolved its ideology based on its interpretation of *Quran* and *Sunnah* and its aim is to establish an Islamic society in conformity with those interpretations. Islam, Maududi asserts repudiate, the philosophy of popular sovereignty and believes in the sovereignty of God and vice regency (Khilafat) of man (Maududi, 1978). Maududi was opposed to the formation of political parties as he felt that the entire Muslim community was itself a party and no further sectarian groups were needed. He had a different political structure in mind, which was different from the present system of representative democracy. Maududi also opposed the concept of composite nationalism. He opposed the demand for Pakistan. For him Islam was a movement, which was not concerned with the national objectives of any particular nation, its aim was the welfare and prosperity of the entire humanity. The main issue for him was whether the system of government would be based on the western democratic theories or on the sovereignty of God. Maududi was far ahead of his time. His interpretation of Islamic principles was very scholarly and he attempted to grasp the very essence of Islam as a religion. Yet, as we have argued, the human social behaviour in reality is far removed from the ideals of any kind. The efforts to give a particular direction to the process of social change have generally not been very successful. Both Maududi and modernists are making the same mistake. They believe that a transformation of millions of minds precisely in the same direction is possible. In actual practice, the agenda for change is constructed by different segments of elite to suit their own interests. The inconsistency of the development agenda in Bangladesh is therefore obvious and its outcome would be no different from the attempts to create an ideal society in India and Pakistan. The state shall strive to promote the welfare of the people, by securing and protecting a social order in which justice, social, economic and political, shall inform all the institutions of national life, is a slogan to keep the unending process of economic development and political goal of ruling class hegemony alive.

Demographic Profile

Population Growth, 1801-1991

Year	*Population (million)*	*Growth Rate (%)*
1801	14.5	0.67
1901	28.9	0.72
1911	31.6	0.89
1921	33.3	0.52
1931	35.6	0.67
1941	42.0	1.65
1951	41.9	-0.02
1961	50.8	1.93
1974	71.3	2.61
1981	89.9	2.35
1991	111.5	2.17

Source: Experiences with Economic Reform, 1995: 301.

Period	*Crude Birth Rate (per 1,000)*	*Crude Death Rate (per 1,000)*
1881-91	—	41.3
1891-01	—	44.4
1901-11	53.8	45.6
1911-21	52.9	47.3
1921-31	50.4	41.7
1931-41	52.7	37.8
1941-51	49.4	40.7
1951-61	51.3	29.7
1961-74	48.3	19.4
1971-80	—	17.2
1986	38.9	11.9
1994	27.8	8.6

Source: Experiences with Economic Reform, 1995: 302.

Male Intake as a Proportion of Female Intake of Various Nutrients, 1981-82

Age in Years	*Energy (Kcal)*	*Protein (gm)*	*Calcium (gm)*	*Iron (gm)*	*Riboflavin (gm)*
10-12	1.10	1.12	1.19	1.13	1.22
13-15	1.18	1.19	0.98	1.23	1.22
16-19	1.29	1.27	1.34	1.33	1.16
20-39	1.40	1.44	1.32	1.33	1.38
40-49	1.40	1.40	1.65	1.52	1.38
50-59	1.32	1.37	1.39	1.44	1.64
60-69	1.33	1.33	1.22	1.40	1.27
70+	1.52	1.56	1.30	1.41	1.81

Source: Assaduzzaman and Westergaard (eds.), 1993: 200.

Economic Profile

	1991-92	*1995-96*
Agriculture	34.5	30.0
Mining and Quarrying	0.01	0.02
Manufacturing	9.1	9.6
Construction	9.1	5.9
Power, Gas, Water and Sanitary Services	1.5	2.2
Transport, Storage and Communication	12	11.4
Trade Services	8.1	9.0
Housing Services	8.7	9.6
Public Administration and Defense	4.8	5.4
Banking and Insurance	2.0	2.0
Professional and Miscellaneous	13.4	14.9

Source: Bangladesh Statistical Yearbook, 1996: 270.

Growth and Structural Change of the Bangladesh Economy

Sectors	*Annual Rate of Growth %* 1973-84	1984-97	*Share % of The Sector to GDP* 1973-74	1996-97
Agriculture	1.9	2.1	51.0	29.8
Non-agricultural	4.2	5.8	49.0	70.2
GDP	2.9	4.1		
National income	3.2	4.7		
Per capita income	0.8	2.7		

Source: Bangladesh Bureau of Statistics, Monthly Statistical Bulletin, June 1997 and Twenty Years of National Accounts in Bangladesh, 1995.

Labour Force

Year	*Sex*	*Total Population (in '000)*	*Labour Force (as per cent of total population)*
1901	Both	28937	33.3
	Male	14,716	60.6
	Female	14,257	5.1 (6.5million)
1931	Both	35,573	25.2
	Male	18,296	45.0
	Female	17,277	4.2 (7.14million)
1961	Both	50,840	34.3
	Male	26349	56.2
	Female	24,491	10.8 (25.2million)
1981	Both	89,900	28.8
	Male	46,300	52.7
	Female	43,600	3.4(14.6 million)

Source: Hye, 1993: 275.

Total Labour Force (millions)	*1989*	*1990-91*	*1995-96*
Both	50.7	51.2	56.0
Male	29.7	31.1	34.7
Female	21.0	20.1	21.3
Active Labour Force			
Both	50.1	50.2	54.6
Male	29.4	30.5	33.8
Female	20.7	19.7	20.8
Labour Force Participation rate			
Both	74.7	69.6	64.8
Male	79.6	79.6	78.3
Female	85.3	58.2	50.6

Source: Bangladesh Statistical Pocketbook, 1996: 155.

Poverty

Number of People Below Poverty Line

	Absolute number of poor in millions			
	Poverty	*Line I*	*Poverty*	*Line II*
	Urban	*Rural*	*Urban*	*Rural*
1973-74	5.6	57.4	2.0	30.7
1991-92	6.8	44.8	3.8	26.5
Percentage 1973-74	81.4	82.9	28.6	44.3
1991-92	46.7	47.8	26.2	28.3

Source: Bangladesh Statistical Year Book, 1996: 371.

Sectoral Allocation of Government Resources

(percentage)

Sector	*1991-92*	*1995-96*
Agriculture, Water Resources, Rural Development	22.4	19.2
Industries	1.7	1.2
Power and Energy	19.2	12.9
Transport and Communication	14.5	23.2
Physical Planning and Housing	5.0	5.2
Development Assistance to Thana Parishad	3.2	1.9
Social Sector	34.0	36.4
Education	7.2	13.3
Health and Family Planning	7.2	7.3
Others	19.6	15.8
Total (percentage)	100.0	100.0
Total (crore taka)	7150.0	10,447.0

Source: Bangladesh Statistical Year Book, 1996.

Education

Growth of Educational Infrastructure

Type of Educational Institutions	*1993*	*1994*
Primary Schools	49942	66168
Secondary Schools	11095	11019
Madarsahs	6179	5762
Colleges (General)	989	1268
Govt. Medical Colleges	13	13
Medical Colleges (Private)	4	5 (1995)
Engineering Colleges	4	4
Govt. Universities	11	11
Private Universities	6	18

Source: Bangladesh Statistical Year Book, 1996.

Student per Teacher

	1993	*1995*
Primary	63	66
Secondary	33	36 (1994)
College	38	29 (1994)
University	17	36

Source: Bangladesh Statistical Year Book, 1996: 371.

Operating Expenses per Student

(Taka)

	1993	*1994*
Primary	567	475
Secondary	1638	472
College	1146	1485
University		
Govt. Expenditure on Education (per capita)	197	213

Source: Bangladesh Statistical Year Book, 1996: 321.

Health Statistics

Immunization Coverage

Vaccine	*RU*	*RA*	*L*	*UR*	*BA*	*N*
DPT and Polio	Total	Girls	Boys	Total	Girls	Boys
1st dose	81.8	80.0	83.4	86.7	85.5	87.5
2nd dose	76.2	75.2	77.2	88.8	85.9	91.2
3rd dose	73.9	73.0	74.8	81.4	78.7	83.6
Measles	72.3	61.6	73.6	76.5	73.9	78.7
BCG	69.1	68.9	73.6	76.7	75.0	78.1
Tetanus	71.8	73.0	70.7	74.5	76.3	73.3

Source: Bangladesh Statistical Pocketbook, 1996: 342.

Infant Mortality Rate

Year	*Infant Mortality Rate*
1911	205
1921	198
1931	179
1951	168
1961	144
1971	125
1981	128
1989	99
1994	82

* data for 1911-1961 is for the region known as East Bengal.

Source: Centre for Policy Dialogue (1995), *Experiences with Economic Reform*, Dhaka: Dhaka University Press.

Sex-wise Disabilities

(percentage)

Disability	*Total*	*Male*	*Female*
Visual	26.40	23.53	30.30
Hearing	18.5	18.28	18.76
Speaking	14.04	17.10	9.97
Hands	3.40	4.10	2.59
Legs	11.04	12.21	9.50
Mental	4.68	4.66	4.71
Leprosy	1.14	.65	1.81
Goitre	3.94	2.24	6.20

Source: Bangladesh Statistical Pocketbook, 1996: 344.

Nutrition

Consumption Pattern

	Total	*Rural*	*Urban*
Average per day calorie intake			
1981-82	1925	1905	2048
1991-92	2266	2267	2258
Average daily protein intake 1981-82	56	55	65
1991-92	63	62	65

Source: Bangladesh Statistical Year Book, 1996: 353.

Nutritional Status by Gomez Classification

(percentage)

Agency/Year	*Normal*	*Mild*	*Moderate*	*Severe*
INFS/1975-76	3.49	17.68	53.02	25.81
INFS/1981-82	10.0	28.82	46.08	15.10
BBS/1985-86	5.30	33.10	52.0	9.60

Source: Assaduzzaman and Westergaard (eds.), 1993: 211.

Note

1. *Iddat* refers to a waiting period of three months after divorce or the death of the husband under the Sharia among Muslims.

6

India, Pakistan and Bangladesh: A Comparative Analysis

The experts of different disciplines have spent considerable resources in trying to work out theories of development, including economic and social development. The famous economist from Pakistan, Mahbub-ul Haq is credited with the idea of giving a human touch to development by emphasizing education, health and gender related issues in calculating the level of human development. Amartaya Sen from India won the Nobel Prize for his work on welfare economics for more or less adopting a similar approach. The tribe of economists, in particular, is credited with developing models and prescriptions for explaining both the success and failure of development efforts. Yet, as the latest version of the Human Development Report (1999) itself noted globalization, the most recent prescription for speeding up economic development, is creating new threats to human security in both rich and poor countries alike. The relentless pressures of global competition are squeezing out compassion, the invisible heart of human development. Poor people and poor countries risk being pushed to the margin in this proprietary regime controlling the knowledge of the world. After nearly five decades of efforts about 840 million people are malnourished. A vast majority of them are to be found in India, Pakistan and Bangladesh. The overall consumption of the richest fifth of the world's people is 16 times that of poorest fifth. Nearly 1.3 billion people live on less than a dollar a day and close to one billion cannot meet their basic consumption requirements. The share in global income of the richest fifth of the world's people is 74 times that of the poorest fifth. As Sen (1999) noted the complex reality about human development and deprivation remains a mystery even now. The world GDP increased from 3 trillion to 30 trillion in the last 50 years, but the share of poor countries fell from 20 per cent to 10 per cent (HDR, 1999: 25).

A comparative analysis of three countries, which earlier were part of India, would be helpful, not so much in understanding the causes of failure or success, of development efforts, but in providing a summarized account of the development efforts and outcomes. Any attempt at theory building is consciously being avoided since it would become clear in the course of the discussions that social science theory itself is beset with problems, and is generally not helpful in explaining macro realities. Therefore, the very process of trying to transform these realities based on any theoretical framework, remain beset with grave difficulties and falling woefully short of the expectations.

The similarity in the social background of these countries is obvious since they shared the same colonial history and initially a single geographic territory. The regional differences provided some points of departure from this unity, though two major regions Punjab and Bengal were divided to form part of the new nations. The latter again got divided to form two separate nations. The latter division simply put at rest the claim that Muslims and Hindus are two different nations. The politics of power and cultural identities within the same religious category emerged as equally powerful factors in fragmenting human societies. It also laid at rest the theory of religion per se being able to forge a lasting unity among segments of the same religion whose interest are at variance with each other. Simply believing in a common God does not take one very far in structuring 'other' as a friendly neighbour. However, despite sharing a common history and geographical boundary for a long time, there are some characteristics unique to these nations. India remained a multicultural society with a secular constitution; Pakistan's population shared a common God, but significant ethnic differences. It started with a secular constitution but soon converted it into an Islamic one, in an attempt to push the ethnic and economic differences in the background, but failed miserably. Bangladesh is more culturally homogenous as compared to the two. However, the ruling elite in all the three countries has a lot in common and present a marked similarity. For example, the ruling elite in Pakistan was dominated by a feudalistic aristocracy and a group of rich professionals and merchants (Gardezi and Rashid, 1983), and the bureaucracy was trained in West; the ruling elite in India came from feudal background as well, initially at least, which got somewhat changed later with the entry of newer groups seeking their share in the spoils of development. In fact, that has been a major factor of development in India, as it provided more space for other groups to emerge, Pakistan could not do so and remained a closed feudal society. Bangladesh political elite was as feudal in character as was the case with its neighbours, though from a different culture. The bureaucracy in all the three countries had something very significant in common. They came from affluent backgrounds and were generally more close to the west in terms of intellectual underpinnings. USA and UK thus played a major role in shaping the notion of development in these countries with the training of bureaucrats and social scientists involved with development. For example, the Ford Foundation saw its own role as creating and strengthening institutions needed to train man power and develop the knowledge and approaches required for economic and social progress in these countries (Ford Foundation, 1965). It was, therefore, not surprising that in all the three nations, state embarked upon a process of 'development' in line with the thinking in the west.

The central thesis of development in the West, popularly known as modernization theory, is that social change occurs according to a pre-established pattern, the logic and direction of which are known. Social science has been viewed as the science to provide the logic, direction, and technology of social change. As pointed out earlier, immense resources have been spent and continue to be spent on both theory building and project management of development. The myth of the modernization continues since the human societies in recent times have undergone rapid transformations such as the rise of the nation states, industrialization, urbanization, secularization, bureaucratization, and above all rapid expansion of human knowledge. Though these transformations have been unequally distributed in different societies and within societies, there is a systematic way to project that these transformations would effect the common man's life in the near future in a positive way. It is true that these transformations have happened and would continue to happen perhaps at a faster pace than ever, but the consequences of these rapidly happening changes is far from certain. Efforts to recreate Europe in any case can only succeed materially, as all high-rise structures and five star hotels tend to indicate, but that is how far it would go, as the social situation in the countries under review indicate. The hope that these nations would become similar to the western world is neither feasible nor desirable. The theory construction, with one or more factors to describe 'modernization' albeit 'development', should not even be attempted since the very concept is theoretically untenable. Kuhn has noted that proliferation of versions of a theory is a common sign of paradigmatic crises (Kuhn, 1962: 69-72).

Social Consequences of Economic Development

Development is a relative term. Some developments are referred to as 'progressive' while others are termed 'conservative'. Apparently some standard and a sense of direction exist. However, the key concepts relating to 'progress' are rarely reflected upon with any degree of thoroughness. Key words in social analysis and policy, such as social development, participation, emancipation, empowerment, have rarely been clearly defined, or for that matter referred to in indexes. The ultimate objective of development is seen as, to promote human well-being. A major aspect of well-being is defined as economic well-being. Midgley (1995), for example, defines 'social development' as a process of planned social change, with major emphasis on a process of economic development. The primacy of economic is therefore, taken for granted by most thinkers of development, social reconstruction, or social development. The argument here is that the development giving primacy to economic development is feasible and is inevitable, as this thrust would continue to dominate the future efforts in many developing countries. However, the social consequences of economic development are far from clear and difficult, if not impossible, to be given a direction. The evidence from India, Pakistan and Bangladesh indicate that the economic development in the past five decades have not helped the poor and it has not resulted in making society more egalitarian or more gender friendly either. It suggests a rethinking on assuming a positive correlation between economic and social development.

The initial quest for development began by addressing the agenda of economic growth, in India, Pakistan and Bangladesh. All the three nations followed a centralized planning approach to address the problem of economic development. A review of the outcome of development by the official planning documents after four decades admit that the social development has not kept pace with economic development. Social development according to these sources means access to social services such as education, health, and development opportunities for poor sections in particular woman.

The Ninth Five-Year Plan (1997-2002) in India stated:

> "Today, India has a much more developed resource base, in terms of physical and human capital, domestic savings and supply of foreign exchange... The people of India have conclusively demonstrated their ability to build up a nation... The time has now come to extend this spirit to the social and economic spheres in full measure, so that the poorest and weakest will be able to shape their destiny in an unfettered manner. This will require not only higher rates of growth of output and employment, but an all-round human development with stress on social sectors and a thrust on eradication of poverty, minimizing economic disparities and correcting regional imbalances."

In Pakistan, the Seventh Five-Year Plan document (1988-93), with a long-term perspective plan till 2003, stated:

> "Over the course of the last four decades, economic development in Pakistan has been directed by a pragmatic effort, in securing initial national survival and subsequently, attending to the task of providing basic social necessities, however the process only indirectly addressed the higher social and political objectives. Now that the economic foundations are firmly established, it is time to be more sensitive to the larger social vision.... Presently we are very far from the realization of that vision, largely because of difficulties in arriving at a consensual view of common objectives between a strong modernizing elite and the relatively poorer, traditional mass of common people."

The planners after their initial optimism and excitement have realized that there would always be a gap between the objectives of the plan document and what would be achieved on the ground. They have, therefore, began to admit the failure and project some superficial reasons for the same such as the one mentioned above, to sustain the hope in the planning process. The similarity of the arguments in the countries reflects, the way the bureaucratic mindset work. But, the merit of some of the claims such as success in providing basic necessities and attempts to change the social and political realities, without specifying the strategies are obvious. Further, it is not true that no effort in that direction was made earlier, it was, but the efforts failed to alter the overall economic, social and political situation, for the simple reason that bulk of the population remained outside the scope of economic development process, and the efforts made for social and political emancipation. The social situation of mass poverty and deprivation from an economic viewpoint has not changed even now and therefore, there is not much hope for any substantial change in future.

This is what comes out in the brief description of the social reality in these countries. The outcomes of development projects in these countries are not very different, despite the fact that they tried different approaches to achieve the same development goals. The fact remains that the differences were marginal, as pointed out earlier, and only referred to the generation of resources, the question of distribution of resources and creating a mindset compatible with the changes envisaged remain unresolved since the theory had very little to offer in that area.

For example, the state in Pakistan emphasized foreign trade based on the export of raw materials and industrialization geared to the production of consumer goods and was more flexible in welcoming foreign goods and investment. It paid considerably less attention to poverty alleviation as an objective in its development planning. India despite accepting western development goals and strategy followed a Nehruvian approach of socialist development. It did invest considerable resources in developing education and health services and trying to undertake rural development projects as well. Pakistan in particular from the very beginning and Bangladesh after trying with socialism initially adopted a more capitalist approach. Throughout the development efforts during the past five decades 1950-2000, defense, agriculture, industry and infrastructure development accounted for the bulk of government efforts in their search for greater economic prosperity in these countries, with marginal differences in emphasis on one or the other sector. However, whereas in India the same leadership in terms of individual actors as also the political party remained very stable and firmly in place for a long time, the leadership in the other two places underwent radical and sudden change periodically. All the three nations followed a centralized planning approach to address the problem of economic development. The objectives were almost similar as indicated earlier, though the emphasis was on economic development some effort at developing social services was made.

After nearly five decades of efforts, economic development did take place but the major share of the material wealth generated was monopolized by the elite, and the poor masses remain outside the scope of economic development. The similarity of the outcome of efforts during the past five decades is obvious. Pakistan has a much smaller population than India, it followed a more open door policy of economic development than India, it got more financial support from the Muslim countries in terms of employment for its workers of various categories. In India democracy remained firmly in place, whereas it was never firmly in place in Pakistan as it had long periods of military rule. Bangladesh also is still struggling to retain its democracy. The internal strife also in all the three countries is high with recurring violent conflicts. A sizeable population is below the poverty line and illiterate. The status of women in terms of literacy, social, economic and political participation continues to lag behind and is a cause for concern in academic circles and in five star conferences in all countries. Despite low status of women from a western perspective the family as an institution is very stable, divorce rate is insignificant, and above all a caring attitude still can be found particularly in rural areas. The common man is not even aware of such mundane issues. It has more pressing problems to deal with just to survive. The majority of the population still lives in rural areas and has not felt the need for migrating to an urban area. In other words, the need for development is still not a felt need for them.

The so-called strategies for rectifying the situation in future are full employment, national integration to reduce conflicts, rural uplift, social improvement programmes of women and youth, a target approach and technological innovation (Government of Pakistan: 15-16).

The Indian plan emphasizes four themes, quality of life of the citizens, which in fact is (a) new term to giving more attention to education, health, woman's development and in particular providing greater opportunity for weaker sections to participate in economic development; (b) generation of productive employment; (c) creating a regional balance in development efforts or in other words giving more resources to poor states and (d) self-reliance, or lesser reliance on international sources for funding the development.

A comparison of plan document statements over the years would reveal that the sentiments expressed in the recent documents have been present in all plan documents though expressed in different terms. However, the problem is that so far efforts to translate these sentiments into actual results have been failing on account of a number of factors. The problem in fact is lack of a theoretical framework to transform macro social realities in a given direction. The economic theory of development can promote economic growth but it cannot redistribute the benefits of economic growth. The planning process itself raises many issues, which are discussed in greater detail later.

Development is visualized as a process for total 'transformation' of a traditional society. Such a society is characterized by a higher control over natural resources, which are exploited for maximizing the material need fulfilment, based on scientific knowledge. The preference for urbanization reflects this approach. It assumes certain superiority of urban social organization as well, over the rural lifestyle. This is the dichotomous mode of viewing rural areas as a repository of 'folk' culture and regarding cities as the seat of what Redfield called 'urban' culture. It assumes cross-cultural typologies of social system characteristics and a linear model of evolution from folk-local traditions to urban-western ways of life.

This approach raises some issues about the relevance of these typologies for developing countries and about the validity of polarities derived there from. The test question in this case is whether the urban communities acquire the characteristics associated with modernization such as a change in their reproductive health behaviour. Further, whether this is solely a function of urbanization associated with better education, health and economic development or is it associated with religious/cultural belief and practices. The modernization theory does not offer any suggestions about the level of each, education, health, and economic development, at which the interface with religious and cultural beliefs and practices becomes interactive, either in negating or reinforcing them. Further, the issue that all cultural traditions as compared to European tradition, view reproductive health as a non-issue is far from settled. If that be so the possibility of achieving any breakthrough in improving reproductive health will have to wait, till the goal of universal urbanization accompanied by westernization is achieved. Modern medicine, the transistor and television and a modern bureaucracy are all modern traits, however, whether or not such modernization implies eventual modernity is problematic. Rapid social change in one sphere may serve only to inhibit change in others (Huntington, 1965, 1968a).

A study (Qadeer, 1974) of household size in urban and rural areas in India, Pakistan and Bangladesh found that there was little difference in each of the three countries. The little difference that is discernible is in both directions. Indian urban areas had slightly smaller households, while similar households in Pakistan and Bangladesh were a bit larger. The average household sizes for Mumbai, Kolkata, Delhi and Chennai were 4.7, 4.7, 4.6, and 5.4 as compared with a village near Kolkata 4.6 and a village near Baroda 5.3. Karachi and Dhaka had 5.3 and 5.8 as the average household size. Let us now take a brief look at the existing realities in other spheres in these countries to put the entire discussion in a wider perspective. We shall then return to conclude our understanding of the outcomes. A comparative analysis of the three countries is presented below to compare their records of changes in economy, income distribution, poverty alleviation, health and educational status of the population etc. It is interesting to note that India has a number of characteristics which makes it different from the other two yet the outcome in some respects are not very different.

HDI, GDI and GEM Rankings

To begin with, we start with the overall comparison of the HDI ranking which is supposed to be an indicator of the level of human development in the country. There are in all 174 countries which are ranked and the one having the highest level of human development is ranked 1 and the lowest as 174. India was ranked 139 in 1995 and improved its position to 132 in 1997, and 115 in 2001; Pakistan was ranked 127 and Bangladesh 132 in 2001, it was ranked 150 in 1997. The GDI rank captures the achievements in basic human development adjusted for gender inequality, whereas the GEM measures gender inequality in political and economic opportunities. In case of GDI we find India improving her position in 1997 to be ranked 112 against the earlier rating of 128. Pakistan also improved its record to be ranked 116 against an earlier ranking of 131 and Bangladesh came closer to Pakistan by reaching 123rd position in the GDI ranking. However, it is interesting to note that Bangladesh is ranked higher than both India and Pakistan in GEM ranking. Though the Indian position remains stagnant during the two years at 95, Pakistan declined to 101 from 100 and Bangladesh also declined to 83 from an earlier ranking of 80 in 1995. This may be largely due the fact that Bangladesh has 9.1 per cent women in parliament compared to 8.3 in India and 2 per cent in Pakistan. Similarly, the percentage of female professional and technical personnel in Bangladesh is fairly high at 34.7 per cent compared to 20.5 both in India and Pakistan. It is surprising that the number of female administrators and managers is lowest in India 2.3 as compared to 4.3 in Pakistan and 4.9 in Bangladesh.

The life expectancy at birth was almost similar in India and Pakistan in 1998 but life expectancy declined to less than 60 in 1999 in Pakistan. It is still lower in Bangladesh. The interesting fact being that female life expectancy is slightly higher both in India and Pakistan and it is almost same for male and female in Bangladesh. Despite a low record in efforts in improving the status of women in general, as the female literacy rate indicate, which is lowest in Pakistan a mere 24.4 per cent, the female life expectancy at 65.1 years was highest in Pakistan till 1998. The female life expectancy in 1999, was given as 59.5 which was lower than male figure of 59.8 years in Pakistan. The combined, first second and third level gross percentage of school enrolment is also lowest only 28 per cent in Pakistan, while in India it is 47 and Bangladesh 30. The female share of earned income also is lowest in Pakistan, 20.6 per cent compared to 23.1 in Bangladesh and 25.4 in India. In Pakistan, only 2 per cent seats in Parliament are held by women, compared to 9.1 in Bangladesh and 8.3 in India. The participation of Muslim women in politics in Bangladesh is contrary to what the trend is in India and Pakistan. It again puts a question mark in assuming a straight forward relationship between religion and social behaviour of Muslim women. The percentage of female professional and technical workers which is highest in Bangladesh, as indicated earlier is another indicator in that direction. The higher contraceptive use in Bangladesh, indicates that religion as a factor in case of Muslims is not the only factor responsible for low acceptance of birth control measures. Further, it also may be a reflection of the fact that, the response of the common man undergoes a change, as the same factors in cumulative terms, produce a different behavioural response, when the population status changes from minority to majority. However, as we have argued earlier, theory building remains the most difficult task in explaining human behaviour. Contrary to what the data may suggest in Bangladesh, it contradicts it in case of Pakistan, which incidentally has the lowest contraceptive use among the three countries under review.

General Characteristics

Population

India has a far larger population as compared to Pakistan and Bangladesh. It had nearly 966.2 million people in 1997 (now over 1 billion) compared to 620.7 in 1971. Pakistan nearly doubled its population during the period to reach 144 million mark from 74.7 million in 1971. Bangladesh was not far behind with 122.7 million in 1997 from 76.6 in 1971. The annual population growth rate was highest in Pakistan at 3 per cent per annum. The dependency ratio was highest in Pakistan at 83.8 followed by 69.9 in Bangladesh and 65 in India. India has the largest number of old people as population above 65 was 4.1 per cent compared to 3.2 in Bangladesh and 3.1 in Pakistan. Pakistan expectedly has the highest fertility rate of 5 per cent and the lowest contraceptive prevalence rate of 17 per cent. It is significant that Bangladesh have a higher contraceptive use than India. Pakistan has a higher percentage of urban population nearly 35.4 per cent compared to 30.8 in Bangladesh and 27.4 in India. There are numerous explanations available about the high growth of population in these countries, one of them being education of women and improving her status in society. It is a mute point why the efforts in that direction have so far been negligible in Pakistan, rather lukewarm in India and Bangladesh. The governments have right from the beginning realized the problem, but were not in a position to put any definitive efforts and policy in place like China. Even now, the efforts of whatever variety are not likely to produce any dramatic change in these countries. They are very similar in this respect despite, the differences in size and culture. The discourse about the importance, future implications and strategies to tackle the rapidly growing population would continue.

Demographic Trends

Country	*India*		*Pakistan*		*Bangladesh*	
Total population, millions	*1971*	*1999*	*1971*	*1999*	*1971*	*1999*
	620.7	992.7	74.7	137.6	76.6	134.6
	1230.5	2015	204.3		183.2	
Annual population growth rate % 1975-99	2.0		2.8			2.4
Urban population	1975	1999	1975	1999	1975	1999
As % of total	21.3	28.1	26.4	36.5	19.4	23.9
Dependency ratio, 1997	65.0		83.8		69.9	
Population aged 65 and above, 1999, as % of total	4.9		3.7		3.1	
Total fertility rate %	1975	1995-2000	1975	1995-2000	1975	1995-2000
	5.1	3.3	7.0	5.5	6.8	3.8
Contraceptive prevalence rate %	48		24		54	

Source: Human Development Report, 2001.

Structure of Economy

India is huge as compared to Pakistan and Bangladesh as far as the size of the economy is concerned, with a GNP of 421.3 billion US $ in 1998 compared to 63.2 billion of Pakistan and 44 of Bangladesh (WDR, 1999-2000: 230). The annual average growth rate was highest in India 6.1 per cent. compared to 5 in Pakistan and Bangladesh. The average growth rate in South Asia was 5.9 during 1997-98. However, during the last 20 years 1975-95 the average growth rate was 6 per cent in Pakistan, 5 in India and 4.4 in Bangladesh. It indicates that Pakistan's economy did fairly well despite the frequent political changeovers. Does it mean that a stable democratic system has no correlation with economic growth. In per capita GNP Pakistan was highest with 480 US$ followed by India 430 and Bangladesh 350. Measured in terms of PPP$ the GNP was 1,660.9 billion in India followed by 204.9 in Pakistan and 137.7 in Bangladesh. The per capita GNP of 1,700 in PPP$ terms in India, therefore, was higher than 1,560 in Pakistan and 1,100 in Bangladesh (ibid).

The difference in the per capita GDP in India 465 (calculated in terms of US $1987) and Pakistan 417 were nominal but Bangladesh 218 was comparatively poor in 1997. The per capita GNP was marginally higher in Pakistan 480 compared to 430 in India in 1998. However, the GDP calculated in terms of PPP$ the per capita GDP of 2,209 in Pakistan was higher than India 1,422 in 1995. It is interesting to see that per capita GDP in PPP$ terms in India and Bangladesh in 1960 was almost same at 617 in India and 621 in Bangladesh and they have been growing almost at the same pace, with India in 1995 at 1,422 as compared to 1,382 in Bangladesh (HDR, 1998: 149). In 1988, the per capita GNP in US$ was 350 in Pakistan, 340 in India and 170 in Bangladesh. But in PPP$ it was 1,790 in Pakistan, 870 in India and 720 in Bangladesh (HDR, 1991: 153). This, however, could well be an error in calculation. The current income disparity between the poorest 20 per cent and richest 20 per cent is almost same in India (5 times) and Pakistan (4.7 times), and 4 times in Bangladesh. In 1988 also the poorest 40 per cent has an income share of 19 per cent in Pakistan, 20.4 in India and 22.4 in Bangladesh and the ratio of highest 20 per cent to lowest 20 per cent was 5.8 in Pakistan, 5.1 in India and 4.2 in Bangladesh (HDR, 1991: 153). The Gini coefficient reflecting the inequality of income between the rich and poor during 1970-85 was 0.42 in India, 0.36 in Pakistan, and 0.39 in Bangladesh. The Gini Index was 31.2 in 1996 in Pakistan followed by 29.7 in India and 28.3 in Bangladesh. It is interesting to note that the poorest 10 per cent consumed 4.1 per cent of the total income in all the three nations, whereas the highest 10 per cent consumed 27.7 per cent in Pakistan, 25 per cent in India and 23 per cent in Bangladesh. This perhaps accounts for the higher income inequality in Pakistan. The poorest 20 per cent consumed 9.2 per cent in India and 9.4 in Pakistan and Bangladesh. Similarly, across all other income segments there appears to be a similarity in all the three countries (WDR, 1999-2000: 238-39). It is difficult to give a very convincing explanation for such similarity in the distribution of income among the three countries, but perhaps it reflects that: (i) the economic resource distribution among the different segment of the population in the undivided India was almost same in different regions; (ii) it has not changed during the subsequent years despite whatever development efforts, change in political elite and their religion and ideology. In 1998, the structure of economy reflecting the share of different segment in the GDP provides an interesting insight that it is almost same in all the three countries. There is ample evidence to suggest that the planning efforts in the three countries were not exactly similar in all respects, yet the similarity in outcome is striking. The only logical conclusion one can draw from this is, that certain changes are inevitable, as the process of economic development unfolds, driven by national and international development forces, where the overall ideology is liberal in character. The fact, whether the government is democratic or autocratic have not made much of a difference in the economic outcome. Even the size of the population and the cultural factors do not seem to have made much of an impact on the structure of the economy. Yet, the poverty level of the countries is different with Bangladesh being the poorest. It is equally interesting to see, however, the nature of savings and investment patterns. The gross domestic investment is lowest in Pakistan, 15 per cent of its GDP compared to 24 in India and 21 in Bangladesh. Same is true for domestic savings which is 10 per cent of GDP in Pakistan, 20 in India and 15 in Bangladesh (HDR, 1999: 182-83). Yet, the per capita income and growth rate is comparable to India and better than Bangladesh; saving is a matter of habit among certain castes in India, while the Muslims and people of Punjab are known for their consumption patterns. The saving habit in India has lead Krishna Raj to evolve the now familiar term of 'Hindu growth rate'. The central government expenditure as percentage of GDP was 23 in Pakistan as compared to 16 in India. As a result, the budgetary deficit was –7.9 in Pakistan as compared to 4.9 in India. There was not much difference in terms of tax revenue which was 11 per cent of GDP in India and 13 in Pakistan. Government consumption was lowest in Bangladesh at 4 per cent of GDP compared to 12 in Pakistan and 10 in India.

Size of the GNP and GNP Per capita

Country	*GNP billion $ 1998*	*Growth rate % 1997-98*	*GNP per capita 1998*
India	421.3	6.1	430
Pakistan	63.2	5.0	480
Bangladesh	44.0	5.0	350

Source: World Development Report, 1999-2000: 230.

It is obvious that in terms of size of GNP India is a giant as compared to the two countries. The growth rate is however comparable in India and Pakistan, Bangladesh being the lowest. The structure of economy in terms of contribution to the GDP is very similar, with the service sector becoming a major contributor in all the countries. The private consumption is highest in Bangladesh and the government consumption lowest 4 per cent as compared to the 12 in Pakistan and 10 in India. The gross domestic savings was highest in India and lowest in

Pakistan, indicating that Pakistan has been more influenced by market values.

Distribution of Income

It is interesting to see that income distribution depicts a similar distribution across all classes with only minor differences in the share of the richest 20 per cent. It is not surprising, therefore, to find Gini Index showing marginal difference with 31.2 having highest inequality to 28.3 in Bangladesh as the lowest. The similarity across classes may reflect that the class structure before separation into independent countries have continued to be unaffected by the change of national boundaries. In other words, very little has changed during the past 50 years among the general location of the common people.

Country Gini Index	*Poorest 20%*	*II 20 %*	*III 20 %*	*IV 20 %*	*Richest 20 %*
India 29.7	9.2	13.0	16.8	21.7	39.3
Pakistan 31.2	9.4	13.0	16.0	20.3	41.2
Bangladesh 28.3	9.4	13.5	17.2	22.0	37.9

Source: WDR, 1999-2000: 238-39.

The data reflects that though over the years per capita income has registered a change which is significant yet a substantial percentage of population in these countries suffer from what is termed acute poverty. In absolute terms nearly 360 million people in India, since Indian population has now crossed a billion mark, nearly 43 million in Pakistan and nearly 35 million people in Bangladesh are absolutely poor struggling for their survival, and if we assume another 15 per cent or so who would be just above the poverty line then people who are simply poor and surviving without much hope of a high level of social mobility would be around 50 per cent of the total population. Such a large number of poor people on the one hand and a fairly large segment of upwardly mobile, consumer goods rich segment creates the real problem. There are nation's within a nation, entirely different from each other in value orientation, dependent on each other, yet at war with each other. These are the consequences of economic development resulting in wide disparities and generating new tensions. The World Bank report noted that the disparities between rich and poor are growing despite economic growth. What is interesting to note, is the similarity in the percentage of poverty on the basis of the national poverty line. If the figures are correct it simply prove that planning in the country, the system of government, and the investment in social services, had very little to do with at least the percentage of population remaining below poverty line in these countries, as there were wide variations with respect to these in India, Pakistan and Bangladesh.

Size and Structure of the GDP

		India	*Pakistan*	*Bangladesh*
GDP (million $)	1980	186,439	23,690	17,430
	1998	383,429	63,895	42,775
Agriculture	1980	38	30	34
	1998	25	25	23
Industry	1980	24	25	24
	1998	30	25	28
Manufact.	1980	16	16	18
	1998	19	17	18
Services	1980	39	46	42
	1998	45	50	49

The similarity in the structure of economy is also quite striking with only minor differences. Agriculture and industry contribute around 50 per cent of the GDP and the services the remaining. Manufacturing is about 16-18 per cent within the overall industry sector and does not appear to be growing at a fast pace. The fertilizer use in agriculture is growing and it is surprising that it is still slightly higher in Pakistan and even in Bangladesh compared to India. In fact, fertilizer use is highest in Bangladesh and tractor use is lowest in Bangladesh, and highest in Pakistan.

Kg. per hectare of Arable and Permanently Cropped Land

Country	*Fertilizer Consumption*		*Tractors in Use*	
	1970	*1999*	*1970*	*1999*
India	13.7	99.1	0.6	9.1
Pakistan	14.6	111.7	1.1	14.5
Bangladesh	15.7	140.5	0.2	0.6

Source: HDR, 2001: 58.

Poverty in India, Pakistan and Bangladesh

Country	*India*		*Pakistan*		*Bangladesh*	
	Rank	*Value*	*Rank*	*Value*	*Rank*	*Value*
Human poverty index, 1997	59	35.9	71	42.1	73	44.4
Population below income poverty line per cent	$ 1 a day	NPL	$1 a day	NPL	$ 1 a day	NPL
	52.5	36.0	11.6	34.0	28.5	48.0

Source: Human Development Report, 1999; Ninth Five-Year Plan, Government of India, 1997-2002.

The poverty calculated on the basis of national poverty line in India, Pakistan and Bangladesh, indicates that Bangladesh has the highest percentage of poor people among the three, but based on dollar a day poverty line, India has the highest percentage of poor people. In absolute terms, India has the highest number of poor people.

Rural poverty in India is spread across all the occupation groups. Self-employed in agriculture and allied activities have 38.50 per cent of the rural poor, followed by agricultural labourers (23.32%), non-agricultural labourers (15.80%), self-employed in non-agriculture (15.01%), salary earners (5.66%) and others (1.71%) (Pant and Patra, 1998). However, there are large inter-state variations in distribution of rural poor across occupation groups in Andhra Pradesh, Gujarat, Kerala, Maharashtra and Tamilnadu. Agricultural labourers are the poorest compared with the self-employed in the agriculture sector. In Bihar and Haryana poverty is evenly distributed across self-employed in agriculture, agricultural labourers, non-agricultural labourers and self-employed in non-agriculture sector. Punjab and Kerala has poverty greater among non-agricultural labourers. In Andhra Pradesh, Bihar and north-eastern region poverty is concentrated among self-employed in non-agriculture group (Pant and Patra, 1998).

In Pakistan, the population below the national poverty line on the basis of a survey conducted in 1991 was estimated to be 36.9 in the rural areas and 28 per cent in the urban areas. In Bangladesh the official figures of poverty based on poverty line indicate that nearly 47.2 per cent population was living in poverty. There was only marginal difference in rural and urban poverty reflecting the mass scale nature of poverty. The poverty line was at about the same level in the 1980s and 1990s as in the early 1960s (Amin, 1997: 217). The vast majority of the poor continue to live in rural areas.

In India and Pakistan, the facilities which are generally considered as indicators of development, such as telephones, television sets and computers are quite at par, but Bangladesh is way behind on these indicators. It may be a reflection of the lack of materialism which is fairly high in India and Pakistan compared to Bangladesh. An alternative interpretation could be weak infrastructure development in Bangladesh. Whatever, be the level of achievement or failure, and the nature of explanations for that, but the fact remains that it is difficult to exercise any control over the dimension and nature of change. In fact barring minor changes in the nature of economic resource availability, nothing much has changed in the society, in all the three countries in the overall sharing of economic resources.

Per 1,000 People, 1997

Country	*India*		*Pakistan*		*Bangladesh*	
	1990	*1999*	*1990*	*1999*	*1990*	*1999*
Telephone	6	27	8	22	2	7
Cellular mobile	0	2	0	2	0	1
Televisions	—	69	—	65	—	7
Fax machines	0.1	—	1.2	—	—	—
Personal computers	—	2.1	—	4.5	—	—

Sources: World Development Report, 1999-2000: 266-67; Human Development Report, 2001: 62.

Health

The people in all the three countries are now expected to live longer than they were three decades earlier, however, the overall health scene is better in Pakistan. The life expectancy at birth, which was 49 in 1970 became 64.4 in 1998 and has declined to 59.6 in Pakistan (HDR, 2000 and HDR, 2001). It was 62.9 in India in 1999, whereas in Bangladesh it was much lower at 58.9, it was only 44 in 1970. All the three countries have reduced the number of children dying before reaching the first birthday. In case of India it has come down to 70 per thousand from 130, in Pakistan it has come down to 84 from 118 and in Bangladesh it was 81 in 1997, 79 in 1998 and 58 in 1999, compared to 148 in 1970. In case of Bangladesh, it is a remarkable improvement to have a child mortality rate of 58 from 79 a year earlier. It suggests a remarkable improvement on a number of fronts like immunization, availability of nutrition, improvement in weight at birth and so on. However, considering the economic, political and social conditions in Bangladesh, it is difficult believe that such improvements can occur in a year. Infant with low birth weight percentage is highest in Bangladesh, 50 compared to 33 in India and 25 in Pakistan. The percentage of children under age 5 found under weight for their age, 56 is also the highest in Bangladesh compared to 53 in India and only 26 in Pakistan. The logical conclusion appears to be a shift in data. The number of children dying before their 5th birthday has come down to 136 per thousand from 183 in Pakistan, 108 from 206 in India and 109 in 1997, 106 in 1998 and 89 in 1999 from 239 in Bangladesh. Obviously, the change in Bangladesh has been far more encouraging compared to Pakistan and India, despite the fact that Bangladesh is still the poorest of the lot. However, on the other hand, people not expected to survive, to cherish their 60th birthday, is lowest in Pakistan at 27 per cent of the total population compared to 30 in India and 38 in Bangladesh. This may be due to the fact that there are lesser incidence of TB cases and pregnant women with anaemia in Pakistan, compared to India. It could only mean that nutritional levels are better in

Pakistan. But, the recent decline in life expectancy is contrary to these indicators. Looking at all these figures with no accompanying explanation makes one very wary of these figures. It becomes a rather risky affair, to form your conclusions based on data, you do not fully understand.

The index of cigarette consumption per adult 1984-86 = 100 has become 72 in India during 1993-97, 85 in Pakistan and 87 in Bangladesh (HDR, 2000), which means the smoking habit is declining. However, HDR, 1999 has provided data earlier for 1971-72 to 1992 reflecting an increase. Similarly, Malaria cases per 1,00,000 are also lowest in Pakistan at 54 compared to 56 in Bangladesh and 275 in India. Similarly, TB cases per 1,00,000 population were only 3.1 in 1997 which rose to 60 in 1998, in Pakistan, 52 in 1997 and 58 in 1998 in Bangladesh and 136.9 in 1996, 118.3 in 1997 and 115 in 1998 in India, in 1996 (HDR, 1999:174; 2000:192; 2001: 164). The number of persons with disability is 4.9 per 1,00,000 population in Pakistan compared to 0.2 in India and 0.8 in Bangladesh. The total number of persons suffering from HIV/AIDS is estimated to be 4.1 million in India, compared to 64,000 in Pakistan and 21,000 in India (HDR, 2000:192). Nearly 52 doctors and 32 nurses were available to 1,00,000 population in Pakistan compared to 48 doctors in India and 18 doctors and five nurses in Bangladesh. The number of people having access to safe drinking water has increased in India to 88 per cent in 1998, compared to 88 in Pakistan and 97 in Bangladesh and people living in more sanitary conditions is 61 per cent in Pakistan compared to 31 in India and 53 in Bangladesh (HDR, 2001: 160). Except for the fact that both Bangladesh and Pakistan have a slightly higher urban population and the size of population in India being very large, it is difficult to account for these differences. Maternal mortality rate during 1980 to 1999 was 410 per 1,00,000 live births in India and 440 in Bangladesh (HDR, 2001: 168). The figures for maternal mortality in 1990 were 340 per 1,00,000 live births in Pakistan, 570 in India, and 850 in Bangladesh (HDR, 1998:157). However, the government spent on an average only 0.8 per cent of the GDP on health during 1990-97 in Pakistan, 0.7 per cent in India and 1.2 in Bangladesh (WDR, 1999-2000: 242-43).

Nutrition

The daily per capita supply of calories show an increase in India and Pakistan during the period 1970-1996, whereas it declined in Bangladesh. Per capita supply was 2,078 in 1970 in India, which increased to 2,415 in 1996, in case of Pakistan it became 2,408 from 2,198 in 1970, whereas in Bangladesh it declined from 2,177 in 1970 to 2,105 in 1996. Daily per capita supply of protein was low in Bangladesh at 45 grams, compared to 58.6 in India and 59.9 in Pakistan. Same was true for per capita supply of fat which was 23.2 in Bangladesh compared to 65.6 in Pakistan and 44.2 in India. Food consumption as percentage of overall household consumption was highest in Bangladesh at 59 per cent compared to 52 in India and 37 in Pakistan (HDR, 1999: 213).

Environment Degradation

The annual average rate of deforestation was highest in Pakistan at 3.1 per cent during 1980-90 and 2.9 per cent during 1990-95 in Pakistan, compared to Bangladesh where it was 1.8 in 1980-90 and 0.9 in 1990-95. India has increased its forest cover by 1.1 per cent during 1980-90 and retained its forest cover during 1990-95 as it is (HDR, 1999: 207).

The net result of some of the gains in the health sector appears to be a higher growth rate of the population and people living longer than they were earlier. For many poor households, it means feeding more people for a longer period of time. The women in these poor households have more children on their hands. These children are unable to or do not want to go to the school. Some of them work instead in a natural way along side their parents but others are forced to earn a living in more hazardous circumstances. In general, one-way of looking at more children surviving is to see them suffering for survival instead of dying before their first or fifth birthday. One is free to decide which way to interpret it and whether it could be called 'development'.

Education

The adult literacy rate in India, 34 in 1970 increased to 53.5 in 1997 (65.38 in 2001) as compared to Pakistan where it increased from 21 in 1970 to 40.9 per cent in 1997. The HDR, 2001 gave literacy figure for India to be 56.5 in India in 1999, that to in respect of population 15 years and above. Bangladesh has the lowest literacy rate of 38.9 per cent (40.8 in 1999). In other words, nearly 75 per cent male population became capable of reading and writing as compared to 54.16 per cent woman who acquired the same skills in India (Census, 2001). In comparison only half the male population (50%) and one out of four women (25%) acquired literacy levels in Pakistan and nearly the same number in Bangladesh. Similarly only one in four girls (28%) was going to school as compared to one of the two boys (58%) (HDR, 1999: 140) in Pakistan compared to two out of three boys (62%) and one out of two girls (47%) in India. In Bangladesh 30 per cent girls and 40 per cent boys were attending school HDR, 1999: 140). The government was spending nearly 3.4 per cent of the GNP on educating people in India compared to 3 per cent in Pakistan and 2.9 per cent in Bangladesh. Nearly 66 per cent of this expenditure was for promoting primary and secondary education and 13.6 per cent for promoting higher education in India and the trend was not very different in Pakistan, 77.3 per cent and 13.2 per cent though Bangladesh spent more on primary and secondary 88.6 per cent and only 7.9 per cent on higher education.

In recent times most eminent development economists including Amartaya Sen have been emphasizing the importance of promoting education for accelerating the pace of development. However, continued low enrolment ratio and nearly 50 per cent population remaining illiterate scores the point that people in general are not interested in the 'education' being offered. Many studies have noted that the education was largely irrelevant to the needs of the people. People in rural areas who are generally engaged in agricultural activities for earning a living have felt that 'school education' create difficulties for them at several level.

For example, the educated boys would prefer white-collar employment rather than working in the field or carrying out other agriculture related activities. They would prefer to migrate to urban areas and their cultural preferences for food or clothes may change. The education generally expands the need but it may or may not expand the resources. Lack of success in finding suitable employment or poor wages may generate frustration and relationship problems.

Female children are in particular not sent to school since the parent do not want them to interact with their male counterparts. The people in general in India, Pakistan and Bangladesh view maintaining close vigil on their daughters to preserve their sexual morality and the family ties. The concept of freedom is, therefore, almost non-existent for females. The cultural norms are more closely enforced at the family and community level informally in rural areas. The school education is generally seen as disturbing the cultural norms. For example, early marriage of females is a common practice, which clashes with school education. The logic for such arrangements is greater emphasis on the well-being of the family and the community. The early marriage releases a lot of anxiety for parents. If the majority of girls get married in the community at the right age it is expected to cause less problems than when there are a large number of girls unmarried in the family. In other words the 'individual' is given very little space in the construction of the 'social well-being' in the case of females within the family and the community. The education can and does effect this construction which has far reaching implications both for the individual and the society. The result of the transformations which the 'school education' is capable of introducing in society can be viewed from several perspectives. But, in the cultural milieu of these countries so far, particularly the common man has viewed the changes caused by school education with good deal of apprehension. As a natural consequence, the school education has not been an immediate priority of the common man if they have not rejected it out of hand.

Resource Use Imbalance

It is interesting to note that the percentage of government expenditure on education as GNP has been stagnant at 3.4 from 1985 to 1996 in India. It showed a marginal increase from 2.5 to 3 in Pakistan and from 1.9 to 2.9 in Bangladesh. In contrast military expenditure has been highest in Pakistan 6.5 in 1985 declining to 5.6 in 1996, compared to 2.5 per cent of GDP in India and 1.7 in Bangladesh. Expenditure on health has been the smallest – 0.7 in India, 0.8 in Pakistan and 1.2 in Bangladesh – in 1996. There has been a lot of debate on the subject as the donor countries offering development assistant to these countries have been insisting on increasing the amount spent on social services to 20 per cent of the grant. These countries have maintained that this is an internal matter for them to decide. However, over the years, there has been a decline in the development assistance being received by these countries. The resource imbalance is likely to continue as the state is gradually likely to withdraw from the provision of social services, and also from exercising any control over the economy. Secondly, the resources needed to attain even the minimum standards of creating an infrastructure of service delivery for education, health and housing are very large and beyond the capacity of the state. The rough estimates to strengthen primary education in India vary from 450 billion to 550 billion Indian rupees.

Country	*India*		*Pakistan*		*Bangladesh*	
Public expenditure	1985	1996	1985	1996	1985	1996
on education as % of GNP	3.4	3.4	2.5	3.0	1.9	2.9
Health as % of GNP/GDP	1960	1996	1960	1996	1988	1996
	0.7	0.5	0.3	0.8	—	1.2
Military expenditure	1988	1996	1988	1996	1988	1996
as % of GDP	2.5	3.4	5.6	6.5	1.7	—

Source: Human Resource Development Report, 1999.

Note: The figures for expenditure on health in 1960, is as percentage of GNP whereas for 1996 it is as percentage of GDP. See original source for details.

Gender Gaps in Economic Activity

Yet another difference in the cultural context of these countries is the way the women's participation is viewed by the society. The non-participation of females in the economic, political and social activities have generally been well documented in the whole of South Asia. A number of explanations are being offered to explain the same. It is generally considered undesirable from a development perspective that a substantially large percentage of human resource remains unutilized or under utilized for economic production. An implication of this is that it is over utilized for reproduction. So, instead of adding to goods, it is enlarging the consumption, thereby creating huge short falls in availability of resources. Therefore the simple economic logic demands full utilization of human resources for productive purposes. Yet, there is a different cultural orientation as mentioned above, which views females as different from males and prescribes very different roles for females. The logic of the other perspective usually termed 'traditional' is generally misunderstood in the western world. This logic focuses on the social or group relationship rather than on individual freedom which is the corner stone of the 'modernization' albeit westernization. It, therefore, is not surprising to find that only 29 per cent women in India 20 per cent in Pakistan and 44.4 per cent in Bangladesh are economically active. The Bangladesh figures, reflecting the higher quantum of female economic participation in India and Pakistan also refute the largely held assumption of Muslim orthodoxy preventing women's participation in economic development. It shows that traditional views are mediated by other factors. This shows how difficult it is to explain a complex social reality within a given theoretical framework. Putting women behind closed doors or veiling of women has an interesting history. The practice is said to have originated among the high-ranking noble men at a time when the rulers were known for their large 'Harems'. No good-looking woman was considered safe from the king. The noblemen, therefore, started hiding and veiling their women. But the fact remains that Islam provides for maintaining a distance between the sexes. The idea is to regulate individual freedom and in particular to regulate sexual relations. The general logic is that if man has to love and provide for his child, he must be sure of fathering the child. Therefore, exclusive right over the female body is considered a necessity. The polygamous nature of man, is acknowledged and provided for, though with due restrictions. The general trend is to assign females roles within the household although no specific role allocation is prescribed in the holy text. In India, too, the customary practice has been similar, in all these respect, except for allowing polygamy under the formal laws. The social structure generally assigns household roles to women and to prescribe taboos on sexual relations to regulate the same. The different cultures in India, Pakistan and Bangladesh exhibit similar practices even today and deviations cause a great deal of turmoil. The public report on basic education in India (Probe, 1999) brings out some of these prejudices. The economic aspirations in a growing economy on the other hand put pressure on the household to allow greater freedom for economic participation. The economic participation is bound to raise several other issues, which were earlier put on hold. The rights of the women, under international pressures, and in the changing economic conditions are assuming greater importance and her status vis-à-vis men in the household is being reconstructed in certain pockets. The economic participation of women in different socio-economic strata some how poses different dilemmas for the women. The point is, even when the women on account of recent transformations are allowed to work, it may not alter the earlier oppressive reality which the economic development was aiming to accomplish. It may at least in some cases lead to more problems. The so-called prescriptions of women's development have so far addressed elite segments and have failed to address the common person. In some cases like, the middle class and lower-middle class, the education and employment of women have posed more problems for them as the corresponding change in social norms and in particular men's attitude have not kept pace. This has resulted in conflicts and harassment for women in the families and at work place. Pakistan is however considered to have followed a less women friendly policy as compared to India and Bangladesh.

Country	*India*		*Pakistan*		*Bangladesh*	
Female economic activity, 1997	Rate %	As % of male rate	Rate%	As % of male rate	Rate %	As % of male rate
	29.0	50.3	20.8	40.3	44.4	77.2
Female unpaid family workers	—		33		71	

Source: Human Development Report, 1999: 233-34.

Conclusion

Although the countries have differences in size and level of sophistication of bureaucracies and an elite diverse in orientation, the process of development raise issues, which are similar. The people in these countries have characteristically regarded development and modernization projects with a considerable measure of suspicion. Although motivation for these feelings varies from person to person and region to region, it derives basically from two sources. The first is the cultural values particularly in the matters of giving primacy to institutions of social control such as family, caste and religion. The second is the general belief that macro policies and programmes are not in tune with grassroots realities, and hence fail to change these. A large portion of writings on planned development including micro-level investigation of projects, acknowledge that efforts at development have failed due to local, cultural, environmental, and or social conditions (Foster, 1978: 320). The impression one gets, after looking at the way development process have folded in these countries, that attempts at economic development was the central objective through industrialization and infrastructure development and it continues to be so. The development approach was different, in the degree to which, the state was allowed to manipulate and control the economy. In all the three countries growth in gross domestic product was significant. What Myrdal (1968) pointed out remains true even today that despite growth things have not changed for some people. Sociologically speaking, as Madan (1994) put it, changes have taken place in society but society has not changed, and that is true for all the three countries. As Dreze and Sen (1995) noted in the context of India the task Nehru had identified remains largely unaccomplished. The areas of achievements identified by them are elimination of substantial famines, though the scarcity of drinking water continues, a stable democracy and a large scientific community. The last two are confined to India as Pakistan and Bangladesh continue to struggle to stabilize their political system. But to believe that things overall have improved is an illusion of sorts. The widespread economic poverty remains a major reality.

Many studies (Ahluwalia, 1978, 1985; Saith, 1981) have focused on the relationship between rural poverty and agricultural performance. Saith (1981) has challenged the view that increases in agricultural production has reduced poverty. Gaiha (1989) has argued that despite its obvious importance in designing anti-poverty strategy, the distinction between chronically poor and temporarily poor is seldom emphasized. He also argued that an income/expenditure rank (or level) is a poor predictor of the chronic poverty of a household. It is not a low per capita income but low variation in it over time in absolute terms. This low variation he argued was on account of low/negligible endowments (e.g., cultivable land, labour power, skills) and without any possibility of augmentation. A number of prescription of all kind economic, political and social have been advanced to augment these, the most recent being Dreze and Sen (1995) who lament the neglect of provision of public education, health care and other services aimed at the augmentation of capacities for economic participation. As many have pointed out the problem of subject orientation continue to distort the truth. Provision is a complex phenomenon to begin with. Who shall provide, what and to whom and on what basis, with what consequences, remain an unending debate in all the countries, with no end in sight. The whole process revolves around negotiating these issues within a close circuit, though others are trying to get accommodated and some do find a space. But then there is a limit to the numbers and the type who could be accommodated.

As a study which looked into the outcomes of development in four Asian countries including India and Bangladesh noted, the model of development supported by western countries not only failed on its own terms but also caused fundamental damage to the possibility of these nations mobilizing their own resources and shaping their own destinies. These countries had two options; to pursue a path of future development in conformity with their own philosophy of life or to follow the model of western development. The Indian philosophy cutting across all major religious communities in India, is rooted in a non-materialist, 'other world' approach, which is an anti thesis of the Christian spirit and capitalism. The 'present', in the context of Indian philosophy, is assumed to be a short and transitory phase. The ties to the 'present' should be kept to a minimum by keeping the consumption level low, and consciously rejecting the material comforts, including that of body. This philosophy, would reject industrial development and an expansion of needs, that is why Gandhi, steeped as he was, in Indian philosophy rejected industrialization. The economic growth per se, therefore, would not have been pursued and no need for any technological development felt. The second option was, what these countries followed, to think of a development, which believed in the present and did every thing to control its future. This model obviously gave economic growth a central position and accordingly the success of the model had a direct relationship with the growth of technology employed for production, and the size of the GDP. India, Pakistan and Bangladesh all have succeeded in enlarging the GDP, with only minor differences in growth rate. The Nehruvian model helped India, in thinking in terms of self-reliance to some extent. Its socialist values helped in providing quality education to a small segment of population, which is now paying dividend. The educated elite has contributed to develop indigenous expertise in many areas. A major area was agricultural development to achieve self-sufficiency in food and building infrastructure, roads dams etc. Unfortunately, it failed to make any major breakthrough in the industrial technology, but the current developments in information technology has given a major boost to the economy. Both Bangladesh and Pakistan have not been able to achieve this. The quality of higher education in Pakistan and Bangladesh is not comparable to India. The intellectual base in India and a wider base of professional elite, and more growth-oriented centres like Bangalore, Mumbai, Chennai, Hyderabad earlier and many more emerging in recent years, have helped in spreading the scope of economic development, whereas in Pakistan and Bangladesh it remained more limited in its coverage. However, sociologically what is interesting is, that despite these differences and difference in size of population, language, religious rituals and gods, the distribution of income across different strata is remarkably similar, as also the percentage of people below the poverty line.

The other similarity lies in the social values of the people, in all the three countries, the common man has rejected western values, in particular that of giving greater space to individualism and consequently greater space to female freedom. The male control over female bodies, the core of gender discrimination, have as a result, not changed at all. The idea of female empowerment has not found favour at any level, including among the educated elite. Religion continues to ritualize the lives of people and influences behaviour significantly. The rituals and the relationships are still predominant in the psyche of the ordinary people. The life in all the three countries goes on at its own pace and on its own terms and logic, uninterrupted even by earthquakes, droughts and cyclones. For the simple reason that the majority still believe in mere survival and is not trying to hegemonies the future. The elite in these countries is getting threatened, as it is unable to control the common people, the only significant outcome of economic development. It is inventing new symbols steeped in religious and cultural traditions to evoke passions, to create new constituencies. The World Bank predictions are hinting at an increase in conflicts within nations rather than between nations, yet the relations between the nations under review are not likely to change in the near future. Contrary to expectations, the economic development seems to be supplementing the growth of religious fundamentalism in these countries, along with a sense of despondency about the future.

Comparative Statistics

General Characteristics

Country	*India*				*Pakistan*				*Bangladesh*			
	1995		*1997*		*1995*		*1997*		*1995*		*1997*	
HDI rank (*L174)	139		132		138		138		147		150	
GDI rank (*L163)	128		112		131		116		140		123	
GEM rank (*L102)	95		95		100		101		80		83	
	M	*F*	*M*	*F*	*M*	*F*	*M*	*F*	*M*	*F*	*M*	*F*
Life expectancy at birth in years	61.4	61.8	62.3	62.9	61.8	63.9	62.9	65.1	56.9	57.0	58.1	58.2
Under-5 mortality	*1960*		*1996*		*1960*		*1996*		*1960*		*1996*	
	21		14		22		12		20		14	
Adult literacy rate % M/F 1997	M	66.7	F	39.4	M	50.0	F	24.4	M	49.4	F	26.1
	1970		*1997*		*1970*		*1997*		*1970*		*1997*	
Total	34		53.5		21		40.9		25		38.9	
	Male		*Female*		*Male*		*Female*		*Male*		*Female*	
Combined first, second, and third level gross enrolment ratio %	62		47		56		28		40		30	
Share of earned income %	74.6		25.4		79.4		20.6		76.9		23.1	
Real GDP per capita (PPP$)	902		2,389		701		2363		767		1320	
Seats in parliament held by women %	8.3				2.0				9.1			
Female administrators and managers %	2.3				4.3				4.9			
Female professional and technical workers %	20.5				20.5				34.7			

Source: Human Development Report, 1999: 140.
*L-lowest rank

Economic Profile

Country	*India*		*Pakistan*		*Bangladesh*	
GNP billion US$	357.4		64.6		44.1	
GNP annual growth rate 1975-95	5.0		6.0		4.4	
GNP per capita US$, 1997	370		500		360	
GNP per capita annual growth rate, 1997	2.8		3.1		2.0	
Average annual rate of inflation	1985-96	1996	1985-96	1996	1985-96	1996
	9.0	6.3	9.2	10.5	6.1	3.5
GDP US $ billion, 1997	381.6		61.7		41.4	
Agriculture as % of GDP, 1997	25		25		24	
Industry as % of GDP, 1997	30		25		27	
Services as % of GDP, 1997	45		50		49	
South Asia GDP 505.4 billion US$	Agriculture 25		Industry 29		Services 46	

Country	*India*		*Pakistan*		*Bangladesh*	
Consumption as % of GDP, 1997	Private 70	Govt. 10	Private 78	Govt. 12	Private 81	Govt. 4
Gross domestic investment as % of GDP, 1997	24		15		21	
Gross domestic savings as % of GDP, 1997	20		10		15	
Tax revenue as % of GDP, 1997	11		13		—	
Central government expenditure as % of GDP, 1997	16		23		—	
South Asia gross domestic investment 23	South Asia gross domestic savings 18		South Asia budget deficit–7.0		Central government expenditure 23	
Overall budget deficit, 1997	-4.9		-7.9		—	

Source: Human Development Report, 1999: 182-83.

Country	*India*		*Pakistan*		*Bangladesh*	
GDP per capita (1987 US$)	1975	1997	1975	1997	1975	1997
	251	465	222	417	134	218
Real GDP per capita (PPP $)	P 20 %	R 20 %	P 20%	R 20%	P 20%	R 20 %
	527	2,641	907	4,288	606	2,445
Real GDP per capita (PPP$)	1960	1995	1960	1995	1960	1995
	617	1,422	820	2,209	621	1,382
	Rank	Value	Rank	Value	Rank	Value
Human poverty index, 1997	59	35.9	71	42.1	73	44.4
Population below income poverty line %	$ 1 a day	NPL	$1 a day	NPL	$ 1 a day	NPL
	52.5	36.0	11.6	34.0	28.5	48.0

Source: Human Development Report, 1999.
*P-Poorest, *R-Richest

Country	*India*		*Pakistan*		*Bangladesh*	
Exports as % of GDP, 1997/US $ million	12 (44,107)		16 (10,009)		12 (5,075)	
Imports	16 (59,230)		21 (12,955)		18 (7,656)	
Net foreign direct investment US$ million	1985	1997	1985	1997	1985	1997
	106	3,264	131	800	1	145
Net official development 1997 assistance received US$ million	1991	1997	1991	1997	1991	1997
	2745	1678	1371	597	1889	1009
AS % of GNP	1.1	0.4	3.1	1.0	6.0	2.3
External debt as % GNP	1985	1997	1988	1997	1988	1997
	19.2	24.9	46.1	47.5	31.8	35.1
External debt US $ million, 1997	94,404.2		29,664.5		15,125.3	

Source: Human Development Report, 1999.

Health Services

Country	*India*		*Pakistan*		*Bangladesh*	
Life expectancy at birth (years)	1970	1997	1970	1997	1970	1997
	49.1	62.6	49.2	64	44.2	58.1
Infant mortality rate (per 1,000 live births)	130	71	118	95	148	81
Under 5 mortality rate (per 1,000 live births)	206	108	183	136	239	109
People not expected to survive to age 60	30 (as per cent of total population)		27 (as per cent) of total population		38 (as per cent of total population)	
Maternal mortality rate	570 per 1,00,000 live births		340		850	

Country	*India*		*Pakistan*		*Bangladesh*	
Immunization of 1 year old %	TB	Measles	TB	Measles	TB	Measles
1995-97	96	81	90	74	91	62
TB cases per 1,00,000 population, 1996	136.9		3.1		52.6	
People with disabilities % of total population, 1985-92	0.2		4.9		0.8	
Doctors per 1,00,000, 1993	48		52		18	
Nurses per 1,00,000, 1993	—		32		05	

Source: Human Development Report, 1999: 170, 174.

	India			Pakistan			Bangladesh		
People not expected to survive to age 40 as % of total population	15.8			14.3			20.8		
Population without access to	*SDW	*HS	*SA	*SDW	*HS	*SA	*SDW	*HS	*SA
	19	25	71	21	15	44	5	26	57

Source: Human Development Report, 2000: 170.
*SDW-safe drinking water, HS-health services, SA-sanitation

Education

Country	*India*		*Pakistan*		*Bangladesh*	
Net enrolment ratio as % of relevant age-group	*P	*S	P	S	P	S
	77.2	59.7	—	—	75.1	21.6
Female enrolment ratio	71.0	64.8	—	—	69.6	15.6
AS % of male ratio	86.0	68.0	—	—	87.0	58.0
Public education expenditure as % of all levels 1993-96	*P and *S	*H	P and S	H	P and S	H
	66.0	13.7	77.3	13.2	88.6	7.9
As % of total government expenditure	11.6		8.1		—	
As % of GNP	3.4		3.0		2.9	

Source: Human Development Report, 1999:178.
*P-Primary, S-Secondary, H-Higher
Figures for total government expenditure refer to expenditure on all levels of education and the same is true for expenditure on education as percentage of GNP.

7

Search for a Civil Society

The project 'development' was a logical consequence of the end of the colonial rule in India. The expansion of social sciences and the newfound faith in the development models advocated by the West to convert the 'primitive' into a 'modern' civilization lent support to these efforts. The leadership which lead the struggle for independence from colonial rule was very progressive in its thinking and had a first hand understanding of the grassroots reality of India. It ensured during the process of formation of the nation state, a democratic system of governance and that the state commits itself to the creation of a new society, where the poor are at the centre of the agenda for 'development'. The plan documents and the political manifestos of different political parties provide ample evidence for this. However, as we noted earlier, not much was known in the 1950s, about what is to be done to create the new society, which would do justice to all and particularly to the poor. The key issues at that time were seen as mass poverty, illiteracy and poor economic resources of the country which were not even sufficient to feed and clothe the millions. The main emphasis in creating the new society in the initial stages was on economic development and to some extent on development of social services. The idea of development was also initially conceived as national development, signifying the integration of different groups as part of the nation state rather than as independent political/ social units, in 'developing' countries particularly those of South Asia. The state was expected to be the key actor and coordinator of efforts to create a civil society.

'Civil society' is a term, which has no precise meaning yet.

Hobbes and other political theorists used the term to denote the coming into being of a society governed by rules of conduct to facilitate social functioning, the main concern being the creation of a system of governance and distribution of power among different stakeholders. The 'civil society' discourse is addressed by social science disciplines in what Habermas (1987) termed as the subject-centred context. The political scientists pose the problem in the context of state sovereignty versus the individual liberty. The sociologists are concerned with social action, social movements and moral values necessary for creating social order, while welfare discourse constructs the 'civil society' to enlarge the scope and efficiency of social welfare services and protection of human rights of the weaker sections. The central concern in these conceptualizations is social construction or reconstruction. Also reflecting a confidence in their own expertise to be able to offer solutions having first posed and diagnosed the problem.

The discourse on 'civil society' thus operates at two levels of abstractions, there are those who interpret society to be beyond any grand design of reconstruction and therefore logically closed to any attempts at creating grand alternatives (Berlin, 1997). The post-modernist discourse rejects the possibility of any social engineering to reconstruct it in a given framework. The argument is that the consequences of any 'modernity' project remain uncertain in view of lack of any social theory and obvious limitations of what the science can do to guide human actions and behaviour (Madan, 1998: 234). They suggest emancipation from emancipation (Pieterse, 1992). The committed followers of 'development project' on the other hand, continue to invent projects of hope, and expect 'civil society' to reform, both the state and society. Civil society discourse in this sense is aimed at providing legitimacy to a renewal of faith in the capacity of society to plan its own destiny either through technological change or revolution. The failure of efforts made so far are attributed to state and demand for its withdrawal are posited from economic and social sector to allow greater freedom to other actors including markets in pursuing the task of reconstruction of society.

The Birth of the Civil Society

The idea of 'civil society' was given currency by Hobbes (1960) who defined it as the readiness of each individual to forgo his or her quest for self-preservation and mutually and voluntarily agree with each other to forgo that quest individually and to appoint an individual or assembly to provide security for all. He was, therefore, referring to the formation of a social order and a mechanism of governance. Rousseau, on the other hand, believed that the first man who after fencing off a piece of land, took it upon himself to say "this belongs to me" and found people simple-minded enough to believe him, was the true founder of 'civil society'. The point is, once men begin to seek personal possessions, the very idea of right comes into being, and further the inequality of talent and skills among people inevitably leads to an inequality of fortunes. Wealth also enables some persons to enslave others; the very idea of wealth and possession excites passions, and gives rise to conflicts and turmoil in society. This leads in turn to a demand for a system of law to impose order and tranquility. The rich specially voice this demand, for while the state of violence threatens everyone's life, it is worse for the rich because it threatens their possessions also. In Rousseau's own words:

> "Such was, or may have been, the origin of 'civil society' and laws, which gave new fetters to the poor, and new powers to the rich; which destroyed natural liberty forever, fixed for all time, law of property and inequality, transformed shrewd usurpation into settled right, and to benefit a few ambitious persons, subjected the whole of the human race thenceforth to labour, servitude and wretchedness". (in Cranston, 1968:21)

The term 'civil society' thus refers to the coming into being of a social order based on law. The establishing order gives birth to a state or a centre of power having the authority to make laws and enforce them. The process of making and enforcing laws generate the need for protection of human rights of weaker sections. The central concern being, arriving at a socially just arrangement between members of a society on the one hand and the members and the state on the other, for sharing freedom and economic prosperity, having consented to surrender their individual rights to the state. The nature and functions of state in political science discourse becomes the key to the creation of civil society. The state was meant to provide protection to people, who had appointed it, and the theorists agreed that the sovereign must have enough power to provide such protection. The assumption was that the state actors would use power in a judicious manner and the subjects would abide by the law. Hobbes felt that men must choose, either they were ruled or they were free; they could not be both; liberty went with anarchy and security with civil obedience. Rousseau accepted Hobbes' argument about sovereignty being absolute but felt that it was possible to retain the sense of freedom, if people could retain some values. He, however, felt differently from Hobbes and Locke that sovereignty was transferred from people to the ruler, he felt that sovereignty not only originates in people it ought to stay there. The authority according to Rousseau is based on conscious and vocal assent. In that sense every state action in the final analysis is subject to approval by the people. It gives the right to people to dissent and protest. Civil society, in this sense, is seen as a public sphere of collective action between the family and the state that coexists in a complex relationship of creative tension with the state.

The state became a major component of life by the middle of the twentieth century. It was projected as the key factor in shaping the future of emerging third world countries and the social transformations therein. The cold war era gave boost to the concept of welfare state and projecting state as the God. The transition from colonial state to a nation state also played a major part in defining both the new state and the 'civil society'. The colonial state following Hobbes, took its sovereignty for granted and hence believed in the complete obedience on the part of its subjects, in order for the state to provide them security of person and property. The idea that people of the colony were inferior to the ruling elite, which the state represented, and the need for reforms to improve their status, further separated the colonial state from the people. The question of relations of state and subject was unilaterally decided and enforced in 'the interest' of the subjects on authority of the Queen. As a consequence, legally the colonized inhabitant was a subject with highly circumscribed civil and political rights. Economically, the colonial subject was a unit of labour, in religious terms an ignorant awaiting redemption through Christianity. The state domination over its civil subjects was near total and subsequently leads to social movements to reconstruct the state and its relations with the society it governed.

During the later part of the colonial rule, the rise of nationalist self-assertion gradually promoted an era of political dissent and social movement, which according to some scholars is considered as the birth of 'civil society' in India. It can be taken as the starting point of the very idea of social reconstruction in India. The process of generating a societal response, by uniting a large section of a diverse population, for achieving a specific change, was a grand new experience, generating hopes for many more changes to follow. The general connotation is to rearrange an oppressive structure, in this case colonial state, to make society more humane and just. Subsequently the source of oppression may be identified as economic relations, gender relations, religion or caste. The reconstruction design would have to specify these and the alternative design with evidence of their greater human friendliness, rather a difficult task not easily accomplished.

The political scientists in their discourse on social transformation are generally concerned with issues such as, the process of state formation, the functioning of institutions of the state, political stability, its philosophy and role in the area of economic development and state society interface etc. No definitive answers to any of these issues have so far been possible. Social theorists have used either society or state centred theoretical models to offer an explanation. Unfortunately by using the state or society as an organic entity, the discourse operates at a level of general abstraction, which do not do justice to either the dynamics of state or society. Both 'state' and 'society' remain complex sites and the dynamics of their functioning is difficult to theorize. The discourse to construct an ideal state and society so far remain inconclusive and beyond the realm of social theory.

The post-colonial state in many developing societies, including India, Pakistan and Bangladesh, was given the unfinished task of restructuring of society, by expunging the 'traditional' and replacing it with a 'modern' one. The state thus was not only concerned with the distribution of power, it was expected to redefine the economic and social relationships. It has to evolve a new social policy framework for its subjects and a framework for defining its relations with the world at large. The subsequent debates in civil society discourse began by addressing themselves to evaluating the state action to redefine economic and social relations or in other words its social policy framework. The state policy, institutional mechanisms for implementation of policies and the state actors were reviewed and assessed. The obvious conclusion was discovery of a gap between ideal and the actual situation.

The Weberian traits presumed in the design of the modern state – impersonality of office, uniform application of rules, predictability of behaviour, rationality of organizational structure, etc., to achieve its goal of creating social justice, were highly idealistic. The state which emerged in the post-colonial nations was a perfect model of shared hegemony. The ruling elite exercised unrestricted domination over society, justified through claims of reconstructing the future in the larger interests of the subjects. The process of reconstruction integrates all stakeholders except the poor. For example, the bureaucracy, the intellectual class, the NGOs, the media, and the corporate world are allocated a share for keeping the hope alive and making it possible to govern. The process of state formation in a democratic polity allows for widening the elite circle to give the impression of opportunity for social mobility. The system works perfectly, so long as all actors remain constitutional in orientation, and do not violate the rules of the game. In actual practice, neither the formal hierarchy inherited from the colonial state nor organizational norms of discipline, whether derived from bureaucratic ethics or from ideological rectitude, suffice to control and motivate the key operatives in the security, political and administrative apparatuses. The gap between the ideal and the actual outcome is inevitable.

The need to redress this anomaly results in the search for new actors for carrying on the "project of making society just and humane". The hegemony of 'state', therefore, began to be questioned and the civil society discourse continues.

The state functioning in the area of social service delivery in particular takes centre stage as the democracy becomes the norm in the process of state formation. The civil society discourse in this context is targeted to question the role of state in the delivery of social services (Azarya, 1994:85). The concern is to reach the target groups in society more directly, circumventing state channels that proved corrupt and inefficient. The need for of an 'active civil society' manifests in NGOs the power to represent various groups in society, and provides international donors an alternative to the state. The focus of the discourse here is allocating a greater space to the NGOs in delivery of social services and mediating the social policies of the state in particular for protecting the human rights of the weaker and vulnerable sections of society (Desai, 1999).

Though there is some merit in the state becoming insensitive and inefficient the alternatives suggested also pose problems. As Vassavi et al (1997) noted, the administrative approach to education, initiated during colonial times, focused on supply-side factors like increasing the number of schools, establishing pre service training centres, control through the inspection system etc. The limitations of this approach have been exposed by the persistence of the problem of illiteracy, poor grade completion rates, high proportions of girls in the category of the 'never-enrolled' and weak participation of groups that had traditionally been outside the formal education system. This has resulted in a shift of focus on demand-side factors and in particular to, the role of the community or users of education. The suggestion to form village level education committees (VEC) and standing committee on education in Panchayats, to supervise the educational service and its use is an offshoot of this change. The suggestion for VEC would also create problems as various stakeholders, such as teachers, bureaucracy and panchayat members would find it difficult to synthesize their different perspectives. And that this would lead to tensions between stakeholders rather than improving the efficiency of schools. This is a good example of the duality, the desirability of a remote and inaccessible state apparatus for governance and the problem of it becoming inefficient and insensitive in the process. On the other hand more informal and easily accessible peoples organizations carry the risk of becoming too politicized and whimsical and therefore incapable of wielding power judiciously (Vassavi et al, ibid). Creating democratic organizations cutting across caste and class boundaries is a fairly difficult task. Entrenched differentiation and lack of a sense of community lead to a lack of interest among the people in working and organizing for local and collective interests (ibid). Implications of these in India are significant since many of the NGOs seek to build upon an assumed community consciousness and capacity for organizing at the grassroots level, particularly in rural areas. This is particularly true with reference to programmes where economic benefit is not an immediate output.

Desai (1999) expects the 'civil institutions', or non-governmental organizations, to protect the human rights of the vulnerable groups of society such as women, children and schedule castes and tribes etc. She, however, refrained from stating the reasons for allocating such a role for NGOs or for terming them as 'civil institutions' in place of NGOs. The idea of state allocating some space to the NGOs was based on an appreciation of the NGOs success in empowering the community (Garain, 1993). The explanation was that a large section of the population either did not benefit from development initiatives or became further marginalized due to inappropriate development experiments. Although Garain has not attempted to define either empowerment or community, we assume that what he meant was that NGO programmes resulted in some benefits to some households in a given neighbourhood. Narayana (1991), on the other hand, noted that voluntary organizations have been preferred on various assumptions regarding their approach, organization and behaviour patterns. However, voluntary organizations everywhere and in particular in India, suffer from serious handicaps and problems. He noted that voluntary organizations relied on a single source for funding, and is therefore bound to stagnate and decline in due course. The technical and professional competence of the staff was inadequate. Vivian (1994), in her study of NGOs and sustainable development in Zimbabwe, noted that the assumption that NGOs would succeed in finding solutions to complex problems where the state has failed is unrealistic and counterproductive. Zaidi commenting on poverty elimination through NGOs felt that despite good intentions such projects are narrow in focus and not consistent with the living conditions of the beneficiaries (Zaidi, 1997). The terms used NGO and voluntary organization, are seldom defined, the two may not be synonymous nor the terms may refer to organizations similar in all respects and necessarily working for inducing social change.

In the past two decades voluntary/NGO sector in many countries has undergone a major change. It has become more financially stable by using both the state and international resources. The expansion of government social service sector, and the dissatisfaction with the services over the years, both has helped in making the voluntary sector resource rich and offering it a credibility it lacked earlier. Its resourcefulness has enabled some large size NGOs to acquire a permanent status of 'development brokerage' both nationally and internationally. The NGOs are the major recipient of the resources earmarked for poverty alleviation, and in the process have become development brokers between the state and the international donors and poor. They often use their position to influence grassroots organization to give up political struggles. This has resulted in conflicts and divisions between the grassroots, making them weak politically (Lopez and Petras, 1994). During the 1980s and 1990s, the NGOs proliferated in Latin America, and their role as planners and implementers of development programmes expanded dramatically. This has allowed state to assume less responsibility for the welfare. International donors have contributed to this change. However, the evidence is not clear that NGOs have been more successful in poverty alleviation than state agencies (ibid). More importantly, there is evidence that the combination of state reorganization and the emergence of NGOs as implementers of development assistance has contributed to undermining grassroots organizations representing the interests of poor people (ibid). The impression that NGOs were working for the peoples and have linkages with people's organizations and interests have lead to de-politicization of the grassroots peoples organizations.

Commenting on NGO success stories, Werlin (1991) noted that the successful sustainable development initiatives are generally assessed in a case study framework, rather than analyzed at a broader level. The lessons to be learned from case studies are limited – generalizations drawn from one are often directly contradicted by the results of another, consequently there is little real understanding of the conditions necessary for the success of the initiatives. Existing formulations of the voluntary welfare sector therefore are problematic and reflect a lack of clarity about the voluntary sector and its relationship to the state (Ostrander, 1985).

The voluntary organizations although they are non-profit

in terms of their tax status, may accumulate surpluses. In fact a study of some of the leading NGOs in India would reveal that, initially they had no assets but have acquired huge assets including land and buildings over the years. In contrast to earlier NGO ideology that was typically hostile to government, leading advocates of voluntary sector are now more amenable to a partnership with state and corporate sector. They believe that the expansion of government in social services, far from being a threat to voluntary sector has become a boon to the voluntary sector.

The recent rise of NGOs is not an accident. Over the last fifteen years and particularly since the collapse of the communist bloc, development policy and aid transfers have come to be dominated by a New Policy Agenda (Robinson, 1993; Edward and Hume, 1995). It has three underlying assumptions, economic, political and managerial, relating to effective welfare provisions, flowing from the new economic policy agenda. First, the state should enable the market but remain outside the economy to accelerate the economic growth. Secondly, the NGOs and grassroots organizations (GROs) are seen as promoting democracy and the third, it is more cost-effective for state to provide welfare services to the poor through the NGOs, as its cuts administrative costs. The impact of these assumptions on quality of services and continuity are a matter of debate. The belief that the NGOs are cost-effective may or may not be true but it is clear that the organizational capacity of NGOs is very restricted. It cannot replace the state.

The normative ambitions and competency claims of the non-governmental sector fall well short of guaranteeing their own security of tenure or their routine operations. Accountability does not flow simply from the organization to the members, but is also reciprocated by the members to the organization. All actors in any development intervention including the beneficiaries play an important part in ensuring accountability and transparency. The members of the organization and beneficiaries are more important tools of effecting accountable behaviour than formal structures. The issue is can accountability be enforced and if so how?

In India, in particular, several debates have taken place around the subject. The debate reached a crucial stage when during mid eighties the then Prime Minister took an initiative to set up a national body for monitoring the NGOs. Although there is a sort of consensus on the need for being accountable, there are wide differences among the various stakeholders for defining the accountability and the methods of ensuring it. Despite the fact that the voluntary sector in India has been in existence for a long time and the state has recognized its potential from the beginning by allocating it some space in the delivery of welfare services, it has not developed a sustainable base. Its major weakness lies in its complete reliance on government or other funding sources for its existence. The quality of NGOs extends from very poor to very effective on a continuum, which is very wide indeed. The need for a code of conduct under such circumstances is obvious. During the 1980s, India was not having good relations with the US and some apprehensions about the sources and motivations of foreign funding were very prominent. In 1986, the possibility of developing a code of conduct and a body to enforce it was vigorously debated. Some supported the move, particularly those in academia and the state, but the NGOs themselves were critical of the move, which they saw as a form of extending state control. The criticism has some validity since the state-voluntary sector relationship was already creating tensions in some places due to corrupt officials. The state has by now already lost much of its credibility, for not being efficient and transparent in its dealings. The usual comment was that the state would do well, to put its own house in order, before sitting in judgement on others. Very few actors in the development sector, are either equipped to deal with accounts or rules for keeping records. Most of them believe that following any rules is not necessary, since their intentions are noble, and following rules means delay. But this only refers to financial accountability, the most important aspect of accountability is what is the outcome of any project and who it has benefited.

Thus though the idea of accountability was accepted but no mechanism to practice it could be evolved.

Let us now look at what the accountability as such refers to in greater detail and at some experiences of projects dealing with development issues.

Sreen (1995) identifies three levels of accountability, viz., financial, project outcomes and social. Though the first two are self-explanatory, the third is not clearly spelled out, except that it expects the NGOs to contribute to policy development on social issues. Development of policy is a complicated task as we have argued earlier. A local grassroots NGO, engaged in service delivery would find it difficult to comprehend the larger social issues. However, social accountability should refer to taking a look at the social implications of the NGO activity, is it promoting conflict or making individuals, groups and communities more cohesive? Many of the NGO activities have often resulted in promoting conflict within groups or between groups and communities. A good example is, the school education leading to alienation from indigenous cultural values, or even simple education resulting in migration from villages, and religious education leading to greater tensions between communities. The question of development with respect to tribal people in India, Maori population in New Zealand and indigenous people in USA and Australia is a glaring example of social accountability not given its due importance. Sreen in her study focuses on accountability measured in terms of improvement of quality of life, which she measures in terms of higher economic rewards leading to female education, better nutrition and better clothes. Other social benefits are seen as, greater self-reliance, prestige and participation of women in decision-making. Sreen is not aware that in many communities where girl education was successfully promoted, it led to a situation where many girls were unable to find a suitable life partner as most of the men in the community were not well educated. Same was the case with more self-confident women who ended up living alone as they found it difficult to surrender to the demands of a highly patriarchal society. The loss of family in the west is a direct result of more individualized attitudes both among male and females and yet the women end up on the losing side with teenage pregnancies and single motherhood. The social accountability is a complex phenomenon and an NGO would do well to be aware of the kind of social change it is promoting and with what results. Though the successful experiences even in case of income generation are very few, the linkage between poverty and empowerment is also not a linear one. Amin (1997), in her study of poverty and *purdah* in Bangladesh, noted that while a link between poverty and *purdah* is assumed, there are two opposing schools of thought. One views poverty as a potent agent of change that decreases the practice of *purdah*: the other views *purdah* as a dominant and resilient institution that exacerbates the impact of poverty rather than being ameliorated by it. The essence of the first poverty-seclusion association in the context of Bangladesh is that when families are poor they are forced to allow greater freedom to women to work outside the home. On the other hand there are studies which indicate that as the family become prosperous women are confined to the house, as it lowers the prestige of the household, if women work outside and come in contact with other men.

However, the crucial question is do the NGOs have enough expertise and willingness to ponder over these issues before they embark on a development project. Looking at the profile of NGOs in India, Pakistan and Bangladesh it would be unrealistic to presume it to be the case. Looking at the 'development' projects run by NGOs, it is not surprising to find that projects are generally driven by an impressionistic understanding of problems and the solutions. In most cases, it is the availability of funds and the agenda of the funding agency that determines their work area and goals. The staff is inadequate and poorly trained. As a study (Khan, 2000) pointed out there is a wide gap between the understanding level of the key functionaries and the way they define their objectives and that of the lower level functionaries. Alphonse (1990) in her study found that the programmes of the organizations were not in tune with the objectives laid down. For example, the empowerment was the objective but the programmes concentrated on service delivery. As Rao (1998) noted that the state during the past five decades concentrated on relief measures and did not attempt any structural change. The capacity of NGO and voluntary sector to address macro issues in the development agenda appear to be highly restricted.

The sociological discourse in order to create a just and humane society locates the central problem in the arena of the source of moral values and action in society. The central concern here is developing norms and social institutions to create social order. Unlike the political discourse where the state is the central concern to create order, the sociologists are concerned with creating a moral society. As Robson (1976) queried is it possible to have a welfare state without a society which believes in welfare. The question can be posed somewhat differently by looking at the capacity of the state to induce change in a society. A sociologist may argue that we need to look at the process of socialization to explain moral rather than the actions of the state. It is social institutions and consequent social action, which concern sociologists in the context of morality. Morality in this sense has been a central theme in the sociological discourse, till recent years. However, the recent trend in sociological discourse is to reject the notion of morality (Giddens, 1991). Giddens believes that modernity is based on control and reflexivity and pushes moral questions into the back regions of life, as modernity has 'dispensed' with tradition and 'ultimate truths' (Giddens, 1991:202; 1994b: 79-87). To understand the question of morality it is necessary to take note of the central tension in modernity. This is the tension between the normative and the real, between what should be done and what is actually done (Flyvbjerg, 1998:200). First, it is difficult to develop a universal rational foundation for the functioning of any institutions. Even Hegel and Marx have been unable to develop, the much sought after rational and universal foundation for social institutions. Most contemporary philosophers and social scientists have accepted the consequences of more than two millennia of failed attempts to establish a universal constitution of philosophy, social science and social organizations (ibid:212). Second, rationality demolishes the institutions by giving freedom to individuals to act as per their own norms and aspirations. It thus negates the process of consensus building among the groups to make it possible to evolve any norms and to enforce these norms. Giving individuals the power and freedom to act based on individual norms dilutes the possibility of a shared system of values governing human behaviour. Machiavelli (1984: 96) commenting on good governance, states: "one can make this generalization about men: they are ungrateful, fickle, liars and deceivers'. People know how to be tribal and democratic at the same time, to use democracy for personal or group ends (Flyvbjerg, 1998a). The actors can reverse their own roles in a democracy as Young argued earlier. The dilution of the tradition thus creates a lot of open space for the actors to formulate their own ideas about social and moral issues, including justification for the use of power.

Synnott (1992:80) noted that body signifying material pleasures have no intrinsic meaning. Populations create their own meaning and thus their own bodies. Ideas about what the body is, what it means, its moral value and the values of its constituent parts, the limits of the body, its social utility and symbolic value, in sum, how the body is defined both physically and socially, vary widely from culture to culture and have changed dramatically overtime. The central point is the part that culture plays in defining a reality. All cultures evolve a framework to evaluate and categories, the material and the sensual. All cultures try to balance the individual and his human nature for material needs with the social responsibility in particular towards the family and the community at large. How important the material is has always created a dilemma for the philosophers. Body and soul are in Plato's dualism, not only separate but opposed and equally ranked. He insists that the body is a 'hindrance' to the soul, an 'impediment' and an 'imperfection', distracting and preventing us from getting a glimpse of the truth. It enslaves us and shackles us (Plato, 1963:66, 47,50). The conflict between body and soul is therefore built in, permanent and total. Nonetheless, he explained that a beautiful body is the first step on the way to absolute beauty and God. Thus for Plato and Socrates the body may lead to or away from God. Aristotle (384-322BC) shows the same dualism in his remarks that we must take care of the body 'for the sake of the soul', and that intellect more than anything else is man. This duality can also be interpreted as economic versus the social. We may ask is it economic deprivation that leads to social disintegration or the abundance of wealth? The economically developed nations gave primacy to body and individual freedom and witnessed the collapse of social institutions such as marriage, family and religion. In their case the body took them away from god. Whereas in developing countries the god is still firmly in place and so is the case with institutions of marriage and family. Women in India, Pakistan and Bangladesh are in particular socialized to negate the material to fulfil their 'moral' obligation by remaining focused on serving the male and the family. This is simply done by declaring the body of a woman as sacred, to be controlled and protected. A polluted woman consequently has no place in society. The morality is in place for women as the statistics on drug use, alcoholism, crime and broken marriages indicate. This morality is being questioned now as part of modernization, the issue is, who controls a woman's body? Tradition created norms and institutional arrangements and succeeded in making it part of the human psyche, which resulted in spontaneous compliance. The secular creates rules, but is not capable of making it part of the human psyche and thus faces problems in compliance. The body creates the greatest hurdle for the secular law.

Through centuries, thinkers have addressed the difference between two forms of human behaviour, one governed to a great extent by verbally formulated rules, maxims or hypotheses, the other shaped to a greater degree by non-verbal events that affect the organism, often resulting in knowledge that is hard to report verbally. Conscious and unconscious knowledge has been given many names, such as 'linguistic formulations of knowledge' versus 'intuition' (Smolensky, 1988), 'declarative' versus 'procedural' knowledge (Lewicki, Hill and Bizot, 1988) or 'explicit' versus 'implicit' knowledge (Berry and Broadbent, 1988). On the other hand, there is still no agreement as to whether unconscious learning and knowledge exist at all (Overskeid, 1994b) and if it does, how it should be referred to (ibid, 1995). This obviously denotes the difficulty of theorizing about human behaviour and denotes the difficulty of constructing 'social' or moral by controlling human minds and emotions through a secular format.

As Fields (1995:IV) notes 'moral' is often synonymous with 'social' in Durkheim's work, in which 'individual' stands opposed to 'moral' because of his/her egoist passion and sensuality. This uncertainty is logical since the outcome is unpredictable. The savage lives by rules one imposes on oneself and there is no 'other', and the construction of morality is neither needed nor attempted. Rousseau was stating the obvious when he realized that the passion comes with the society, where 'other' is created and defined. Man becomes wicked in the society of fellow men. The sociability is a facade, the outer mask, to project a public image. A naked person is closest to the state of nature, but the quest for civility makes one social and superficial. But yet one hopes, at the same time that by becoming a social being in the fullest sense, man can realize man's true nature. This hope is based in the ultimate ideal of achieving a state of nothingness through a conscious process of learning. Both are ideal states, mere dreams which some can achieve but none can become a social norm. Both defining 'moral' and creating it poses many problems for social science theory.

Conclusion

The initial formulations of welfare society/civil society, denoted industrial societies with highly developed universal state social services. More recent conceptualizations stand in direct contrast to this formulation. The term now denotes a high degree of individual responsibility and rejects extensive collective responsibility, particularly as exemplified by state provided benefits and services. The new concept emphasizes the responsibility of family and community in the west. The state provision is rejected on the plea that it fosters dependency, weakens the social structure and encourages bureaucratic inefficiency (Herman, 1991). The alternative proposed was a pluralist approach through voluntary, commercial, and informal sectors and state only providing the services, which these sectors fail to provide (Davey, 1987). Interestingly, this shift took place in early 1980s in New Zealand, a developed economy as compared with India, Pakistan and Bangladesh, with a population of only 3.5 million. The pre-colonial indigenous society in New Zealand consisting of Maori population believed in decentralized tribal autonomy and the organic solidarity of kinship. Prior to the coming of the white settlers Maori society had a complex caring system based on tribal networks (Herman, 1991). These networks were destroyed as the development project pursued by the white, state sponsored services and market took over. The Maori protests in 1980s asserting that they have been adversely affected by the development in New Zealand were used as an argument to cut short the state responsibility. However, few people are able to appreciate the Maori logic. The Maori culture is similar to cultures of the Indian sub continent, and is non-materialistic in orientation. It still believes in the collective well-being and simple level of need fulfilment. The cultural traditions are oral and informal. One of the basic losses of Maori culture is the youth. It has been trapped between two opposite cultures. The Pakiha tradition pushes them towards an individualist, achievement oriented, highly competitive society. The Maori culture is an anti thesis of this formulation. The result is a confusion of identity. They end up in prisons, in de-addiction centres, welfare homes and reform centres. The Pakiha welfare system analyses it with reference to lack of education and economic skills. The basic failure, however, was that the 'development' agenda of the Pakiha variety relying on social services, was totally ignorant of the cultural traditions and needs of the Maori people. From a purely sociological perspective too, it took over their economic assets and political power to construct their future and in turn provided remedial services in dealing with poverty and it never could do anything to check inequality of income or wealth (Oliver, 1989:4; Herman, 1991: 8). To be fair to the ruling elite, economic theory have so far not discovered any model of redistribution, which has worked to reduce inequality. In addition in 1980s the New Zealand economy faced the usual problem of stagnation, high inflation, growing unemployment, a drop in export demand and a rising balance of payment crisis (Collins, 1989:188). A new economic policy was the inevitable outcome and consequently a cut back in the role of the state. The welfare state was seen as undue interference in the exchange between family and economy (Halsey, 1981:21). The rising expectations of people in the mean time made more demands on the welfare state. The failure of the state thus led to a criticism from both left and the right, though for different reasons. The concept of a plural welfare mechanism with emphasis on voluntary sector, particularly looking beyond the conflict with commercial sector, was advocated (Hadley and Hatch, 1981: 101). Hadley and Hatch were trying to make the democracy more participatory by giving the beneficiary the right to decide and get it through self service, with little help from the state or any collective societal effort. The last two points self-service and collective responsibility are then reinterpreted as 'community' responsibility than 'social' responsibility. The 'community' here is seen as the old network of close ties in small populations in a local rural area in the early eighteenth century. A revitalization of community spirit and consequent care, the development project replaced with 'formal institutionalized care', was again sought as the caring was found wanting. But, the possibility of community care in a society which emphasizes individualism and competition, duality and conflict and where the social movements have never gone beyond particular campaigns or single issues was rather remote. The community participation in any programme of wider concern, largely has not evoked a very positive response and more so in deprived areas. The direct beneficiaries participate while the community remains passive.

The important point is that the story is so familiar, while it is unfolding in a very small society with no population pressures, and with much better education and health systems in place, than are to be expected in India, Pakistan and Bangladesh even in the next five decades. The cycle of development project, going from notion to notion, to justify continuance and legitimacy of different political elite, driven by the economic greed and individual power, in different periods of history, seems to convey a definite pattern. It continues to raise hope and come up with an explanation for failure, rather than accepting the simple truth that there is a limit to what man can achieve and construct.

8

Conclusion

Documenting social change during the last fifty years or so in the life of the three nations poses many issues. The analysis would include changes in the economic, social and political arena in these countries, and its implications for the common person. For example has the poor nations been able to increase their wealth, and if so has it helped the common person to have more space to participate in decisions that significantly affect them. More importantly, can the common person live in peace without fear of physical or cultural violence? In other words, has the society in these nations become more cohesive and conflict free? It may also be relevant to study the sociological significance of these changes. In particular, the impact of economic well-being on the social attitudes, values and consequent change in social relationships at different levels.

The specific objective of increasing the GNP has been achieved to some extent, as there has been economic progress in all these nations as we discussed earlier. The changes in economic well-being within a society, as a poor country undertakes the process of increasing its wealth are bound to generate social tensions as Apter rightly anticipated (Apter, 1963). The modern state system during the colonial rule functioned as a booster and promoter of private enterprise (Waseem, 1994), and it failed in managing mass scale poverty during the period after independence. The state focused itself more on enforcement of laws related to preservation of private property rather than social and moral issues. Consequently, in all the three countries, the process of generating economic prosperity has inevitably created tension at all levels of society. Tensions are increasing in families, workplace, in the community and between communities. As we have noted incase of India, Pakistan and Bangladesh that the elite has largely appropriated the benefit of economic development and the benefits have not been filtering down to all segments. This incidentally has been happening in almost all countries where economic development process was initiated. Conflict among various groups within these countries has increased, as different groups struggle to garner scarce resources. The caste and class disparities, rural urban divide, the regional disparities and gender disparities have all made people in general to become restless and suspicious of each other. It is not that the economic disparities did not exist earlier, they did, but what has changed is the perception of people, who they are and their economic share in society. The earlier explanations of poverty and deprivation rooted in the '*karma*' theory are no longer acceptable. The presence of material goods and services has increased and it has affected the sense of deprivation and changed the perception of need of all segments of society. As has rightly been pointed out by studies it has generated a sea of expectations. In the absence of opportunities for a large number of people to participate in the process of economic development the ensuing tensions are inevitable.

Economic Development

The data from India, Pakistan and Bangladesh regarding economic development indicates that GDP per capita has nearly doubled in the last twenty years or so. In India, for example, it rose to US$ 465 in 1997 from 250 in 1975, in Pakistan 417 from 222 and in Bangladesh 218 from 134. As is generally the case, the middle class has expanded and has got more benefits as compared to the poor class in all countries. The mid 20 per cent income group has had a share of between 16-17 per cent, the 2nd 20 per cent from the top around 21-22 per cent and top 20 per cent 39-40 per cent share of the national income, in all the three countries.

The 20 per cent poor at the bottom got only around 9 per cent of the national income. Further, the poor in rural areas benefited much less in comparison to poor in urban areas. A good indicator of that is the increase in real wages. While the wages have shown some increase in urban areas, the wages in rural areas have not registered any significant increase. The availability of work has also been vastly different in rural and urban areas. These differences can also be noticed across regions and across gender categories. The contribution of agriculture in the GDP has been continuously declining, in India it declined from 41.3 in 1981 to 29.7 in 1996, in Pakistan it declined from 53.2 per cent in 1950 to 24.2 in 1996. In Bangladesh the share of agriculture declined from 51 in 1974 to 30 per cent in 1996. In all countries, the majority of population still continues to be dependent on agriculture for its livelihood. Just to give an example of decline in agriculture a report about agriculture sector in Kerala noted that in the agriculture production sector, the mild recovery in 1980s was limited to cash crops like rubber, while the major food crops like rice has been declining steadily since the mid-1970s. The steady decline in the price of rubber and coconut during the second half of the 1990s has taken the agricultural sector back to a state of stagnation (Mohanakumara, 2002). The nature and degree of decline and stagnation may differ from state to state, but the general nature of decline or stagnation is quite uniform throughout the country, particularly in case of small and marginal farmers. The economic assets of the poor has not shown any increase, the availability of land, economic skills or work opportunities, have been declining over the years. In some areas the decline in real wages of rural workers was ten per cent or more. In India nearly 75 per cent population gets a share of 56 per cent of the national income, compared to 44 per cent consumed by the 25 per cent urban population (Pradhan et al, 1998).

Desai (2001), using data from National Sample Survey 38th, 43rd and 50th rounds, examines the changes in the size and composition of the households in India. While doing so, some of the observations are important to take note of: (1) income data is difficult to collect; (2) most researchers ask just one question, what is or was your household income in any reference period; and (3) finding such data for several points in time is all the more difficult. Similar problems can be faced with consumption data. (*Note*: Near-poor households are defined as those whose income is less than twice that of poverty line; lower-middle are those households whose income is more than twice the poverty line but less than four times that of poverty line; and upper-middle households have an income of four times or more that of poverty line.)

Desai (ibid) noted that from 1983 to 1993 the number of people below poverty line has declined substantially from nearly 49 per cent to 31.6 per cent, whereas there is a significant increase in the percentage of near poor people which rose from 37.5 to 48.6 there is some increase in the lower-middle category of about 5 per cent but the increase in upper middle is slightly less than one per cent. He further sums up that even the consumption levels of the upper middle at 1993-94 prices were around Rs. 1,000 per person which is not very remarkable. The analysis based on the national level data sums up the economic progress story of India. We have indicated earlier that the income distribution patterns being so remarkably alike in the three countries, it is logical to assume that it can be taken to apply to Pakistan and Bangladesh as well. Desai also noted in her study that the share of households listing their primary source as agriculture or production workers or artisans in the upper middle class was declining.

The following conclusions can be drawn from this scenario:

(1) Despite economic growth, the share of the poor has either remained stagnant or improved so marginally that its overall impact is insignificant.

(2) The disparities between poor and rich have increased over the years.

(3) The absolute number of the poor has been increasing despite some decline in the percentage of poor below poverty line, and it runs into millions.

(4) Economic growth rate going up significantly is not a distinct possibility, there are indicators that it may decline or continue to show an uneven record over the years.

It all leads to only one logical conclusion: there is very little possibility of any significant change taking place in the lives of millions of people either below poverty line or just hovering around it in the three countries under review.

Social Development

As indicated earlier, there is no universally accepted definition of social development. The need for the term arose to change the focus from economic aspect of development in the planned efforts to people's participation in it or the percolation of the benefits among the wider society. The political compulsions also forced the state to do something to facilitate the participation of middle class in the economic development in the emerging nations. Social development as a new approach to development was expected to provide better social services, including education, health and employment. The strategies to change social relations, attitudes and practices in accordance with the requirements of an industrial society, as Apter (1963) indicated, can broadly be classified as the socialist approach and the democratic approach. These reflect the state attempts to alter existing social roles, attitudes and values and general life styles of people. A good example is the approaches used by Soviet Union and other European nations. Soviet Union introduced the changes swiftly by drastically altering the pre existing social framework, whereas in other European nations the process took a long time and changes were more piecemeal. Commenting on the approaches adopted by the developing nation states he noted that while some states have adopted a more autocratic approach, others paid more attention to democracy, pluralism and individualism. He predicted in the context of newly emerging states including Pakistan and India (Bangladesh had not come into being by then), that no matter which model they adopt none would be able to become like the western European nations. He emphasized that industrialization and modernization are different phenomenon and it is difficult to achieve both. He noted that new nations are short of capital and skills and hence industrialization process cannot be used by these nations to resolve role changes or increase material welfare for the entire society.

The current state of affairs in India, Pakistan and Bangladesh support what Apter argued. The economic, social and political environment on the one hand, and the cultural and psychological traits in India Pakistan and Bangladesh on the other, are vastly different from the European nations. One of the most important differences lies in the fact that in most European countries the population growth is either stagnant or negative, while in all developing countries the population continues to grow at a rapid pace. In the three countries under review socio-economic differences have increased on account of development. The urban-rural divide is very pronounced. People in rural areas manage their lives with bare minimum resources in very natural surroundings, where modern technology, markets, schools and hospitals, etc., are not playing a significant role in their lives. Yet not very far from this scenario, people are living in an industrialized urban society, having better access to health, education and employment opportunities. This is not to say that there are no differences within the urban population as far as access to health and education is concerned. Social development, as an attempt to convert the former into a later variety of human existences, is still a distant dream. The fact that nearly 65 per cent or more people, in India, Pakistan and Bangladesh, are in the former category, clearly indicates that it is a huge task and even this limited goal of social development has not been achieved so far. As we indicated earlier that the possibility of common people in general and the rural poor in particular to have the same facilities of education, health and employment, as is the case with a small urban population is rather dismal even in the next millennium. The other issue still debated is, although the debate is losing ground, is it desirable? Certain features of the rural society; more stable relationships, a lower crime rate, a generally peaceful and nature friendly environment, and the non-material lifestyles of these people are considered highly desirable. In other words many would want to retain these. Not surprisingly, school education and other economic and more precisely the material changes are seen as threatening these features. It is here that the term 'social development' defined in terms of access to greater opportunities poses problems. Gore (1965) while conceptualizing social development in India, has 'some thing more than economic, social and political development' in mind. The framework of defining social development in India, Pakistan and Bangladesh is rooted in preserving the collective and relegating the individual to a subservient position, which the current economic, educational and democratic development contradicts. This confusion makes the term 'social development' as problematic as the term 'modernization'. However, the key to understand the 'social' is, the manner in which relationships are structured in a society between members and between members and the state. The cohesiveness of a society depends on a harmony between, individual, group and societal interests and the possibility of members being able to reconcile their individual choices in the context of the family, community and society. The norms governing the roles and status of different members are clearly defined and structured. Deviations up to a point are expected and accommodated. The social functioning of the society rests on these arrangements. The traditional societies valued faith, obedience and hierarchy. The positions and roles were ascribed, strongly legitimated by religion. The need for dialogue was neither felt nor evoked since it was generally understood that man cannot be expected to know everything. The general belief is that sovereignty belonged to god not the man. The education and political development question everything but as Giddens (1991) noted the rational cannot provide all the answers. Developing alternative source of legitimization of social status, roles and hierarchy is posing a severe problem on the one hand and finding justification for moral on the other. As a consequence, the society is in turmoil both in developed as well as developing nations. Social development in societies, where deviance is on the rise poses serious problems of definition. The economically developed societies are credited with the decline of institutions such as family, marriage and religion, which have affected the social relationships in significant ways. The social values in developing countries are still significantly different from those in the western world and therefore they are reluctant to accept individual freedom in particular, though they are being pushed in that direction by the economic development.

Let us recapture the point made earlier by reverting to the efforts made in India to promote social development. The idea of modernizing the 'traditional' society in India, Pakistan and Bangladesh, poses some simple questions. The terms 'modernization' and 'tradition' are not precise enough to be used to denote societies as modern or traditional as we argued earlier. In other words, the culture of the rural people or any group need not be portrayed as unacceptable, to be changed to conform to the norms of an industrial society. Secondly, the economic, educational and political developments have not kept pace with each other and as a result do not result in overall social development as anticipated. As we have noted that economic development has pushed a section of the population from below the poverty line to just above the poverty line but they are still poor. At the same time, educational development have pushed a section of earlier literate to become secondary school graders. Yet it has not enlarged their economic share in any significant manner. It may in fact have alienated them from their traditional work. The political development has changed their perception of rights including economic rights. The result is a loss of contentment and a sense of growing deprivation. These changes thus are not complementing each other but are rather creating more tensions and frustrations. The promise of a socially just society is part of the constitution in many new states, but continuing lack of means to attain the ideal is pushing these societies towards invoking religion, caste and other primordial loyalties to seek power, in absence of any secular logic for explaining continuing failure. The capacity of the state to affect any far-reaching changes in the social structure at any level, as also to defuse the conflicts, in the countries under review, has been getting weaker and weaker in the years under review.

Political Development

Political development in the context of development referred to the emergence of a democratic state in place of the feudal structures of power. The first stage of putting in place a democratic form of governance obviously is the framing of a constitution and developing and maintaining institutional arrangements, which sustain the democratic process. As the history of political development of these countries reveals, that only India succeeded in putting in place the necessary institutional arrangement which could at least sustain the democratic system of holding periodic elections at different levels, and continue to be governed by democratically elected governments. Pakistan and Bangladesh could not even achieve this despite being much smaller in size. This is not to say that there are no political institutions in Pakistan and Bangladesh. The judiciary and the press exist in both these countries and both are governed by a constitution. The professionalism of its members on the one hand and the general political texture of the country on the other, however, determine the independence and strength of these institutions. The conditions in Pakistan and Bangladesh in this respect are far inadequate as compared to India. Though the political texture is fast declining in India as the political ideology and ethics are losing ground, and criminalization of politics is gaining ground. Centre-state relations have created some tensions in India as well but Pakistan's political development could never take off because of its inability to resolve the same as Samad (1995) noted. The development of an independent judicial system and freedom of press have contributed a lot in India's political development, whereas in Pakistan the judiciary and press have not been able to play the same role in promoting and preserving democratic practices. The process of political development in India seems to be going through a decline. The declining percentage of voters in recent elections is a clear indication of the common person losing faith in the political system. In the past several elections at the Centre, no single party is able to get the necessary political mandate to form a government. This is reflective of the decline of the national parties such as Indian National Congress, which ruled for more than three decades, and inability of any other political party to emerge as an effective alternative to it. The growth of regional parties and religious orientation of some political parties has further compounded the political development agenda, which is threatening to subvert the constitution, which has so far survived with some modifications, the change of governments.

In Pakistan and Bangladesh, the religion has played a major role in political development. By playing a decisive role in determining the nature of political elite, the power of political parties and the role of the state, religion has posed far greater problems in promoting a democratic state. One of the characteristics of the modern democratic state is its secular character. Pakistan has already declared itself an Islamic state and Bangladesh is not very far from doing so. The religious orientation to politics negates the principle of equality, as all religions have pronounce gender biases, and discriminate between the faithful and the non-believer. The religious nature of state create tensions in inter-state relations as the states following other religions or no religion, are constructed as 'other' and generally projected as enemy of the society and the state. Many conditions imposed by donor nations in particular are unacceptable to these nations, creating a dilemma for the state, which needs resources. If it complies with the public religious sentiments the economic progress lags behind creating tensions at home. If it ignores the religious sentiments it creates problems of governance and may result in the ruling political elite losing their power. India, Pakistan and Bangladesh, all are facing the dilemma but more so in Pakistan because of it being officially declared as an Islamic state. In case of Islam, the law becomes given, as the sovereignty lies with the god and not the man. The role of the state has by necessity to conform to the major tenets of Islam. The guidelines on the issues relating to gender and in dealing with non-believers have to be complied with. As such treating everyone as equal before the law poses problems. The maximum brunt of religious orientation to politics is borne by the women, as their social position and roles get defined, leaving little scope for change.

The recent political development in India where some political parties are trying to promote Hindu religious ethos aggressively and yet being forced to follow a secular constitution after coming to power is creating additional tensions, besides the misuse of power in general. The use of religious symbols is likely to continue in India in absence of other political goals, particularly in states, where regional parties based on language or other regional identities have not emerged. Creation of a Hindu state in India does not appear feasible because of the size of minority population on the one hand and non-acceptance of Hindu ethos in general in secular domain by a sizeable elite among the Hindus.

As the political development was expected to contribute to social development, the modern state was expected to create a just social order by radically altering the social relations as we noted earlier. To make it possible for the common person to not only participate, in the process of transformation of the society but also design the economic system, keeping their own stake in mind, yet ensuring a fair deal to all. This duality of inclusion and exclusion also created tension for the modern state in India, Pakistan and Bangladesh. Although modern state no where was able to provide the space to common person to share power in the real sense of the term, but the political compulsions made the ruling elite to give some space to common person. The political development thus was expected to enlarge the base of political participation by allowing different segments of population to get some space to articulate their ideas about governance of the society. It also meant that the right to organize and express concerns would not only be available, it would also lead to development of a culture of dialogue, discussions and resolution of issues through such a process. The possibility of a dialogue begins with respective self-images of different social groups and how they construct 'the other'. If the 'other' is constructed as significantly different, the possibility of a dialogue is restricted. The trend of different social groups being able to negotiate and share power is becoming weak as the differences and suspicion of each other is growing particularly among elite. As Apter (1963) noted what took Europe a long and slow process of development spread over centuries cannot be reproduced in these nations in a matter of decades. The process of political development has been more complicated in Pakistan and Bangladesh as compared to India because of historical reasons. The bureaucracy and military in Pakistan and Bangladesh played a crucial role in shaping the political system rather than the political elite, as was the case in India. As La Porte, Jr. (1993) noted the bureaucracy in Pakistan believed that if you allow the politicians to debate the issues, they ended up agitating the masses and creating problems of governance in the process. General Ayub Khan agreed with this formulation and produced his own constitution in 1962, providing little power to the civilian politicians whom he appointed as ministers. The elite bureaucracy and the general himself as president exercised control in the system. The election of democratic representatives was indirect (ibid). In India, it was the political elite which shaped the constitution and subsequently protected it as well, despite some critical moments. However, the political development lead to the emergence of different stake holders enjoying some space in India, whereas less so in Pakistan and Bangladesh, where the old elite remain entrenched by maintaining their hegemony over the political power. The state is still controlled by the elite but the changing nature of ruling coalition changes the beneficiary status of the small section, which has the capability to manipulate the state. In conclusion the conditions for real democratic behaviour do not exist in the countries under review, despite the political freedom of five decades or more. The polity in India, Pakistan and Bangladesh conceived theoretically to serve the 'civil society', has in fact emerged to dominate civil society (Nandi, 2000).

It is ironical that state was considered and still is considered, as the key actor in promoting 'economic well-being' of the common person. The capacity of state institutions to control or service vast population, particularly those in the rural areas, has generally been overestimated. Even in smaller countries compared to India, Bangladesh and Pakistan, the links between the elite and the common person in the villages, are non-functional if not non-existent. Further, there are divisions among people based on caste, religion or culture, which are beyond the power of the state to manipulate at will. The relations between state and common person, at times wrongly termed as civil society, are problematic at best and the term 'welfare state' is a complete misnomer in the context of India, Pakistan and Bangladesh. The failure of the state in achieving the desired economic standards and provision of social services is now being reassessed, and consequently questions are being posed about the future of the role of state throughout the developing world. The recent emphasis on economic reforms is a major shift in recent years in redefining the role of the state.

The Role of the State and the Planned Change

Let us return to the recent discourse, the role state should play in the economic development. In India, Pakistan and Bangladesh, right from the beginning, it was assumed that the state would play a major role in social development. The capacity of the state to play a major role in economic development has become suspect in recent years. Yet, it is assumed that the state can succeed in widening the scope of beneficiaries in economic development, by improving its efficiency and functioning in collaboration with NGOs. It is still expected that state can control corrupt practices and become more transparent in its functioning at all levels. These assumptions are not based on a sound understanding of power positions and consequent human responses as shown earlier. State planning of whatever kind is an exercise in futility. Whatever little success it has achieved is in increasing the size of the economy and infrastructure development, however it has achieved little in influencing social values and consequent human responses to changes. The assumption that the state or any other organization would be able to generate and sustain any particular social response was short lived as the experiment in the socialist countries indicated. The institutionalization of social values, as Berger indicated, is a long-drawn process. Social theory lags far behind to explain social action fully, the possibility of any predictable courses those societies may follow to generate particular social values and direct social action universally is rather remote.

The centralized planning is a strategy that India in particular and Pakistan and Bangladesh to some extent adopted as a means to achieve social justice. But, as we indicated earlier, so far no model has been found to alleviate mass poverty, provide educational and health services and other social changes successfully, within a given time frame. As an alternative compromise the politically convenient version of strategies to eliminate poverty and other social goals conceived by ruling elite is given to the planner. The planning for change, therefore, commences on a false note. Planning is supposed to be an exercise in instrumental rationality. That is the existing reality is objectively analyzed and accordingly decisions taken to achieve targets in the context of resources available. The feasibility of each decision is to be assessed before hand, if the planning is to be successful. The history of Indian planning is full of anecdotes where decisions taken were not based on facts. For example, a simple issue in planning is to anticipate your resource base and the size of the problem to be tackled. The planners have seldom any clarity about both. This is true in case of even physical targets of setting up education and health facilities. The more complex issue of the social change that education is expected to accomplish is a different matter. The state planning, therefore, as the analysis of different sectors shows, in the countries under review, seldom succeeds in achieving the objectives. More importantly, as Patnaik (2000) noted, the class interests underlying state actions, produces changes in class configuration which in turn gives rise to policy shifts, which obviously are not necessarily concerned with objective facts or interests of common person per se. Besides the implementation failure is a foregone conclusion as, (i) facts on which the plan is based are collected and interpreted by inefficient persons, (ii) the time taken to collect the facts is so long that the facts become obsolete, and (iii) finally, the implementing agencies are incapable of implementation on account of the strategic action of private actors (Chakravarty, 1987). Chatterjee (2000) further elaborating the implementation failure raises the issue of the modalities of knowledge and implementation. All three conditions mentioned by Chakravarty as responsible for faulty implementation denote the manner in which the planner, representing the rational consciousness of the state, can produce knowledge of the objects of planning. A plan, which does not correctly estimate the capacities of the implementing agencies, is bound to fail. The issue is therefore not merely the facts but how they are formulated, interpreted and legitimized. Chatterjee feels that these agencies act in determinate ways according to specific kinds of signals. He further noted that the rationality of planning practices a self-deception for its own survival. The state as a planning authority can promote the universal goal of economic development by harnessing within a single interconnected whole, the discrete subjects of power in society. As Chatterjee pointed out this simply cannot be achieved, since the best efforts to secure 'adequate information' leave behind an unestimated residue capable of upsetting the implementation of the plan. But, to me, the problem is not the residue but the ambiguity of construction. Very often facts are referred to without stating the meaning in specific terms. The construction of terms such as modernization, development, empowerment and the meaning attached to each are left to the individual actor. This vagueness helps both, the planner and the critique to justify their own version without even contradicting each other. Since most of the time they are conceiving different realities and are incapable of communicating their meanings to each other. The macro restructuring of social realities remain theoretically unresolved to date, despite the development of social sciences.

State and Economic Reform

The most recent attempt towards social structuring as noted earlier is the attempt at structural adjustment to promote more economic growth. The main idea is to downsize the role of state in economic matters. This shift in thinking is a recent phenomenon in India, whereas the policy was in place in Pakistan and Bangladesh since the very inception of these countries. The shift and its impact in India are interpreted in different ways. First, as Bardhan (2000) noted, there is the rosy view that crucial reforms have taken place and more could follow if there is political will and stability. The pessimistic view is that only the peripheral issues have been tackled and that central issues have been stalled and cannot be done as the political situation is not favourable. A good example of this is the crucial area of labour law reform. The intermediate position is that a slow process of reform is in place and would continue. The important point, however, is that in Pakistan and Bangladesh, where state has never played a key role in the economic affairs of these nations, the growth rate of economy or its impact on poverty has not been very different. The debate about growth rates and poverty elimination which the reforms have accomplished and its long-term implications both social and political, remains inconclusive, as different versions by different economists and researchers, from different disciplines, quoting different data, continue. Discussions and studies trying to highlight the change in the social character of Indian State and the possibility of changes in social policy continue (Nandi, 2000; Chatterjee, 2000; Kohli,

2000). Nandi pointed out that state is dominating rather than serving the people, and Kohli noted the centralizing tendency of the state and the resultant powerlessness of people. More importantly, Kohli (2000) highlights the tension between growth-oriented policy measures and redistributive goals, which are difficult to resolve. The dilemma of investment and consumption has been an old phenomenon, which Apter (1963) has highlighted by noting the problem of inadequate capital in the new states. So more or less the same facts, which were known or anticipated, are being re-discovered after almost half a century of attempts at economic and social development.

Modernization of Tradition

The contemporary societies in India, Bangladesh and Pakistan are still predominantly traditional if we use framework for modernization developed by Smelser (1964), in the sense that the demographic, economic, educational, religious and political structure is much like that which existed centuries ago. Yet, he would consider them on the way towards modernization, though they differ considerably in the point and time of departure, the stage they have reached, the pace, orderliness and the path their development follows, as well as in the end result for which they strive. Smelser draws on a differentiation model to provide an analytical framework for the study of modernization. He studied the process by which the major social functions gain structural independence. According to him, the crucial link between differentiation and modernization lies in the fact that for every social function there is a distinct set of structural conditions under which it is optimally served. He tries to demonstrate modification of social structure by looking at economy, family, religion and stratification. For purposes of analyzing the relationship between economic growth and the social structure, he cites example of technological change from simple and traditional techniques towards the application of scientific knowledge, in matters of agriculture from subsistence to commercial production, in industry from human power to use of machines, etc., in ecological arrangements the change from village to urban centres. While he focused attention on changes in economy and family or other social units, Inkeles (1964) concentrated his studies on man. He argued that if people had an attitude of openness to new experience, independence from parental authority and took an active part in civic affairs they could be termed as modern. It is obvious that modernization is a term, which is being used to indicate a preference of some kind of social, economic and political behaviour by some over other types of behaviour. The western bias has generally been acknowledged and the term though still in use, is not universally accepted as relevant in either describing a society or an individual, as we argued earlier. However, the two issues central in evaluating social development of a society, the concern with gender equality and a secular worldview in the developing world, are generally accepted as important in making societies more tolerant if not entirely conflict free. Both have in recent years evoked a great deal of intellectual debate, in the context of development of a society.

However, since our efforts at development in the early fifties westernization was seen as a precondition to the emergence of a modern state in the sub-continent and for bringing about radical and lasting changes in Indian society (Srinivas, 1966; Mukherji, 1958; Majumdar, 1955). They further believed that westernization promoted secularism. Yet many others carried and still do an ambivalent attitude towards modernization. As Madan (1994) pointed out many Indian intellectuals over the years have suffered from what he called 'split consciousness'. Nehru held the British rule responsible for most of India's current miseries and yet conceived a modern India based on western socio-political thought and institutions. To be fair to those who favoured modernization, they generally were wanting to modernize the physical or economic aspect of the society. They also preferred a democratic polity over a feudal state yet they were very ambivalent about any change in some of the social arrangements. This dualism of wanting to modernize the material, while clinging to the traditional moral is nowhere more pronounced and evident than in the discourse on women's issues in India and in the whole of the Indian sub-continent. While some space has been conceded to women, particularly in economically well off households, to receive education and to work full time, the overall position of women in the social structure and their social evaluation has not changed. The birth of a girl child still causes gloom and efforts to prevent the birth of a girl child are increasing with the increase in material prosperity, as the 2001 Census data on sex ratio from the developed states in India indicate. As a woman activist puts it, in the village a woman's life is in many ways valued at less than an animal's. The logic is simple, it takes money to replace an animal, whereas to replace a woman is not only easy but also under certain circumstances even remunerative (Kishwar and Vanita, 1991).

The way feminist in the sub-continent construct women's issues, indicate their concern with material issues relating to women; the heavy work burden, several unwanted pregnancies at short intervals, still births, miscarriages, infant deaths, lack of sufficient food and poor health. The consequent policies and programmes, therefore, are designed to address these issues. The more important issue of social construction of woman and the space allocated to her to construct herself has still not been given adequate space in the discourse on empowerment of women. The reasons are obvious – the freedom for women to construct herself, is seen as threatening the family, community and society. In effect it is threatening the male, though it is never acknowledged and she is portrayed as the weaker sex, who needs protection. The family in India occupies a very central place in the life of an Indian woman, and she devotes all her life and energy into working for its well-being. The more recent interpretations of empowerment of women prescribing individual freedom find the family as a trap to restrict the freedom of women. On the other hand, examples from the western society of teenage pregnancies, broken families and single parent households leading to juvenile delinquency are cited to justify the control over women. But, the assumption that the social health of the family and society is so dependent on women has not lead to a higher social status for her. This creates a dilemma for feminists, as the individual space versus collective good of the family, remain unresolved. So, as a compromise, the debate now seems to posit responsibility for men to preserve the family and social health of the community and to glorify women as mothers. In practice, however, the continued relegation of woman as a cheap and expendable commodity continues, irrespective of caste, class and religion in these countries. An educated and economically active woman has to pay dowry, accept a subordinate position in the family hierarchy or be declared an out caste. If she chose to command her right over her own body, her own family would sign her death warrant. Education and economic participation of woman increases this risk. The traditional seclusion of women from technology and economic skills therefore was and still is a well-planned strategy of controlling woman. It is interesting to note that woman still are not supposed to touch the plough or drive a tractor or operate any kind of machinery in many parts in these countries. In many areas, she is still not supposed to ride a bicycle. In some religious groups, even in educated families, women cannot enter kitchen or carry out other functions during menstrual cycle. Giving many female characteristics a negative and evil image is part of the process of social institutionalization for domestication of women, in the three countries under review. Further, while the feminist want her to participate in economic development, they are still not prepared to free her from her family commitments. By the age of 25-29 years, more than 90 per cent of women are married in India, Pakistan and Bangladesh. A sizeable percentage, about 30 per cent females, gets married while they are still in their teens (i.e., 15-19 years). The mean age at marriage for female, around 13 years at the beginning of the century, has shown an increase in recent years, to reach 19 years in India for example. The Child Marriage

Restraint Act, 1976 raised the minimum age at marriage of girls to 18 years from 15 years and for boys to 21 years in India, but no such law is there in Pakistan and Bangladesh. This was intended to prevent child marriages, early marriage of girls and consequent early pregnancies and thereby curtailing fertility at young ages and birth of premature babies. It was also expected to lead to higher education and higher work participation rates for women. Not much has happened as planned.

Literacy overall has shown substantial increase from 16.7 in 1951 to 65.38 in 2001. The sex differentials in literacy, however, have been throughout consistent and pronounced. Over the last five decades (1951-2001), female literacy has gone up substantially from 7.9 in 1951 to 54.16 in 2001 in India (Census, 2001). However, literacy in rural areas is way behind. Only 30.6 per cent females are literate in rural areas compared to 64.1 per cent in urban areas. The literacy figures have improved, since in the 1991 Census the population below seven years of age is excluded to work out the percentage, which earlier was not done. In Pakistan and Bangladesh the female literacy is around 24 and 26 per cent respectively. There are wide regional variations too, ranging from near universal literacy in Kerala to 20.8 per cent female literacy in Rajasthan. Similar regional variations are found in Pakistan and Bangladesh. Rural-urban differentials in literacy are also wide. Female literacy in rural areas is still very low and is less than half of the literacy rate in urban areas, in the countries under review.

Though school enrolment ratios have been rising, high rate of drop-outs, particularly of girls still continues to be a major problem. During 1993-94, little more than one-third (39%) of the number of girls enrolling at the primary stage dropped out before completing primary level. More than half of them (about 57%) dropped out before completing upper primary levels. Of the remaining 43 per cent who reached the high/higher secondary stage, another 10 per cent dropped out before completing the school stage. Thus, only about 32 per cent of girls entering the primary stage reach the end of schooling in India. Information about Pakistan is not available while in Bangladesh 69.6 per cent of all primary school-going age girls enrol at primary level, this percentage declines to 15.6 per cent at the secondary level.

Employment of women is taken as an index of their economic status in society, especially with reference to equality. According to the census data in India, the work participation rate (i.e., the proportion of employed or total workers to population) of females steadily rose from 14.22 per cent in 1971 to 19.67 in 1981 and to 22.27 in 1991. However, the HDR, 2000 estimated that 41.8 per cent females over the age of 15 years, in India were economically active in 1998, compared to 34.4 in Pakistan and 65.8 in Bangladesh. They constituted 49.3 per cent of male economically active population in India, compared to 40.5 per cent in Pakistan and 76.2 per cent in Bangladesh. During the 1991 Census, conscious efforts were made to count women workers more completely and remove their invisibility. This could be one of the reasons for the increase reflected in the work participation rates between 1981 and 1991 in India. Much of the fluctuation in figures is also on account of the change in the definition of work.

Women's employment in the organized sector has almost doubled and about 62 per cent of these women were employed in the public sector and the rest in the private sector. As compared to women in the organized sector, the representation of men is almost six times more. About 56 per cent of women's employment in the organized sector is in community, social and personal services, 16 per cent each in transport, storage and communication and financing, insurance, real estate and banking services. Of the total employment of women, the organized sector employment forms only 4 per cent, whereas, for men, organized sector employment constitutes 10 per cent of total employment in India. It is surprising to note that percentage of female administrators and managers are lowest in India around 2.3 per cent compared to 4.3 in Pakistan and 4.9 in Bangladesh. India and Pakistan have the same percentage of women as professional and technical workers around 20.5 per cent, whereas

Bangladesh has 30.7 per cent women working in professional or technical jobs.

The flow of benefits to women in the three core sectors of education, health and employment was to be closely monitored and the general belief was that the approach has now moved from development to empowerment in India and Bangladesh. The myth of empowerment becomes obvious as the sex ratio continue to decline in India in the age-group of 0-6. The sex ratio is a more potent indicator of how gender free a society is. Generally, the sex ratio should indicate a balance between male and female population and its increase or decline. It is interesting to note that the gap is increasing with development efforts to improve health and the child mortality rates. It was 972 females per thousand males in 1901, which has declined to 927 in 1991. Though this figure has improved somewhat in 2001 but the sex ratio in the age-group of 0-6 has further declined from 945 in 1991 to 927 in 2001. The decline has been more acute in economically more progressive states such as Haryana, Maharashtra, Gujarat and Punjab. Punjab with the highest per capita income has the lowest sex ratio of 793 females per 1,000 males in the 0-6 age-group. The sex ratio steadily declined over the decades, except for a marginal increase between 1941 and 1951 and 1971 and 1981 when it rose to 934 from 930. It declined to 927 in 1991. The adverse sex ratio for women needs to be seen against other indicators of falling death rates for men and women, higher child survival rates and the improvement of life expectancy, which is more significant for women than for men. As per the development hypothesis, improvement in health care should have contributed to a more favourable sex ratio.

Sex ratio in Pakistan and Bangladesh exhibits a cultural similarity and is calculated as 105 males per 100 females in Pakistan and 106 males per 100 females at birth in Bangladesh in 2001. What is interesting to note is that at 65 years and more the sex ratio further declines in Bangladesh to 119 males per 100 females and in Pakistan it improves as it reaches 96 males per

100 females. It is also interesting to note that in many Muslim countries the sex ratio at birth is around 105 males to 100 female children, which increases phenomenally in the age-group of 15-64. For example, in Qatar, it is 243 males, Kuwait 177, UAE 173, and Saudi Arabia 141 males per 100 females. This could only mean that a large number of women are migrating out, there is no indication of a higher female mortality rate in these countries. Looking at the world population data more male children are born as the sex ratio is generally around 105 males to 100 female (*World Population Report*, 2000).

In conclusion, the Indira Gandhi Institute in Mumbai records a dismal picture of women empowerment in the last fifty years (Dev, 1997). It noted that barring only few women in the middle and upper strata of the society, women by and large remain deprived – in work opportunities, in access to markets, in ownership of productive resources, in education, science and technology, in all those things that makes it possible for a human being to experience the freedom and participate in and enjoy the fruits of economic development. The old economic policy did not do any good either for the poor or women, but it had good intentions. The new economic policy simply believes in the survival of the fittest and is neither interested in closing the gap between classes or between genders. Tension between democracy and development, rather than economic development, is evident in the formulation of policy, in setting developmental priorities and in controlling the outcomes of biases in development (Krishnaraj, 1998). Development of women is weak in Pakistan and Bangladesh compared with India. The gender development index was 0.533 in India, 0.466 in Pakistan and 0.459 in Bangladesh in 2001 (HDR, 2001). The rural Pakistan like India is as feudal in character as it was when the development efforts commenced in 1950s. Social policy with reference to women in Pakistan has changed with the frequent change of governments. Differences in ideological orientations of the governments particularly how they construct women in the social order and her consequent status and role, account for these shifts. The Zia-ul-Haq government implemented an Islamization programme in 1979. As part of the programme various laws relating to women known as "Enforcement of Hudood Ordinances" were introduced. Although Weiss felt that these efforts on the part of the government resulted in expanding the woman's movement in the country, it does indicate how an Islamic state would construct women's position in society. The officially formulated image of women play a significant role in re-enforcing or negating the traditional construction of images of women in the economically less developed countries, with a large segment of population still rural in character. The symbolic representation of women is done first to define the cultural identity, and then it is redefined to indicate a movement towards 'modernization', signifying education and economic participation. Pakistan, India and Bangladesh all have gone through the process of such symbolization, though they are very sure of what they want. They have accepted the universal logic of reform in the existing status of women but are unable to accept the logic of gender equality. The first significant change occurred in Pakistan, in the form of Muslim Family Law Ordinance in 1961, during the military rule of Ayub Khan, regarded as the first attempt to provide protection to women by regulating divorce and polygamy. It provided for registration of all marriages and eliminated divorce solely by repudiation *(talaq)*. The written permission of wife (wives) is to be obtained and brought before an arbitration council, for permission to remarry. To what extent it can be enforced on the ground is another matter, but it was a step in the direction of reform. In India even this has not been achieved in case of Muslim women on account of political compulsions of a different kind. While in India the spread of education and access to mass communication has made minor inroads, the mindset in India, Pakistan and Bangladesh, with the growth of religious orthodoxy, remains unchanged towards women, as the studies of women in these countries indicate. The situation of women in rural areas is very different, with respect to access to education and health and as far as the rituals of *purdah* and their economic participation is concerned. The urban women in Pakistan and Bangladesh, like their counterparts in India, are gradually becoming economically active and better off in terms of education and access to health facilities. Yet educated women do not have the social freedom, mobility and independence. The self-image of an educated woman is not very different from an illiterate woman. The women generally accept an inferior social status in the family and are amenable to social control. The dominant belief is that the woman is created to serve the family, a sentiment dominant in India, Pakistan and Bangladesh alike. Female children are in particular not sent to school since the parent do not want them to interact with their male counter parts or work outside the house. The women in particular are not free to choose their spouse. The parents want to exercise this right in conformity with the social norms and to marry her as per their own convenience. The prime consideration is the notion of social approval. The logic is that the marriage is between families and not between individuals. The people, therefore, in general, in Pakistan, view maintaining close vigil on their daughters to preserve their sexual morality and the family ties, a social responsibility, a trend found in India and Bangladesh as well. Bangladesh, with a predominantly Muslim illiterate population, faces a crucial dilemma in pursuing change with respect to gender issues. The reproductive role of women is given high priority and any women either unable or unwilling to deliver, is looked down upon. Ironically this is happening in countries with huge populations where enormous resources are being spent on curtailing the birth rate. Social preference for marriage and fertility at an early age remain firmly in place.

As Kaviraj (2000) noted in the context of India, the durability of the basic morphology of social arrangements of the village community is remarkable. The elements in these arrangements often changed, but the relations did not. Modification of the gender relations is definitely not under consideration in these countries in general, particularly in rural areas. The state has remained marginal to the fundamental process of every day life of society. The intense everyday repression of social order could not be directly attributed to the state structure. These are to be seen as the impersonal functioning of the structure itself. The state cannot rectify these, because it has no control over the source of its creation, to a great degree religion. The various political parties have been using religion in India, Pakistan and Bangladesh, as a tool, to capture power. The state's capacity to reform the 'social' constructed by religion has diminished rather than increased during the past decades in these countries. The opinions on what state efforts have delivered differ and often vary from little to great change in the status of women. The truth, however, is indicated by the title of a book, *Modern Myths and Locked Minds*. The myths of what development efforts have achieved or will achieve notwithstanding, the society in India, Pakistan and Bangladesh continues to be highly male oriented. There appears to be a consensus among social institutions such as family and religion on: (a) maintaining a hierarchical structure, and (b) to control the women and her product. The woman is still looked at as a commodity to serve the needs of a male society. The concept of integrating women's issues in public policies ignores existing class and gender inequalities. de Beauvoir (1949) argued that a woman is not born, she becomes one. Men define her, as distinct from a man and assign her definite role status as distinct from men. To reverse this trend a woman must negate her femininity. In India, Pakistan and Bangladesh, even the urban educated woman does not appear to be contemplating it, even though they may be economically independent. An issue often raised is the relevance of the western paradigm of women's development in the sub-continent and the possible alternative. The concept of gender equality is not differently arrived at. The possibility of its acceptance in these countries remains rather remote, so long as religion and family continue to play a powerful influence in these countries. The efforts at empowerment of women would only accentuate the gender conflict, particularly in upper strata of the society, where women empowerment would be more pronounced, as the male psyche remain largely unchanged.

Let us now turn to the discourse on secularization. The quest for modernization of social values as we argued earlier, has not been clearly defined and at best remains vague. As Madan (1994) noted, the need for modernization was accepted without any real discussion of the meaning, scope and the outcome of planned efforts. With the expertise of social relations, social scientist was expected to help define, control and direct social changes and speeds up the process of making India comparable to Europe. The basic premise was an acceptance of Indian culture as being decadent and consequently to be replaced by a more vibrant and achievement oriented culture. The assumption was that the stagnant cultures fail to grow and die a natural death. The contact with a more vibrant culture like that of Europe could become the engine of social change. A noted anthropologist, D.N. Majumdar (1955) defined 'development' as the impact of 'advanced' upon 'simple and passive' societies, though he could see that this process of development was not, however, an easy one. It raised several tensions and social intervention was needed to do something about these tensions, conflicts and burdens placed upon the weaker societies. Yet, he noted that the tribes when they came in contact with Hindus society seemed to be losers on all fronts – cultural, social, and psychological, if not on the economic front (Majumdar, 1955; Madan, 1994). The issue often debated is, whether the tribal absorption into a more dynamic culture a problem or is it a natural process of inevitable change. Majumdar referred to cultures as dominant' and 'decadent' without hesitation, and emphasized that 'decadent' cultures could hardly hope to survive except by "surrendering their values and even identifying completely with the dominant culture". Individual adaptations to change occur more easily in material culture but changes in non-material aspect (a) take a long time, and (b) may never be accepted as a preferred behaviour. Gandhi and Nehru advanced similar arguments for maintaining openness in viewing and interacting with other cultures to assimilate the desirable. The societies where religion still is a dominant force do not permit such freedom. The ambivalence is inevitable, as the material glitter is too powerful to resist. The material change looks so logical yet pose issues which are not easily resolved. Migration to urban area is a good example. The need for better material prosperity is accepted yet freedom for women is not, similarly a change in the family hierarchy is not contemplated. The loss of community is felt but accepted in due time. The need for a higher material status promotes self-orientation and diminishes the ethics of collective good. The self-orientation questions the established norms, the very base of the social structure. The family is considered the key to happiness in the societies under review. As Bose (2002) recently pointed out family support for elderly is very high in oriental societies and low in western world. For example, the search for competent help when one is sick involves multiple discussions among family and friends about possible causes and explanations for the problem, and making a decision about whom to consult. People view health and illness holistically and seek resolution of both physical and mental aspects of distress, by consulting practitioners of different types of medicine (Sweetser, 1993). Choosing a spouse is similarly not left to the individual since the marriage is not seen as an individual affair, it is considered a family affair as it involves others. Individual's freedom to action in any field is simply considered irrelevant and undesirable in all the countries under review irrespective of the religion. The agenda of making individual free of all social ties which some western sociologist felt was the most significant change of the last century is still not firmly in place in these societies. The presence of the idea and its partial acceptance has so far caused more problems.

The quest for economic development in line with western societies, therefore, poses several problems. The implications of economic change were misread, and it was hoped that the expansion of economic and material wealth would not disturb the social values. As is well known economic change has the potential to induce change in social and moral values, as the studies of urbanization and industrialization indicate. In particular it radically influenced the social institutions of religion, family and marriage in the western society. The globalization some feel would create a global culture, with two main features: (a) a materialist orientation, believing in here and now, and (b) a belief in individual rights, whereas others think that globalization would coexist with a multiplicity of cultures. The power of religion and family is still very visible and substantial for a very large section of the people in India, Pakistan and Bangladesh. The society in these countries is struggling to hold on to its traditional arrangements, with respect to women, caste, religious identity and family, while economy has undergone a change. The point is will further changes in economy, that is globalization, would further impact the cultural aspect? And would that imply social development? In other words what aspects of social arrangements are in the process of change and its implications for future social structure in these countries?

Modernization, as we noted earlier, clearly favours a decline of the given categories. You are not born a Hindu or Muslim, you become one and similarly you are not born a woman you become one. The concept of modernization expects one to move in that general direction. Individual should exercise the right in choosing what he or she wants to become. The secular constitution of India provides for this change. In actual practice society expects individual to accept the category allotted by birth as final. It neither tolerates change of religion or a change of gender. The power of the category remains as strong as ever. The religion may not be as powerful in Europe as it is in India, Pakistan and Bangladesh, but it still exists as a category, and continue to influence individual and community responses.

Gandhi had immense faith in religion to generate moral values and the thinking of the common person in India, Pakistan and Bangladesh is no different. But moral is defined as control over women and her product in the feminist theory. Feminists argue that moral theory is based on male experience because morality is defined as a public realm rather than as private or concrete and particular. The important point to note here is that the moral development of women is different from men but run parallel to that of men (Gilligan, 1982). However, the common person practices religion as a vital support system, which for him/her is a guideline for dealing with day-to-day realities or deprivations. As McKim Marriott in her study of an Indian village noted, the 'little tradition', her term for the grassroots cultural practices, poses no problems as it is considered personal. As a logical consequence, they are not under obligation to impose it on 'other', and neither they feel threatened by the presence of 'other'. The elite has other ideas as far as religion is concerned. The political development in India, Pakistan and Bangladesh has made religion a powerful tool. The 'great tradition', the elite, consider it an obligation to protect the pure textual form of religious traditions and uses the religious symbols to create political constituencies. It launches periodic movements to establish its superiority over other religions to preserve and expand its constituency by projecting a cultural identity superior to others. There is always a gap between what is prescribed or intended in religious texts and the grassroots religious practices. This gap is increasing as the rituals are easy to perform but it is far more difficult to understand the philosophy and almost impossible to imbibe the spirituality, as it means negating the material and the body. It is, therefore, not surprising that in contemporary society in India, Pakistan and Bangladesh, the religion is being used as a political strategy for capturing power and being used as an explanation for preserving the existing social structure.

The values of vast populations living in agrarian societies generally illiterate or semiliterate are difficult to change. Even the most powerful nations have failed to evolve a social consensus on most issues through economic development. The possibility of developing any macro consensus of any kind remains a mere possibility only. But, it is the possibility, howsoever remote, which is keeping the pursuit of an ideal society going in the name of modernization and social development. The social scientists continue to debate the possibility of planned social change, while some think that it can be done and should be done, others advocate an emancipation from emancipation.

In his village studies Majumdar (1955) undertook to examine both selected problems calling for immediate relief, such as water scarcity and those which required long-term efforts. He concluded that villagers were apathetic and immured in timeless inertia and, therefore, the change had to be induced externally. Majumdar did not, however, consider villagers or tribesmen to be irrational, as Madan (1994) noted. There are many social scientists today, who hold the same views as Majumdar did on development and the role of the social sciences, though they are likely to state them, in more sophisticated phraseology and with greater caution, being the wiser for the experience gained. As Madan (1994) noted, that contemporary literature 'exaggerates' change. During the last fifty years or so, Madan feels that the society as an overall framework has not changed. He admits there has been change in the society but not of the society (ibid: 66).

The implications of industrialization and urbanization on social institutions are still far from clear. Madan (1994a) and other studies (Kolenda, 1970; Shah, 1973; Kessinger, 1974; Oberoi, 1993) noted that in studying these very definition of the term such as family poses problems. The consequent generalization, therefore, is a distorted version of social phenomenon. There is a common assumption that the process of industrialization and urbanization has lead to the decline of joint family, giving rise to a nuclear family form. The studies point out, that the joint family was less common in rural areas, and that prevalence of joint families may in fact be on the increase rather than decline, and that the very definition of family and joint family pose problems. Madan is critical of Indian social scientists as they are not using their own understanding and are being guided by frameworks and concepts evolved by western scholars. However, objectivity in social science is a perennial problem, professional training in sociology or anthropology notwithstanding. Some element of subjectivity rooted in discipline or culture is inevitable. Positions would remain relative and subject specific. Social action is generally logical if it is really social in character. The idea of economic and political development as the key to social development came from Europe. It succeeded in both expanding the economic wealth and creating new institutions of political governance, but failed to influence the social values and attitudes of the common people in the developing countries, and thus succeeded in disturbing the ecological balance of the social order. The process of economic development tends to remove women from productive labour and increase sexual stratification. Politically awared mass, without the necessary economic skills and social attitudes, can create more problems and an elite without a secular political ideology adds fuel to the fire in the process of social development. Gore (1965) intuitively felt the need for the ecological balance by defining social development a little more than economic, political and social development put together. The point Madan (1994) and among others Nandi (1983) have argued is that by adopting a foreign framework for judging a society we would be reaching the inevitable conclusion of degrading the indigenous. But the point is that a corrupt state is not a foreign viewpoint, and defining indigenous is difficult in a multi-cultural society. There are several versions of it and the dominant culture may impose its version on 'others' and may even term 'other' indigenous members as outsiders, in justifying the whole or part of the dominant cultural. Nehru undoubtedly had an understanding of all this and had the courage to act. The nature of changes was determined by a host of factors during the last fifty years or so. To pursue a different path of development grounded in our own culture, for example the one advocated by Gandhi, as we noted earlier, would have resulted in other issues coming to the fore. The model would have undergone change, as was the case with the original idea of Mujibur Rehman about the future of Bangladesh. He paid with his life as the other more powerful indigenous elite rejected the idea. Now looking at the history of the options available in terms of known models or ideology of development, as we noted earlier, the choice was non-existent. And, as Apter (1963) noted, it would not have mattered anyway. The choice has to be grounded in economic development, as the process of colonization has set the ball rolling. The human history is a testimony to the body dominating the soul. The Gandhian model was rejected and it became redundant when the process of industrialization commenced, and the elected governments were formed in India. After that there was no going back. The myth of democracy and development has established itself. The history of colonial rule by default determined for the undivided India and later for Pakistan and Bangladesh, the belief in the discourse of progress and democracy, the most potent myths, which continue to dominate us.

Under the garb of democracy, the society in India, Pakistan and Bangladesh remains undemocratic in character. Very recently Indian people have discovered the real truth of the phrase – contempt of court. Nobody has the right to criticize the 'judicial high priests'. It reminds me of the law of blaspheme. The idea is to put certain things beyond the purview of the common person to question, as the law of legitimization requires. Freedom of expression does not mean freedom to question the high priest of democracy. It is the beauty of the western Anglican social institutions, that they are defined in such a way, that they appear so logical and support each other even though in spirit they contradict each other. The parliament and other decision-making bodies including panchayats, judiciary and the bureaucracy are a case in point, as far as democracy is concerned. The democracy at the grassroots in the form of panchayats and family has failed, since we believe in hierarchy and surrender. Democracy without a concept of equality and the courage to dissent is untenable. Yet, democracy in India, in the form of government of elected representatives, has survived despite severe tests. Pakistan has not been able to sustain even that tokenism, while Bangladesh is struggling. The social development associated with change in social structure remains inconclusive. In some segments of society, a little change has occurred, a little space has been conceded to make the hierarchy a little more modest, but the basic institutions of family, marriage, caste and religion have survived and have not undergone any substantial transformation in India, Pakistan and Bangladesh. The construction of woman and her position consequently, has also remained by and large unchanged. The spread of secularism in the sense it is defined and understood in the West has not happened in India, Pakistan and Bangladesh.

The idea of nation state and its cultural identity continue to evoke passions. The most recent example of that is the recent attempt by India and Pakistan to patch up their differences in search of a peaceful coexistence. The public euphoria it generated and the construction of issues at stake by the political and social elite reflects the role religion and culture play in construction of social realities. Within Kashmir the Hindus and Muslim construct the same reality differently. Even at the national level in India, generally though there could be exceptions, the Hindu social and political elite viewed the problem differently from their Muslim counterparts. Views of Indian Muslim elite are closer to their Pakistani counterpart as far as Kashmir is concerned, though not many would propagate them openly. The Hindu elite constructs the problem as an effort on the part of the Muslim population to secede, whereas the Muslim sympathize with the local Muslims, as they feel the Hindu State is giving them a raw deal. They would more readily agree to a third party intervention in Kashmir or to grant it greater autonomy or even unification of two Kashmirs as an independent state. The common people at the grassroots, irrespective of their religion, viewed it differently from the elite. An ordinary youth from a small town in India felt disappointed, as did an ordinary worker in Karachi. They were hoping that the effort would simplify the travel to respective countries, the international boundary represent, restrictions for them to meet their friends and family. They are hardly concerned with the political domination of the territory. The threat of the use of nuclear option has further alienated the masses from the issue. But, the point is that religion still is a dominant factor in constructing a problem or choosing options to resolve it, in the public sphere, in these countries. The planned effort for development in the past five decades has simply generated more material needs, a sea of rising expectations as some studies put it, without being able to provide for the mechanisms to meet these needs. The situation is likely to breed frustration and conflicts. The religion comes in handy in such situations as well. It helps in defining the enemy and also in explaining the material deprivations. As Dreze and Sen (1995) noted the success of development programmes cannot be judged merely in terms of their effects on incomes and outputs unless they focus on the lives that people can lead. The development experts put a lot of faith on two things: the capability of the state, to increase the income levels through development programmes, and to create a political and social environment, which enables people to participate in these programmes. A little modification is likely to be made in the coming years by replacing the state by market and NGOs. The people are gradually being forced to expand their consumption levels and adopt a more market friendly lifestyle. It is ironical that those, who do not wish to opt for a consumerist approach, are termed backward.

For many people in these countries economic well-being is only one part of the overall well-being. Caring and non-materialist values are more important. Economic man usually looks down upon low achievement motivation, while [the] social man advocates it as essential for a good life. Millions of people living in the rural areas prefer a relaxed life style in general, and may not be worried about the future. The present is what matters for them and freedom from emancipation. It is not surprising that they find it logical to reject development projects. The development project as the father of a child labour pointed out creates problem for them. He was referring to a question why he has withdrawn his child from the school. He was not sure what would happen to his son if he studied up to tenth class. The training of making glass products enables his sons to learn the skills to earn their livelihood and keeps the family together as well. Further, more than enough money makes more enemies. He wanted to live in relative poverty but at peace with himself and others.

Similarly, people actually practicing religion are termed primitive. Following tradition blindly may be bad but that does not make all traditions per se bad and to be rejected. However, it is obvious that developing a secular outlook, howsoever defined, does not appear to be theoretically feasible. The debate about secular and religious nationalism has concluded in Pakistan and is about to be settled in Bangladesh but would continue perennially in India. In the prevailing circumstance secularism in Pakistan, Bangladesh and India, is a very distant possibility (the listing of the countries is in order of degree of possibility). Secularism here signifying that those who profess no religion have a place in society equal to that of others, not higher or lower (Madan, 1994; Nandi, 1983). The debate about what is secularism and how it can be achieved remains inconclusive. This is yet another example of the complexity of the task of restructuring the social.

Over the years, the repressive machinery of the state has been immensely enlarged and strengthened. One of the largest areas of government expenditure is the consistently growing investment in the police, the various paramilitary forces, and the army. They have been provided with sophisticated weapons and means of communication and special training for one of their primary tasks – to control the poor. They enjoy near unlimited powers to murder, torture, maim, loot, rape, extort bribes and terrorize. The sight of a government or police jeep entering a village, sends people fleeing into forests and fields in order to escape encountering them. Experience has taught them that a police jeep can mean only more torture and trouble, especially women (Kishwar and Vanita, 1991). The central problem in pursuing social development is the distribution of power among the general members of society. Democratic model is considered a desirable method. Indian Constitution is an excellent example. The difficulty lies in enforcing the constitution. The question of individual freedom versus social control or in other words giving primacy to self or 'other' in the social construction is a dilemma, which is not easily resolved in practice. Social development by all accounts would remain a laudable objective, and the search for a theoretical framework to construct it would continue. As we have noted earlier, the general assumption is that planned social change is possible. But, the possibility of planned change to deliver the economic, political and social in an ecological perspective, to achieve the desired social would continue to elude the theory. We earlier referred to the debate on body and mind in the context of morality and noted that body continues to dominate. Despite the economists' faith in their discipline, they are beginning to realize the difficulty of developing a model which can do justice to economic and political distribution and which works. It remains an illusion to structure an economy, capable of providing a basic economic level of well-being, freedom to participate in political affairs and a society free of an oppressive hierarchy, in the countries under review.

Bibliography

Abbasi, M.B. (1980): *Socio-economic Characteristics of Women in Sindh*, Karachi: Women's Division, Government of Pakistan.

Adnan, Shapan (1988): "Birds in a Cage". Paper presented in a seminar on Women Development at International Union for the Scientific Study of Population, Norway.

Ahluwalia, M.S. (1978): "Rural Poverty and Agricultural Performance in India", *Journal of Development Studies*, 14 (3): 298-323.

— (1985): "Rural Poverty, Agricultural Production and Prices: A Re-examination", in J.W. Mellor and G.M. Desai (eds.), *Agricultural Change and Rural Poverty*, Baltimore: John Hopkins University Press, pp. 59-75.

Ahmed, Ashiruddin (1999): "Accountability by Voters", *Dawn*, 20 November.

Ahmed, Jasim U. (1982): "The Impact of New Paddy Post-Harvest Technology on the Rural Poor in Bangladesh", in M. Greeley and M. Howes (eds.), *Rural Technology, Rural Institutions and Rural Poorest*, Comilla: CIRDAP.

Ahsan, Rosie Majid, Shahnaz Hussain and Ben J. Wallace (1986): *Role of Women in Agriculture*, Dhaka: Centre for Urban Studies.

Albrow, Martin (1996): *The Global Age*, Cambridge: Polity Press.

Ali, Shaheen Sardar (1995): "Women's Rights and Human Rights in Tribal Areas: A Case Study of the Provincially Administered Tribal Areas of Pakistan", in N.S. Khan, Rubina Saigol and Afiya Shehrabano Zia (eds.), *Aspects of Women and Development*, Lahore: ASR Publications.

Alphonse, Mary (1990): "Women Empowerment", Ph.D Thesis: Department of Social Work, Jamia Millia Islamia.

Amin, Sajeda (1997): "The Poverty Pardah Trap in Rural Bangladesh: Implications for Women's Role in the Family", *Development and Change*, 25: 213-233.

Apter, David (1963): "Political Religion in the New Nations", in Clifford Geertz (ed.), *New States Old Societies*, New Delhi: Amrind.

Assaduzzaman, M. and Westergaard Kirsten (eds.) (1993): *Growth and Development in Rural Bangladesh*, Dhaka University Press.

Azarya, Victor (1994): " 'Civil Society' and Disengagement in Africa", in Harbeson, John W., Rothchild, Donald, and Chazan, Naomi (eds.), *Civil Society and the State in Africa*, Boulder: Lynne Reinner.

Bahadur, Kaleem (1978): "The Jamat-I-Islami of Pakistan: Ideology and Political Action", *International Studies*, Vol. 14, No. 1.

Bangladesh Institute of Development Studies (1981): "Rural Industries Study Project", Dhaka.

— (1988): "Bangladesh Handloom Sector Study", Vol. I, Dhaka.

Baqai, M.S. (1976): *Changes in the Status and Role of Women in Pakistan*, Karachi: University of Karachi.

Bardhan, Pranab (2000): "The Political Economy of Reform in India", in Zoya Hasan (ed.), *Politics and the State in India*, New Delhi: Sage.

Barnes, Jonathon (1984): *Aristotle*, Princeton University Press, Bollingen Series.

Bauman Z. (1993): *Postmodern Ethics*, Cambridge: Polity.

— (1995): *Life in Fragments*, Cambridge: Polity.

Bean, Lee L. (1993): "Growth Without Change: The Demography of Pakistan", in J.H. Corson (ed.), *Contemporary Problems of Pakistan*, Boulder: Westview Press.

Begum, Saleha and Martin Greeley (1987): "Women Employment and Agriculture, Extracts from a Case Study", in *Women in Bangladesh: Some Socio-Economic Issues*, Seminar Papers, Vol. I, Dhaka.

— (1988): *The Mechanization of Farm-Level Rice Processing and Displacement of Female Wage Labour in Bangladesh: The Need for and Nature of Effective Policy Response*, Population Council, University of Sussex.

Berlin, Isaiah (1997): *The Proper Study of Mankind*, London.

Bhatti, Mukhtar Ahmad (1988): *Female Teachers in Rural Pakistan: Problems and Remedies,* National Education Council.

Binder, Leonard (1986): "The Natural History of Development Theory", *Comparative Studies in Society and History*, 28 (1): 3-33.

Bosanquet, Bernard (1910): *The Political Theory of the State*, London: Macmillan.

Bose, Ashish (2002): "Face to Face", *Social Initiatives*, New Delhi: National Institute of Social Defence, Vol. 3, No. 11.

Boserup, E. (1970): *Women's Role in Economic Development*, New York: St. Martin's Press.

BRAC (Bangladesh Rural Advancement Committee) (1990): *A Tale of Two Wings: Health and Family Planning Programmes in a Upazila in Northern Bangladesh*, Dhaka: BRAC, Rural Studies Series 6.

Bradburn, N.M. and Orden, R. (1968): "Working Wives and Marriage Happiness", *American Journal of Sociology*, 74.

Bratton, Michael (1994): " 'Civil Society' and Political Transition in Africa", in Harbeson, John W., Rothchild, Donald, and Chazan, Naomi (eds.), *'Civil Society' and the State in Africa*, Boulder: Lynne Reinner.

Burki, Shahid Javed (1993): "Pakistan's Economy in the Year 2000: Two Possible Scenarios", in J.H. Corson (ed.), *Contemporary Problems of Pakistan*, Boulder: Westview Press.

Centre for Policy Dialogue (1995): *Experiences with Economic Reform*, Dhaka: University Press.

Chakravarty, S.R. (ed.) (1994): *Society, Polity and Economy of Bangladesh*, New Delhi: Har-Anand.

Chakravarty, Sukhamoy (1987): *Development Planning: The Indian Experience*, New Delhi: Oxford University Press.

Chakravarty, S. (2000): *Times of India*, January, 1, 2000.

Chatterjee, Partha (2000): "Development Planning and the Indian State", in Zoya Hasan (ed.), *Politics and the State in India*, New Delhi: Sage.

Chowdhary, Naimuddin (1986): "Revaluation of Women's Work in Bangladesh", *The Bangladesh Journal of Agriculture Economics*, Vol. IV (1).

CIRDAP (1988): *Role of Women in Rural Industries*, Vol. II, Dhaka.

Collins, Simon (1989): "Rogernomics: The Economic Aftermath", in Brian Easton (ed.), *The Making of Rogernomics*, Auckland: University Press.

Cranston, Maurice (1968): 'Introduction', *Social Contract*, Rousseau J. J. Tr. by M. Cranston, Hamondsworth: Penguin.

D'Souza, Victor S. (1989): "Economic Development, Social Structure and the Ideal Society", in Pimpley et al (eds.), *Social Development*, Jaipur: Rawat.

Dahrendorf, Ralf (1996): "Economic Opportunity, 'Civil Society' and Political Liberty", *Development and Change*, 27: 229-249.

Das, Gurcharan (2000): "Nation of Thieves", *Times of India*, 23 January.

Davey, Judith A. (1987): *Social Policy Options*, Wellington: New Zealand Planning Council.

Davidson, Basil (1989): "The Challenge of Comparative Analysis: Anti-Imperialist Nationalism in Africa and Europe". Paper presented in a seminar on Relationship between State and 'Civil Society', at Bellagio, Italy.

de Beauvoir, Simone (1949): *The Second Sex*, Bijleveld: Utrecht.

Dereze, Jean and Amartya Sen (1995): *Indian Economic Development and Social Opportunity*, New Delhi: Oxford University Press.

Desai, Armaity S. (1999): "Role of 'Civil Society': The Tasks Ahead for Civil Institutions", XIII John Barnabas Memorial Lecture, New Delhi: National Institute of Public Co-operation and Child Development.

Desai, Sonalde (2001): "A Tale of Two Middle Classes". Paper presented at a seminar on Understanding Socio-Economic Changes Through National Surveys, National Sample Survey Organization, New Delhi.

Dev, Mahendra (1997): "Growth Employment, Poverty and Human Development: An Evaluation of Change in India Since Independence with Emphasis on Rural Area", Indira Gandhi Institute of Development Research, Mumbai.

Durkheim, E. (1958): *Professional Ethics and Civic Morals*, Glencoe, Illinois: The Free Press.

— (1961) [1925]: *Moral Education*, Glencoe, Illinois: The Free Press.

— (1973) [1914]: "The Dualism of Human Nature", in Bellah (ed.), *Emile Durkheim on Morality and Society*, Chicago: University of Chicago Press.

— (1982): *Rules of Sociological Method*, New York: Free Press.

— (1984) [1893]: *The Division of Labor in Society*, London: Macmillan.

— (1995) [1912]: *The Elementary Forms of Religious Life*, New York: Free Press.

Edward, Michael and David Hume (1995): 'Introduction' in Edwards, Michael and David Hulme (ed.), *Beyond the Magic Bullet: NGO*

Performance and Accountability in the Post-Cold War World, Kumarian Press.

Eisenstadt, S.N. (1969): "Reflections on a Theory of Modernization", in Arnold Rivkin (ed.), *Nations by Design*, New York: Anchor Books.

Ellickson, Jean (1975): *Rural Women: A Field Survey*, Dhaka: Women for Women.

Elwin, Verrier (1998): *The Tribal World of Verrier Elwin*, New Delhi: Oxford University Press.

Engineer A. Ali (1997): Bold Court Judgements on Muslim Women, *Economic and Political Weekly*, 32(50): 3189-90.

Ercelawn A.A. (1990): "Absolute Poverty in Pakistan: Poverty Lines, Incidence, Intensity", Draft Mimeo, Karachi: Applied Economic Research Centre, University of Karachi.

Farouk, A. (1980): *Time Use of Rural Women*, Dhaka: University Press.

— (1985): *The Hard Working Poor*, Dhaka: University Press.

Farouk, Chowdhary and Rezaul Islam (1975): Intensification of Homestead Production. Project prepared for World Bank. (Draft).

Feldman, S. (1992): "Crisis, Islam and Gender in Bangladesh: The Social Construction of Female Labour", in L. Beneria and S. Feldman (eds.), *Unequal Burden: Economic Crisis, Persistent Poverty and Women's Work*, Boulder: Westview Press.

Fields, K. (1995): "Religion as an Eminently Social Thing", translators introduction to E. Durkheim, *The Elementary Forms of Religious Life*, New York: The Free Press.

Flyvbjerg, Bent (1998): Habermas and Focault: Thinkers for 'Civil Society'? *British Journal of Sociology*, 49 (2): 210-233.

— (1998a): *Rationality and Power: Democracy in Practice*, Chicago: The University of Chicago Press.

Ford Foundation (1965): *Design for Pakistan: A Report on Assistance to the Pakistan Planning Commission*, New York: Ford Foundation.

Foster, Brian L. (1978): "Development, Modernization and Comparative Parochialism: A Review Article", *Comparative Studies in Society and History*, 20: 319-328.

Friedmann, John (1969): "The Strategy of Deliberate Urbanization", *Journal of the American Institute of Planners*, 34(6): 365.

Gaiha, R. (1989): Are the Chronically Poor Also the Poorest in Rural India?, *Development and Change*, 20: 295-322.

Garain, Swapan (1993): "Training Grassroots Level Workers in Empowering the Rural Poor: The Case of an Indian NGO", *Indian Journal of Social Work*, Vol. LIV, No. 3: 381-392.

Gardezi, Hassan and Jamil Rashid (eds.) (1983): *Pakistan: The Roots of Dictatorship*, Delhi: Oxford University Press.

George, Vic and Paul Wilding (1987): *Ideology and Social Welfare*, London: Routledge and Kegan Paul.

Giddens, Anthony (1991): *Modernity and Self Identity*, Cambridge: Polity Press.

— (1994): "Living in a Post-Traditional Society", in U. Beck, A. Giddens and S. Lash, *Reflexive Modernization*, Cambridge: Polity.

Gilligan, Carrol (1982): *In a Different Voice: Essays on Psychological Theory and Women's Development*, Cambridge, MA: Harvard University Press.

Gore, M.S. (1965): *Some Aspect of Social Development*, Bombay: Popular Prakashan.

— (1968): *Urbanization and Family Change*, Bombay: Popular Prakashan.

Government of Bangladesh (1996): *Bangladesh Statistical Pocketbook*, 1996.

Government of India (1981, 1991): *Census Data.*

— (1997 and 1998): *IX Five-Year Plan*, New Delhi: Planning Commission.

— (1997-98): *Economic Survey 1997-98*, New Delhi: Ministry of Finance.

— *Ninth Plan Document: Economic Survey, 1999-2000.*

Government of Pakistan (1964): *Household Income and Expenditure Survey, 1963-64 and 1968-69.*

— (1987): *VII Five-Year Plan*, Islamabad: Planning Commission.

— (1998): *Economic Survey, 1997-98.*

Greeley, Martin (1987): *Post Harvest Losses, Technology and Employment: The Case of Rice in Bangladesh*, London: Westview Press.

Grieve, Roy H. (1995): "Health for All by 2000", in Grieve R.H. and M. Huq (eds.), *Bangladesh Strategies for Development*, Dhaka, The University Press.

Gudrun, Martius-von Harder (1981): *Women in Rural Bangladesh, Socio-Economic Studies on Rural Development*, Vol. 29, E. Saarbricken, Fort Lauderdale.

Gunnar, Myrdal (1968): *Asian Drama: An Enquiry into Poverty of Nations*, 3 Vols., New York: Pantheon.

Gupta, Anirudh (1994): "Bangladesh: Culture in Politics", in Chakravarty, S.R (ed.), *Society, Polity and Economy of Bangladesh*, New Delhi: Har-Anand.

Gupta, Rahul (2000): "Will Reforms Bring Light", *Times of India*, 23 January.

Gupta, Shekhar (2000): "The Soft Core of the Hard State: The Joke's on us", *Indian Express*, 1 January.

Habermas, J. (1983): *The Theory of Communicative Action*, Vol. I, Cambridge: MIT Press.

— (1987): *The Philosophical Discourse of Modernity*, Cambridge: MIT Press.

— (1990): *Moral Consciousness and Communicative Action*, Cambridge: MIT Press.

Hadley, Roger and Stephen Hatch (1981): *Social Welfare and the Failure of the State: Centralized Social Services and Participatory Alternatives*, London: George Allen and Unwin.

Halim, Abdul and M.H. Ali (1986): *The Effect of Rice Based Cropping System Research on Women in Bangladesh*, Mymensingh Agricultural University.

Halsey, A.H. (1981): "Some Lessons from the Debate: A Sociologist's Viewpoint", in Organization for Economic Cooperation and Development, An Account of the Conference on Social Policies in the 1990s, Paris: OECD.

Haneefa, Deen (1998): *Broken Bangles*, New Delhi: Penguin India.

Haq, M. (1963): *Strategy of Economic Planning: A Case study of Pakistan*, Karachi: Oxford University Press.

Haydar, Afaq (1993): "The Mohajirs in Sindh: A Critical Essay", in J.H. Corson (ed.), *Contemporary Problems of Pakistan*, Boulder: Westview Press.

Herman, Angeline, B. (1991): "The State and Caring: The New Zealand Experience", Unpublished Ph.D. Draft, Massey University, Palmerston North: Department of Social Work and Social Policy.

Hobbes, Thomas (1960): *Leviathan*, Oxford: Blackwell.

Horowitz, I. (1993): *The Decomposition of Sociology*, Oxford: Oxford University Press.

Hossain, M. and Rahman, H.Z. (1997): "Recent Developments in Bangladesh Rural Economy: Implications for Strategies and Policies for Alleviation of Poverty", *The Pakistan Development Review*, 36: 811-836.

Human Development Report (1999), London: Oxford University Press.

Human Development Reports (1998, 1999, 2000, 2001), New York: OUP.

Huntington, Samuel P. (1965): "Political Development and Political Decay", *World Politics*, 17 (3): 386-430.

— (1968): *Political Order in Changing Societies*, New Haven: Yale University Press.

— (1971): "The Change to Change: Modernization, Development and Politics", *Comparative Politics*, 3(3): 283-322.

Hye, S. (1993): "Review of Labour and Employment", in Assaduzzaman, M. and Westergaard Kirsten (eds.), *Growth and Development in Rural Bangladesh*, Dhaka: University Press.

India Human Development Report, 1999, New Delhi: Oxford University Press.

Inkeles, Alex (1964): "Making Men Modern: On the Causes and Consequences of Individual Change in Six Developing Countries", in Amitai Etzioni and Eva Etzioni-Halevy (eds.), *Social Change*, New York: Basic Books.

IOAMR (1998): *Man Power Profile India-1998*, New Delhi: Institute for Applied Manpower Research, p.11.

Islam, Mahmuda (1979): "Social Norms and Institutions", in *Situation of Women in Bangladesh*, Women for Women.

Jafri, A.B.S. (1999), "Towards Grassroots Democracy", *Dawn*, 20 December.

Jain, Sunil (2000): "Hijacking the Indian Economy", *Indian Express*, 1 January.

Jalil, Nasir (1993): "Education in Pakistan: Past Dilemmas and Future Prospects", in J.H. Corson (ed.), *Contemporary Problems of Pakistan*, Boulder: Westview Press.

Jehangir, B.K. (1986): "Women and Poverty in Rural Bangladesh", *Journal of Social Studies*, 34.

Jejeebhoy, Shireen, J. (1998): "Wife Beating: Husbands Right?", *Economic and Political Weekly*, XXXIII (15): 855-862.

Johnson, Norman (1987): *The Welfare State in Transition: The Theory and Practice of Welfare Plurism*, Sussex: Wheatsheaf Books.

Kabeer, Naila (1997): "Women, Wages and Intra-household Power Relations in Urban Bangladesh", *Development and Change*, 28: 261-302.

Kant, I. (1961) [1785]: *Ground Work of the Metaphysics of Morals*, translated by H.J. Paton, New York: Harper and Row.

Kapoor, P. (1970): *Marriages and the Working Women in India*, Delhi: Vikas.

Kaviraj, Sudipta (2000): "The Modern State in India", in Zoya Hasan (ed.), *Politics and the State in India*, Sage: New Delhi.

Kessinger, Tom G. (1974): *Vilayatpur, 1848-1968: Social and Economic Change in a North Indian Village*, Berkeley: University of California Press.

Khan, Aqueel Ahmed (2000): Women Empowerment, Unpublished Ph.D Thesis, New Delhi: Department of Social Work, Jamia Millia Islamia.

Khan, Dilawar Ali (1970): "Planning for the Poor in Pakistan", in R.P. Misra (ed.), *Humanizing Development*, UNDP.

Khan, M. Ali (1997): Comment on Ranis and Stewart, *Pakistan Development Review*, 36 (4): 350.

Khan, Sakina (2000): *Times of India*, 23 January, 2000.

Khaparde, Subhadra (1998): "Alcoholism and Women's Health", *Economic and Political Weekly*, XXXIII (28): 1808-10.

Kishwar, Madhu and Ruth, Vanita (eds.) (1984 and 1991): *In Search of Answers*, New Delhi: Horizon India Books.

Kohli, Atul (2000): "Centralization and Powerlessness: India's Democracy in a Comparative Perspective", in Zoya Hasan (ed.), *Politics and the State in India*, New Delhi: Sage.

Kolenda, Pauline (1970): Family Structure in Village Lonikand, India: 1819,1958, and 1967, *Contributions to Indian Sociology* n.s. 4: 50-72.

Kothari, Rajani (1990): *Rethinking Development: In Search of Humane Alternatives*, Delhi: Somaya Publications.

— (1988): *State Against Democracy: In Search of Humane Governance*, New Delhi: Ajanta Publications.

Krishnaraj, Maithreyi (1998): "Women and the Public Domain: Critical Issues for Women Studies", *Economic and Political Weekly*, XXXIII (8): 391-395.

Kuhn (1962): *The Structure of Scientific Revolutions*, Chicago: University of Chicago Press.

La Porte, Robert, Jr. (1993): "Another Try at Democracy", in J. Henry Carson (ed.), *Contemporary Problems of Pakistan*, Boulder: Westview Press.

Lerner, Daniel (1958): *The Passing of Traditional Society*, New York: Free Press.

Lewicki, P., Hill, T. and Bizot, E. (1988): "Acquisition of Procedural Knowledge about a Pattern of Stimuli that cannot be Articulated", *Cognitive Psychology*, 20: 24-37.

Lewis, W. Arthur (1955): *The Theory of Economic Growth*, London: Allen and Unwin.

Locke, John (1967): *Two Tracts on Government*, in Philip Abrams (ed.), Cambridge: Cambridge University Press.

Lopez, Sonia Arellano and James F. Petras (1994): "Non-Governmental Organizations and Poverty Alleviation in Bolivia", *Development and Change*, 25: 555-568.

Machiavelli, N. (1983): *The Discourse*, Harmondsworth: Penguin.

Madan, T.N. (1976): "The Hindu Women at House, in Indian Women", B.R. Nanda (ed.), *Purdah to Modernity*, New Delhi: Vikas.

— (1994): *Pathways*, New Delhi: Oxford University Press.

— (1994a): "The Hindu Family and Development", in Patricia Oberoi (ed.), *Family, Kinship and Marriage in India*, Delhi: Oxford University Press.

— (1998): *Modern Myths and Locked Minds*, New Delhi: Oxford University Press.

Mahajan, A. (1990): "Instigators of Wife Beating" in Sushma Sood (ed.), *Violence Against Women*, Jaipur: Arihant Publishers.

Mahsud, Alam Jan (1999): "Tribes Without a Right", *The News*, December 22.

Majumdar, D.N. (1955): Introduction, in D.N. Majumdar (ed.), *Rural Profiles*, Lucknow: Ethnographic and Folk Culture Society.

Majumdar, D.N., N.S. Reddy and S. Bahadur (1960): *Social Contours of an Industrial City*, Bombay: Asia Publishing House.

Malik, S.J., Safiya Abbasi and Nargis Sultana (1994): *Pakistan's Economic Performance: 1947-1993*, Lahore: Seema Publishers.

Malinowski, Bronislaw (1945): *The Dynamics of Culture Change*, New Haven: Yale University Press.

Marshall, Peter (1992): *Demanding the Impossible: A History of Anarchism*, London: Fontana Press.

Maududi, Abu Ala (1960): *Islamic Law and Constitution*, Lahore.

Merton, Thomas (1973): *The Asian Journal*, New York: New Directions

Midgley, James (1995): *Social Development*, London: Sage

Mies, Maria (1986): *Patriarchy and Accumulation on a World Scale*, London: Zed Books.

Migdal, S. Joel (1994): "The State in Society: An Approach to Struggles for Domination", in Joel S. Migdal, Atul Kohli and Vivienne Shue (eds.), *State Power and Social Forces*, Cambridge: Cambridge University Press.

Mohanakumara, S. (2002): "From Peoples Plan to Plan Sans People", *Economic and Political Weekly*, XXXVII: 1492.

Moon, Penderel (1961 reprinted in 1998): *Divide and Quit*, New Delhi: Oxford University Press.

Moore, Wilbert E. (1963): *Social Change*, Engelwood Cliffs: Prentice Hall.

Mosse, David, Farrington, Rew Alan (eds.) (2001): *Development as a Process, Concepts and Methods for Coping with Complexity*, New Delhi: India Research.

Muhammed, Fateh (1998): "Socio-Economic and Demographic Characteristics of Illiterate Women", Doctoral Thesis, Department of Sociology, University of Karachi.

Mukerjee, Radha Kamal (1946): *Planning for the Countryside*, Bombay: Hind Kitabs.

— (1951): *The Indian Scheme of Life*, Bombay: Hind Kitabs.

Mukerji, D.P. (1958): *Diversities*, New Delhi: Peoples Publishing House.

Mukund, Kanakalatha (1999): "Women's Property Rights in South India", *Economic and Political Weekly*, XXXIV (22): 1352-58.

Mumtaz, Khawar, and Shaheed Farida (1987): *Women of Pakistan: Two Step Forward, One Step Backward?* Lahore: Vanguard Books.

— (1990): *Women's Economic Participation in Pakistan*, Lahore: Shirkat Gah.

Mungekar, Balchandra (1999): "A Paradox in Maharashtra", *Frontline*, 24 December.

Munir, Muhammad (1979): *1981: From Jinna to Zia*, Lahore: Vanguard Press.

Myrdal, Gunnar (1968): *Asian Drama: An Inquiry into the Poverty of Nations*, Harmondsworth: Penguin.

Nandi, Ashis (1983): *The Intimate Enemy: Loss and Recovery of Self Under Colonialism*, Delhi: Oxford University Press.

— (1988): "The Politics of Secularism and the Recovery of Religious Tolerance", *Alternative*, 13:174-94.

— (2000): "The Political Culture of the Indian State", in Zoya Hasan (ed.), *Politics and the State in India*, New Delhi: Sage.

Narayana, E.A. (1991): "Managing Voluntary Organisations with Limited Finances and Unskilled Personnel", *Indian Journal of Social Work*, Vol. LII, No. 3: 361-368.

Naseem, S.M. (1973): "Mass Poverty in Pakistan: Some Preliminary Findings", *The Pakistan Development Review*, 13(4).

— (1977): "Rural Poverty and Landless in Pakistan", in *Poverty and Landless in Asia*, Geneva: ILO: 46.

— (1999): Good Intentions but are these Enough?, *Dawn, Economic and Business Review*, December 20-26.

Nash, J. and Safa, H. (1975): *Sex and Class in Latin America*, New York: Praeger.

National Sample Survey Organization (NSSO) (1995): *Some Selected Statistics*, New Delhi: NSSO.

Nehru, Jawahar Lal [1946 (1981)]: *Discovery of India*, New Delhi: Oxford University Press.

Nictzsche (1966): *Beyond Good and Evil*, New York: Vintage Books.

— (1974): *The Gay Science*, New York: Vintage Books.

Nur, Najmir Begum (1988): *Pay or Pardah, Women and Income Earning in Bangladesh*, Dhaka: Winrock International Institute for Agricultural Development and Bangladesh Agriculture Research Council.

Oberoi, Patricia (1994): "Introduction", in, Patricia Oberoi (ed.), *Family, Kinship and Marriage in India*, Delhi: Oxford University Press.

Oliver, Hugh (1989): "The Labor Caucus and Economic Policy Formation, 1981-1984", in Brian Easton (ed.), *The Making of Rogernomics*, Auckland: University Press.

Ostrander, Susan A., Stuart Longton and Hon Van Til (eds.) (1987): *Shifting the Debate*, New Brunswick: Transaction Books.

Overskeid, Geir (1994 b): "The Intuitive Mind", *Behavior and Brain Sciences*, 17: 414.

— (1995): "Cognitivist or Behaviourist: Who can tell the difference? The case of implicit and explicit knowledge", *British Journal of Psychology*, 86: 517-522.

Pakistan Commission on Status of Women (1986): "Report of the Women on Status of Women in Pakistan," Islamabad: Mimeograph.

Pakistan Statistical Association (PSA) (1987): *News Letter*, 1986-87: Karachi: Karachi Chapter.

Pant, Devendra Kumar and Patra, Kakali (1998): "Rural Poverty in India in an era of Economic Reforms". Paper presented in the NCAER–IDRC Workshop on Micro Impact of Macro Adjustment Policies in India (MIMAP, India), 1998, NCAER, New Delhi.

Patnaik, Prabhat (2000): "The State in India's Economic Development", in Zoya Hasan (ed.), *Politics and the State in India*, New Delhi: Sage

Pieterse, Jan Nederveen (1992): "Emancipation, Modern and Postmodern", *Development and Change*, 23(3): 5-42.

Pimlico, Berry, D.C. and Broadbent, D. E (1988): "Interactive Tasks and the Implicit-explicit Distinction", *British Journal of Psychology*, 79: 251-272.

Plato (1963): Edith Hamilton and Huntington Cairns (eds.), *The Collected Dialogues*, Princeton University Press, Bollingen Series.

Pocock, J.G.A. (1985): *Virtue, Commerce and History*, Cambridge: Cambridge University Press.

Preston, P.W. (1986): *Making Sense of Development*, London: Routledge.

Probe (1999): *Public Report on Basic Education*, New Delhi: Oxford University Press.

Qadeer, M.A. (1974): Do Cities "Modernize" the Developing Countries? An Examination of the South Asian Experience, *Comparative Studies in Society and History*, 16(2): 266-283.

Quibria, M.G. (ed.) (1997): *Current Issues in Economic Development: An Asian Perspective*, New York: Oxford University Press.

Quraishi, Sarfaraz Khan (1997): *The Pakistan Development Review*, 36 (4) Part I: 323.

Rahman, H.Z. and Hossain M. (1997): "Recent Developments in Bangladesh Rural Economy: Implications for Strategies and Policies for Alleviation of Poverty", *The Pakistan Development Review*, 36: 811-836.

Rahman, Rushidan Islam (1986b): *The Wage Employment Market for Rural Women in Bangladesh*, Dhaka: BIDS.

— (1986): *Impact of Grameen Bank on the Situation of Poor Rural Women*, Dhaka: BIDS.

Ramchandran, Vimla (2000): Women's Empowerment as International Showbiz, *Economic and Political Weekly*, XXXV (15): 1231-2.

Ranis, Gustav and Frances Stewart (1997): "Growth and Human Development: Pakistan in Comparative Perspective", *The Pakistan Development Review*, 36 (4): 332-346.

Rao, V.M. (1998): "Economic Reforms and the Poor: Emerging Scenario", *Economic and Political Weekly*, 33(29 and 30): 1949-54.

Raunaq Jahan (1975): "Women in Bangladesh", in *Women for Women*, Dacca: University Press.

Rawjee, Mariam (1989): "Beyond the Chardiwari", *Herald*, 65 (5): 73-92.

Robinson, M. (1993): "Governance, Democracy and Conditionality: NGOs and the New Policy Agenda", in A. Clayton (ed.), *Governance, Democracy and Conditionality: What Role for NGOs?* Oxford: International NGO Training and Research Centre.

Robson, William A. (1976): *Welfare State and Welfare Society*, London: George Allen and Unwin.

Rose, Nikolas and Peter, Miller (1992): "Political Power Beyond the State: Problematic of Government", *British Journal of Sociology*, 43 (2): 173-205.

Rothchild, Emma (1996): The Debate on Economic and Social Security in the Late Eighteenth Century: Lessons of a Road Not Taken, *Development and Change*, 27 (3): 331-351.

Rousseau, Jean Jacques (1968): *Social Contract*, Tr. by M. Cranston, Hamondsworth: Penguin.

Rudolph, Lloyd and Susanne Hoeber Rudolph (1967): *The Modernity of Tradition: Political Development in India*, Chicago: University of Chicago Press.

Rukanuddin, A.R. (1990): A Country Strategy Paper on Population Welfare Programme in Pakistan. Unpublished paper prepared for UNFPA, Pakistan.

Sadiq, Nafis (1997), *The Pakistan Development Review*, 36(4), Part I:317.

Safilios-Rothchild, Constantina and Simeen Mahmud (1989): *Women's Role in Agriculture: Present Trends and Potential for Growth*, Dhaka: UNDP.

Sahibzada, M.H. (ed.) (1997): *Poverty Alleviation in Pakistan*, Islamabad: IPS.

Saith, A. (1981): "Production Prices and Poverty in Rural India", *Journal of Development Studies*, 17 (2): 196-213.

Samad, Yunas (1995): *A Nation in Turmoil*, New Delhi: Sage.

Seligman, Adam B. (1995): "Animadversions upon 'Civil Society' and Civic Virtue in the Last Decade of the Twentieth Century", in John A. Hall (ed.), *Civil Society*, Cambridge: Polity Press.

Sen, Amartya (1999): *Human Development Report, 1999*, New York: Oxford University Press.

— (1999): *Introduction to Human Development Report, 1999*, New York: Oxford University Press.

SEWA (1989): *Report of the National Commission of Self-Employed Women in the Informal Sector*, Ahmedabad: SEWA.

Shah, A.M. (1973-4): *The Household Dimension of Family in India*, Berkeley: University of California Press/Delhi: Orient Longman.

Sharma, Kumud (1989): "Micro Policies of Natural Resource Management: Marginalization of Poor Rural Women", Occasional Papers No. 14, CWDS, New Delhi.

Shilling Chris and Mellor Philip (1998): Durkheim, Morality and Modernity: Collective Effervescence, Homo Duplex and the Sources of Moral Action, *British Journal of Sociology* 49 (2): 193-209.

Skinner, B.F. (1969): *Contingencies of Reinforcement*, Englewood Cliffs, NJ: Prentice Hall.

Smelser, Neil J. (1964): "Toward a Theory of Modernization", in Amitai Etzioni and Eva Etzioni-Halevy (eds.), *Social Change*, New York: Basic Books.

Smith, D. (1992): "Review Article: Modernity, Post-modernity and the New Middle Ages", *The Sociological Review*, 40(4): 754-71.

Smolensky, P. (1988): "On the Proper Treatment of Connectionism", *Behavioral and Brain Sciences*, 11: 1-74.

Sreen, Poonam Smith (1995): *Accountability in Development Organizations*, New Delhi: Sage.

Srinivas, M.N. (1966): *Social Change in Modern India*, New Delhi: Allied.

Streeten, Paul (1995): "Human Development: Means and Ends", *The Pakistan Development Review*, 34(4): 333-372.

Sweetser, Anne T. (1993): The Plural Medical System and Women's Health in Pakistan: What the Health Statistics Do Not Reveal, in J.H. Corson (ed.), *Contemporary Problems of Pakistan*, Boulder: Westview Press.

Synnott Anthony (1992): "Tomb, Temple, Machine and Self: The Social Construction of the Body", *British Journal of Sociology*, 43 (1): 79-110.

Tahrunnessa, Abdullah (1974): *Village Women as I Saw Them*, Bangladesh Academy for Rural Development, Dhaka: Ford Foundation.

— (1983): *Report on Home Based Agriculture Production in Bangladesh*, Ford Foundation: Dhaka.

Tahrunnessa, Abdullah and Sondra, A. Zeidenstein (1982): *Village Women of Bangladesh: Prospect for Change*, Dhaka: Pergamon Press.

Tipps, Dean C. (1973): "Modernization Theory and the Comparative Study of Societies: A Critical Perspective", *Comparative Studies in Society and History*, 15(2): 199-226.

Tully, Mark (1998): "Introduction", in Moon Penderel (1961 reprinted in 1998): *Divide and Quit*, New Delhi: Oxford University Press.

UNESCO (1985): *Statistical Year Book*.

UNICEF (1993): *Situation Analysis of Women in Children in Sindh*, Karachi: UNICEF.

Vassavi, A.R., P.G. Vijaya, Sherry Chand and Shailesh R. Shukla (1997): "Blueprint for Rural Primary Education: How Viable?", *Economic and Political Weekly*, 32(50): 3181-184.

Vivian, Jessica (1994): "NGOs and Sustainable Development in Zimbabwe: No Magic Bullets", *Development and Change*, 25: 167-193.

Waseem, M. (1994): *Politics and State in Pakistan*, Islamabad: National Institute of Historical and Cultural Research.

Weiss, M. (1994): "The consequences of State Policies for Women in Pakistan", in Myron Weiner and Ali Banuazizi (eds.), *The Politics of Social Transformation in Afghanistan, Iran, and Pakistan*, New York, Syracuse University Press.

Werlin, Herbert (1991): "Understanding Administrative Bottlenecks", *Public Administration and Development*, 11: 193-206.

Westergaard, Kirsten (1983): *Pauperization and Rural Women in Bangladesh: A Case Study*, Comilla: BARD.

— (1993): "Review on Women and Gender Issues", in Assadduzaman M. and Westgaard, Kirsten (eds.), *Growth and Development in Rural Bangladesh*.

Whitacker, C.S. (1967) "A Dysrhythmic Process of Political Change", *World Politics*, 19 (2): 190-217.

White, Sarah C. (1992): *Arguing With the Crocodile: Gender and Class in Rural Bangladesh*, Dhaka: University Press.

Wilensky, Harold L. and Charles N. Lebeaux (1965): *Industrial Society and Social Welfare*, New York: The Free Press.

Winchester, Peter (2000): "Cyclone Mitigation, Resource Allocation and Post-Disaster Reconstruction in South India: Lessons from Two Decades of Research", *Disasters*, 24(1): 18-37.

World Development Report (1999-2000), New York; Oxford University Press.

World Population Report (2000): United Nations Population Division.

Young, Crawford (1994): "In Search of a 'Civil Society' ", in Harbeson, John W, Rothchild, Donald, and Chazan, Naomi (eds.), *'Civil Society' and the State in Africa*, Boulder: Lynne Reinner.

Zaidi, Akbar S. (1997): "Politics, Institutions, Poverty: The Case of Karachi", *Economic and Political Weekly*, 32 (51): 3282-93.

— (1999): *Issues in Pakistan's Economy*, Karachi: Oxford University Press.

Index